NANCY BROWN DIGGS

HIDDEN IN THE HEARTLAND

The New Wave of Immigrants and
the Challenge to America

Michigan State University Press • East Lansing

♾ The paper used in this publication meets the minimum requirements
of ANSI/NISO Z39.48-1992 (R 1997) (Permanence of Paper).

Michigan State University Press
East Lansing, Michigan 48823-5245

Printed and bound in the United States of America.

17 16 15 14 13 12 11   1 2 3 4 5 6 7 8 9 10

LIBRARY OF CONGRESS CATALOGING-IN-PUBLICATION DATA
Diggs, Nancy Brown.
Hidden in the heartland : the new wave of immigrants and the challenge to America / Nancy Brown Diggs.
    p. cm.
Includes bibliographical references and index.
ISBN 978-0-87013-997-0 (pbk. : alk. paper)
1. Migrant labor—United States—History—21st century. 2. Human rights—
United States—History—21st century. I. Title.
HD5856.U5D54 2011
305.9'069120973—dc22
2010051959

Cover design by David Drummond, Salamander Design Inc.
Book design and composition by Charlie Sharp, Sharp Des!gns

Michigan State University Press is a member of the Green Press Initiative and is committed to developing and
encouraging ecologically responsible publishing practices. For more information about the Green Press Initiative
and the use of recycled paper in book publishing, please visit www.greenpressinitiative.org.

Visit Michigan State University Press on the World Wide Web at www.msupress.msu.edu

HIDDEN IN THE HEARTLAND

CONTENTS

ACKNOWLEDGMENTS

I WOULD LIKE TO EXPRESS MY APPRECIATION FIRST TO ALL THE IMMIGRANTS, both documented and undocumented, who were willing to describe their experiences to me. A special thanks to Veronica Aguilar Brown, my neighbor, Spanish tutor, and invaluable link to the Hispanic community. Professor Michael Jerison, chairman of the Economics Department of the State University of New York, Albany, was a great help in explaining the effects of free trade, as was his wife Michele. I am also grateful to all those in so many fields—business, community services, education, government, health care, law enforcement and religion—who shared their insights with me. I hope that this book will offer a clearer picture of the many challenges—and opportunities—as seen by a cross-section of Americans.

PREFACE

" . . . one country, indivisible, with liberty and justice for all."
—from the "Pledge of Allegiance"

MOST PEOPLE WELCOME A SUMMONS TO JURY DUTY WITH ALL THE ENTHUSIASM reserved for a root canal. I was no exception, and yet serving on a jury proved to be a vastly enriching experience. Not only did all the prospective jurors come away with new respect for our system and how it works, but the case itself led me to questions I had never considered before. Those questions are now being raised by scholars, politicians, educators, social-service workers, and ordinary people throughout the country.

The court case in point: two Latino brothers, here illegally and speaking only Spanish, came forth as complaining witnesses against an Appalachian youth, accusing him of assault and robbery. Before the proceedings began, the judge asked if anyone on the jury would be swayed by the fact that the brothers were here without documentation and would need an interpreter in court. No one had a problem with that. Attorneys on both sides repeated the question. We all believed we could act without prejudice.

We found the defendant guilty of assault—it was obvious that one brother had suffered a broken tooth—but not guilty of robbery. It couldn't be proven that he had stolen the gold chain that the accuser had been wearing.

When the judge talked to us later, we had some questions for him. Weren't the brothers afraid to expose their illegal status in a court of law? He explained that they had the same rights as any citizen and that it was not the court's duty to turn them in.

There were no witnesses who could attest to the fight among the young men. They had all scattered as soon as the police appeared. The judge explained that the many illegal immigrants who live in that section of our city frequently change their residences anyway. Hidden away in restaurant kitchens, food-processing plants, construction sites, and gardening crews, they remain the invisible population.

Just how many immigrants, mostly Hispanic, are living in our area without documentation? I wondered. I learned later that there are some 40 million people in the United States identified as Hispanic who have every right to be here, as citizens or legal residents, but another 12 million whose stay is not sanctioned by law.[1] To put the latter figure in perspective, that's more than the populations of Greece, Belgium, Portugal, Sweden, and many other countries in the world. It's almost three times the number of Norwegians or Irish, and about twice that of Israelis in their homelands. It also equals the population of Ohio. Although entry numbers may decline in the face of economic downturns, many of those who are here already are determined to stay.[2] There may be 100,000 illegal immigrants in Ohio alone. That's the size of a mid-sized city like Roanoke, Charleston, or Duluth. What does this huge influx mean for already overburdened schools, social services, hospitals? How does it affect the economy of the area and the employment of American citizens?

What is it like to live in hiding, vulnerable to exploitation in employment, housing, and personal relationships? Not many would have the courage, like the brothers at the trial, to assert the legal rights to which they are entitled. When we ignore laws designed to protect the rights of all, I learned, everyone suffers.

Our country is united by two factors: the rule of law and the English language. Is the presence of illegals undermining these two basic tenets and, as Samuel Huntington would have it, changing the character of our nation, and not for the better? Or, as Sister Maria of Dayton's Hispanic Ministry claims, are their values of family importance and work ethic strengthening our culture?

What have local governments and communities done to meet this challenge? Due to proximity, a porous border, and established family networks, most of this hidden population are from Mexico. So what is our neighbor to the south doing about it?

Most important of all, aided by my fluency in Spanish, I got to know some of those individuals who had risked their lives to come to this, the promised land. I was able to put some faces to those cold statistics.

It was a twist of fate—or the click of the county court's computer—that set me on this course, but it was the challenges raised by the many aspects of immigration that led me to continue. In keeping pace with attitudes and actions, I found it was often the media that best mirrored this ever-changing picture. It is obvious that there are no easy answers, but there are choices. What follows is an objective overview of the situation in all its complexities to consider as we make some difficult decisions.

PART 1

The Promised Land

CHAPTER 1

Getting Here

IMAGINE THAT IN MEXICO YOU'VE HEARD THE STORIES FROM YOUR COUSIN, YOUR brother-in-law, or the neighbor's son about how much better life is in the North. "The streets in America are paved with gold," they say. "Come on up!" If you can't get here by legal means, how would you plan to cross the border?

The best way would be to get yourself a tourist visa and merely stay on when it expires. More than half of those without documentation come over that way. If you don't mind waiting up to a year, negotiating your way through miles of red tape, answering personal questions, and proving that you and other family members have a decent bank balance, that's the way to go. That's what Isabel did. A young widow with an asthmatic child, she left her job as a secretary in Mexico City to earn more money in North Carolina as a chambermaid. Medical treatments back in Mexico for her elderly parents, as well as for her daughter, are expensive, she explains.

Some can't manage that route, though, especially since 9/11 has tightened security, so many come over the hard way—trusting their lives to "coyotes," guides who may or may not be trustworthy. If you're coming to an area with an established community of other immigrants, you may be lucky enough to find someone reliable, but it doesn't always happen, as Luis Herrera will attest from his desert experience.[1]

Events in the very Arizona desert that Luis would cross were the basis for M. J. McGee's research when he wrote his classic article "Desert Thirst as Disease." Published in 1906, it is a graphic account of what happens to the body when it has no water. McGee described the "feeling of dry deadness of membranes" throughout the whole respiratory system, as saliva and mucus dry up in the oven-like heat. The tongue "may cling irritatingly to the teeth, or stick to the roof of the mouth; a lump seems to rise in the throat and starts endless swallowing motions to dislodge it." Throat, ears, and eyes are hurting. As the skin shrinks, the head feels full and there are "throbbing pains in the nape and down the upper spine." Hearing, vision, and judgment are affected; "the sufferer is a walking fever patient, passing or passed into a delirium." And that is just the first, or "cotton mouth" stage.[2]

Luis's Story

Luis knows all about thirst. He is a burly young man, more like a Green Bay linebacker than his smaller compatriots, but even the strongest find it hard to cross the Arizona desert. In March, when Luis and his group of sixty made the journey, temperatures can range as high as the nineties during the day and plunge to freezing at night. In addition to the contingent of young men, there were older men, women of all ages, and children, including a year-old baby.

The group was told that they would be walking in the desert for about six hours, and to be sure to bring food and water for that time. They were to carry nothing else, in order not to slow down their travel. As often happens, not long after their start, their guide claimed that in order to avoid the INS they would take a longer way—a march through the desert that would end up lasting a hellish two and a half days, almost all the way without food or water. It was so hot during the day that when they chanced upon water tanks for animals, they rushed to gulp down the green and slimy water—at least most did. Luis, too afraid of getting sick, merely moistened his lips.

Along the path, the travelers skirted the remains of one man who hadn't made it. His body mummifying in the heat, he had obviously been dead for two or three days. Having been instructed to bring nothing but the clothes on their backs, they were not able to bury him or even grant him the dignity of covering his face. "We were very discouraged," Luis remembers, as the coyote urged them forward.

At night in the desert cold, without extra clothing or blankets, Luis and his companions huddled together for warmth. In order not to be spotted, they were told to wear dark clothes and no white hats. Smoking or whistling were also forbidden. At last they came to a highway to be crossed, where they would wait until late at night when there was no traffic at all. When a car stopped on the road, the guide warned everyone not to move and to keep their eyes closed so the light wouldn't reflect off the whites. Just at that moment Luis could no longer contain the tickle in his throat. It erupted in a loud cough! Everyone held their breath, but fortunately the driver was only someone having car trouble. After waiting for what seemed hours, they were finally alone again.

When all was dark and quiet, the guide called another coyote, who came in about a half hour with two vans. As they were ushered forward, some people were tired and moved too slowly; the guide threatened to leave them behind if they didn't hurry up. The sound of a helicopter caused everyone to push and shove in a vain attempt to squeeze sixty people into the two vehicles. Some had to remain behind, including Luis, who waited anxiously for the coyotes to return. Fortunately there was a big incentive: Luis and his companions had not yet paid them.

At the next step of the journey, the immigrants were loaded into a truck trailer that was "incredibly hot," with no water, let alone air conditioning. After traveling some four hundred miles, they eventually arrived in the Los Angeles area, where they were able to buy plenty of food and drinks, as well as drugs. After spending the night in a safe house, Luis and his group met their new American coyote, an Anglo, who sent them off in different directions. Luis took a bus to Las Vegas where his uncle lived, and later moved on to Ohio to be with friends.

Was it worth the $1,000 that Luis paid to get to California? No, he insists, and he would never take the risk or undergo the agony again. Nor would he advise others to try.

GABRIEL SUAREZ HAD A SIMILAR STORY ABOUT HIS THIRD AND MOST RECENT crossing, in 2004. In his case it was a hailstorm—in August—that almost killed him in the mountains of Arizona. In fact, in March 2006 cold temperatures in the desert were responsible for the deaths of four would-be immigrants. Gabriel's trip, too, was expected to be much shorter than the four days it required. He had brought along enough food and water, or so he thought, but not for such a long period, as the guides altered course to avoid the border guards. Once they arrived at the border, twenty people were packed "like sticks" into a small van, whose driver "drove like a crazy man" to get away from the border.

This dangerous practice of packing as many people as possible into vehicles and driving recklessly to escape the Border Patrol is increasing, according to *New York Times* reporter Randal C. Archibold[3]—nine people died in the recent crash of a Chevrolet Suburban in which twenty-one Mexicans had been stacked "like cord wood," as the Yuma County Sheriff's Department described it.[4] Gabriel tells me that someone he knew in Oaxaca didn't make it on his attempt, dying in the desert and leaving behind a wife and young children.

When Gabriel first came over in 1992, the cost was $1,000, but it has steadily risen. On his last trip it had gone up to $2,000. He explained that there is a sliding scale for the coyote's services, depending upon the difficulty of the crossing. It now costs between $2,000 and $3,000, depending on whether you want to come over fast or slow. The more you walk, the less you pay, for a lot has to be arranged if you choose the fast way.

Although, from the vantage point in Mexico looking toward the green oasis of Quitobaquito Springs, the desert can look almost inviting, you can trust the sign that the Border Patrol has erected on the other side of the fence. It warns in Spanish of the folly of entering the vast area where there is no potable water. "NO VALE LA PENA," "It's not worth it," it says. The desert is a hostile place. Where there is not sand, there is a fine red dust that permeates everything. The animals and plants that live there are uniquely adapted to an environment with extreme temperatures and very little water; people aren't. The plants themselves, prickly cactuses, spiny ocotillos, and thorny trees, have evolved to discourage any intruders. The chollas from a distance look like soft flowering shrubs, but up close one can see that they, too, are covered with needles that seem to jump out at the traveler. Animals also pose a threat. Rattlers, coral snakes, and sidewinders, tarantulas and Gila monsters are out there somewhere. When I camped in the Sonoran desert in April, our guide counted twenty-four scorpions near the campsite. The daytime heat in the nineties, enervating even with ample water, dropped to the chilly forties at night—OK when you're in a sleeping bag and wearing a wool hat, fleece jacket, and sweatpants. Not many immigrants are so well prepared, though—especially when their guides have taken everything away.

Warning walkers to stay out of the desert is one of the tasks of the Border Patrol, and yet at least 200,000 attempt to cross through Arizona's Organ Pipe Cactus National Monument each year alone.[5] Some have put the figure at over three million illegal aliens entering the country annually through our southwestern border states.[6] The extent of the desert borderlands should be enough to deter all but the most desperate—or foolhardy. They face a huge wilderness covering over four thousand square miles; Cabeza Prieta National Wildlife Refuge by itself is as big as the state of Rhode Island. Nevertheless, about a million people have been apprehended every year, and an average of three hundred and fifty have died on the way.[7] It's possible that the death toll has been much higher, numbering in the thousands in Arizona alone; Pima County's deputy sheriff Sgt. Joe Jett estimates that "for every national that makes it, there are probably at least ten that don't."[8] Their families in Mexico may wait and wait and never learn what happened to their loved one.

The dead, like the person Luis encountered, are often left to lie where they have fallen. With no identification on the bodies, they would be almost impossible to trace. Agents don't have time for the mountains of paperwork that recording each death would require, Luis Alberto Urrea explains.[9]

Even a contingent of 17,500 border agents are too few to patrol adequately the six thousand miles of the Mexican and Canadian borders combined, plus the thousands of miles of coastal waters—but they are well trained for their task. Each trainee must complete a nineteen-week resident course at the Border Patrol Academy in Artesia, New Mexico. The challenging curriculum for those stationed on the southern border includes instruction in integrated law, firearms, driving, and Spanish, as well as physical training. An armory of high-tech tools is at their disposal: 6,741 motion and seismic sensors, 413 stationary cameras, 155 mobile video sensors, night-vision goggles, aerial drones, and underground radar equipment. But equipment breaks down, animals set off the motion detectors, and it may take hours for agents to arrive at the trouble spots.[10] The agents know that even if they stop a few—and it's known that the coyotes will sacrifice some in order to distract the guards—many more are waiting behind them. Those used as decoys, who are sent back, may get preferential treatment from the coyotes next time.[11]

It's hoped that the temporary deployment of up to six thousand National Guard troops will ease the agents' workload, although critics, like California's governor Arnold Schwarzenegger, argue that the troops may be needed elsewhere.

Border Patrol agents have seen many a tragedy, including the loss of some of their own—like James P. Epling, who died after rescuing an illegal immigrant from China from drowning in the Colorado River. Or like Kris Eggle, who died in the line of duty, killed by a drug smuggler. The Organ Pipe Cactus National Monument visitor center has been renamed in his honor.

Luis Alberto Urrea reports on the many deaths in the Organ Pipe area, particularly on the Camino del Diablo, "The Devil's Highway," where

all the agents seem to agree that the worst deaths are the young women and the children. Pregnant women with dying fetuses within them are not uncommon; young mothers have been found dead with infants attached to their breasts, still trying to nurse. A mother staggers into a desert village carrying the limp body of her son; doors are locked in her face. The deaths, however, that fill the agents with deepest rage are the deaths of illegals lured into the wasteland and then abandoned by their coyotes.[12]

Urrea focuses on the story of just such an abandoned group. Of the twenty-six who attempted the trip, only twelve remained alive to bear witness to their ordeal and against the guide who left them to die. The teenage gangster is now serving his sixteen-year sentence in an Arizona prison.

Recently one mother deserted by her coyote got lucky when Officer Marisol

Cantu discovered her alone and in premature labor. The baby, automatically a U.S. citizen for having been born in this country, was given the name "Sarai Marisol," after her rescuer.[13]

More common, however, are the horror stories—like that of the nineteen who died when seventy-four immigrants were sealed into an airless 18-wheeler. The victims included a five-year-old child. An assistant U.S. attorney called the driver "the most heartless, evil and cruel" member "of a criminal enterprise that treated people worse than animals on their way to the slaughterhouse."[14]

Rev. Thomas Buechele bears witness to the suffering of those who attempt the crossing not far from his Episcopal church in Bisbee, Arizona. "Borderline property owners," he says, "pick up abandoned backpacks, baby clothes, shoes, empty water bottles, and they grieve as they hope the folks who left them are OK. It isn't a question if they 'made it' or not. The questions are: Are they still alive? Did some coyote rip a child out of its mother's arms and pass the child back across the line because it was making too much noise? Did they get caught by one of the kinder Border Patrol agents? Are they being held at gunpoint by a few wild-eyed, trigger-happy vigilantes? Are they stuffed into stifling hot vans, trucks, or some Tucson or Phoenix bedroom? Are the younger women paying the cost with their bodies?"[15]

Not all border crossers come here freely. Some are "sex slaves," like thirteen-year-old Rosa, who, promised a better life in America, was forced to work as a prostitute when she arrived.[16] Some 15,000 women, many of them young girls from Mexico, are victims of sex trafficking.[17]

In this vast, lawless land, anything goes. "There are bandits that roam the desert now," says Margot Bissell, who is public use assistant at the Cabeza Prieta Wildlife Refuge, headquartered in Ajo, Arizona. "They rob these people at night, attack them. The coyote could care less. He's not going to guarantee anything. He's got their money. That's why, when they get busted, he's the first one to take off. . . . The border's a real scary place on the Mexican side, and people are coming from all *over* Mexico, not just the border towns. Children are being sold in all kinds of awful trades."

She tells the story of the woman who came with her child to join her husband in the United States: "She told the coyote exactly where her husband was, what her whole point was of getting here, so the coyote knew everything he needed to know. Then a couple of guys snatched the child out of her arms and ran to the U.S. Took off! They contacted the husband and said, 'If you want to see your child again, you meet us here with this much money.' He contacted law enforcement and they got him over here, and he met them where they were supposed to be. When they knocked on the door, with the child, of course law enforcement was waiting for them.

"Those kinds of things are starting to take place. It's become a murderous business. It's not just 'Here, give me $4,000 and I'll take you to the U.S.' Now there are many 'opportunistic crimes.'"

Sometimes, though, Margot has to admire the creativity in this "cat and mouse game." Border crossers will brush away their footprints with branches of creosote, or "they'll cut squares of carpet and tie them on the bottom of their shoes, so that their soles don't leave distinguishing signs. You can tell where those footprints are, but they get wiped out, especially if they walk in the arroyos there. It makes it tough walking, but your footprints will be wiped out." A few optimists attempt to cross the desert on bicycle. Margot claims she could open up a bicycle shop with all the new abandoned bikes that are recovered.

Others acquired a school bus and decided to paint on the side, "Ajo Unified School District"—except that they wrote, "Ajo *Unifield* School District." Nobody noticed the mistake until an untold number of trips across the border, when the bus broke down and everybody got off and left it. There are the humorous incidents, like the man in a photograph a friend sent her, who had cut out the seat cover of a van "in such a fashion that he crawled into it, and he was part of the seat. And then the headrest came down over his head, and all that stood out was his legs! I laughed till I cried. How humiliating to get caught . . .

"There have been a number of retired U.S. citizens with their motor homes who have picked up [illegal immigrants] and carried them and got busted. Salt of the earth, sixty-, seventy-year-olds who should know better. You know, 'What are you doing?' It's a lot to resist, anywhere from $2,000 to $4,000, somebody opens their wallet. . . . That's been pretty tough."

What happens to them? "They lose their vehicle to start with. It's confiscated, and depending on what the situation is, probably go to jail, huge fine, humiliation, like the guy in the seat cover."

Not all of those who come to the States cross through Arizona, and yet other crossings are not without their challenges.

José's Story

José was only thirteen years old when he decided to leave the farm in Ecuador to join his half-brother in Ohio. He was aware of the dangers of the trip—he'd heard talk of theft, rape, and even murder—but with no more than the primary-school education his family could afford, "I had no future," he says. José left with a group of five young men, the oldest twenty-eight. He obtained an $8,000 loan from his uncle, from which José was to make a partial payment for plane tickets to the coyotes upon arrival in Panama. The rest would be paid upon completion of the journey. With $250 in his pocket, luggage in hand, and dressed as a tourist, he hoped he didn't look like an illegal immigrant. He had a visa to go through Ecuador and Panama in order to fly from there on to Guatemala, with a change of planes in Costa Rica.

In Guatemala the young men took three different taxis to get to the hotel to which they had been directed. As soon as José and his companions arrived at the hotel, there were two immigration officers waiting for them. They explained that "because of a drug situation on the plane, we have to ask you some questions, but if everything is OK, we'll let you go."

"OK, no problem."

But instead of going to the police station, José remembers, "they took us far away from the city, and then they took their guns out. They searched everything, all our clothes, even our shoes. I had a kind of plastic shield with a picture of Jesus in which I had hidden $20 and they even took that. They took the $250 which I had in my pocket, too. They took everything. Then they dropped us off and they said, 'Go. Just go.' They held a gun on us.

"I never believed in miracles, but I stuck my hand in my pocket, and there was a $20 bill, after they'd searched everything!"

When they found a bus to the city, José asked the driver to change his $20 into local currency. He was given 100 quetzals, when he should have been given 130, as he learned from the taxi driver who took them from the bus stop to the hotel. Two young men in another taxi were robbed, too, as apparently the taxi drivers were connected with the police. Only one of the travelers escaped, because his cab driver had told him to get out a couple of blocks away from the hotel.

Days were spent in Guatemala waiting for their coyote, a woman, to tell them when the time would be right to cross the border. During that time, his uncle sent another $100 for his friend and him to replace part of what had been stolen. While his friend saved his, thinking he might need it later, José spent his "eating and drinking."

Then came a twelve-hour bus ride to the border, where they spent three days at the woman's house. There they were able to do laundry, but with no change of clothes, they would wash only one article of clothing each day.

Finally they were told that all was ready for them to cross the river marking the boundary between Guatemala and Mexico. While the coyotes communicated by signaling each other with lights and whistles, José and his friends, now part of a group of some thirty-five people, were pulled across the river in a plastic boat.

Once in Mexico, they were met by a big pickup truck. In order to "avoid the cops," the driver steered clear of the highways, going through the jungle into the mountains. Traveling only at night, from 9:00 until about 5:00 in the morning, they spent the daylight hours sleeping on the ground in the woods in the mountains, with nothing to eat for two days.

I asked José if he had been afraid. No, he said. He was young and this was an adventure; but, he says, "I saw all the guys crying because they had left their kids and wives behind," certain they would never see their families again.

They were in the mountains for "days and days," he recalls. In all, it took twenty-seven days to go from Ecuador to Los Angeles. At some points, the coyote would bring food to them when they were staying in hotels or safe houses.

At one of the houses, they were joined by about fifty people from another group, so that now there were over eighty. Somehow the Mexican police found out about it, and around 10:00 at night, says José, "Ten cops came and said they were going to take us all in. The coyotes started dealing with them, telling them they only had so much money they could pay. Then they asked everybody to give up their money, whatever they had, so they could come up with more. My friend had to give up his $50, but I had already spent all mine!" Of the three coyotes in the house, apparently their guide was the only one able to come up with the price, because their group of thirty-five was able to leave. "The cops even got her a big car," he says. "We all got in it and went into the town of Moreles. We ate well at the hotel there, and the lady bought us some clothes, Mexican clothes, so we would fit in. We were also taught to speak in a Mexican accent and how to use certain Mexican expressions. Then we took a plane to Tijuana. The coyotes paid the Mexican authorities so that we were not stopped at all. They didn't check our IDs; everything was paid for."

Then came the hard part.

From Tijuana the group took a bus away from the city to very close to the American border, where "the coyote said to get off the bus and cross the highway and start walking to the mountains, all the way up. So we started walking and it was hot. It was really hot that day. These three guys appeared with bottles of water. I thought it was for all of us, but it was just for the coyotes. *We* were the ones who needed water. *We* were the ones who had been walking. We started out at 10:00 in the morning and walked until 3:00 in the morning the next day. We walked all day. I asked one of the coyotes if I could have some water, and she said, 'Just take a sip. Not much.' It was hot the whole day. Everybody was so thirsty," José recalls, so thirsty that when he found a bottle that was half full of liquid and may or may not have been water, he drank it desperately. They had had nothing to eat since a sandwich on the plane two days before, and "that was it."

Because there were helicopters watching the border, José and his companions had to hide in the bushes. From the piles of trash and discarded clothes, it was evident that many had passed that way before them.

After the sun had set, they continued walking for hours. When they could see the lights of San Diego, they knew they had arrived in the United States. Around 3:00 in the morning, they came to a road where three vans were waiting in the dark. With the group crowded into the vans—which had no seats, in order to carry the largest number of people possible—they drove through the mountains with no headlights. José was sure that after all that had happened to him, this was it—he was going to die. He thought of the stories he had heard of cars crashing into the mountains. "Here it was pitch black, and they didn't have the lights on," as they careened down the hairpin curves. It was a valid concern; many have died in accidents as they rush to leave the border, like the man who couldn't control his car at ninety miles an hour on a dusty Arizona smuggling route, or the two-year-old girl crushed to death in a rollover accident.[18]

After an hour and a half of driving, they saw the lights of Los Angeles, where they were able to stay in a safe house and finally wash their filthy clothes. José remembers that he was as tired as he had ever been in his young life.

His uncle sent him money to buy a plane ticket from Los Angeles and, in those days before security was so strict, José flew to Chicago, where he had relatives. From there he took a bus to Dayton. Over a month and seven borders later after leaving Ecuador, he finally reached his destination.

WHY DO THEY COME? SOME, ESPECIALLY THE YOUNG MEN, COME FOR THE adventure. Most are seeking jobs to support their families, including those back in Mexico. According to the values of Mexican culture, "a man *ought* to be willing to sacrifice for the well-being of his family," Richard Alba and Victor Nee report.[19]

Although men outnumber women, those of all ages and sexes do make the trip. Marta, like a number of women, left to escape an unhappy marriage, as well as to seek a better life for the adolescent son who accompanied her. She was frightened; she'd heard about the many deaths that have occurred. Marta was lucky in that the walk across the desert without food and water took only four hours, even though they had to backtrack, but unlucky in that she was forced to leave behind the jewelry she had brought, as well as her suitcase. She had sold everything she owned in order to afford the $3,000 payment to hire a guide for her and her son. She arrived in the United States with just $20 and the clothes on her back. The fee she paid bought her the services of three guides: one to get her across the border, then another one with a car to take her to a safe house, then another to arrange transportation to anywhere in the country—Ohio, in her case. The thirty in her group of mostly men spent one night in Arizona before going their separate ways. No food was provided, and by that time everyone was getting very hungry. One woman had brought along three little tacos, which she insisted that Marta's son eat, because he was the youngest.

Carmen, a pretty twenty-year-old, came to join other family members in Chicago, and later moved farther east to live with her father. She remembers how frightened she was when, again without food and water, they walked in the dark along a narrow cliff-side path. There had been many people in Carmen's contingent waiting to cross at the Arizona border, but in order not to attract attention, they were sent over in groups of six. The small group of those ahead of them had been robbed of everything: money, rings, even tennis shoes.

Even before reaching the border, conditions can be very bad, as those who have come from all over Mexico discover in the towns that serve as staging areas. Roman Catholic bishop Gerald F. Kicanas of Tucson was appalled at the conditions at a guest house in Altar, in Mexico's Sonora State, where at least sixty desperate men, women, and children were "stacked in cots three tiers high, two to a bunk, in a room no bigger than an ordinary bedroom." The conditions seemed to him like those he had read about in German concentration camps. But, he says, "the stench, the filth, the squalor told me this was not something from the past, but the real thing."[20] All for the privilege of paying up to $1,800 to a coyote who might or might not see them successfully across the desert. Not far from the guesthouse, in Sasabe, stands a cross commemorating the known victims who have died along the Arizona border. Those involved in the "No More Deaths" campaign and groups like Humane Borders set out food and bottles of water for desperate immigrants, as do some ranchers, says Rev. Lucie Thomas. But there are others who smash such water bottles when they run across them.

It's not only humans who suffer from the great number of people crossing the desert. Environmentalists condemn the destruction of the fragile desert ecosystem. As Margot Bissell says, "Even driving through it one time damages the Sonoran desert to the extent that it can take up to one hundred years to recover. We have so little rainfall that when you make tracks in the desert, those tracks will stay forever, because there's nothing out there to make vegetation grow."

According to Defenders of Wildlife, Arizona's Cabeza Prieta National Wildlife Refuge, home of the Sonoran pronghorn, suffers from "excessive human presence" and is one of the ten most endangered wildlife preserves in the country.[21] "The pronghorn is a unique creature," Margot explains. "It stays in certain areas. It doesn't cross highways. It's a very, very sensitive creature." For this reason, the U.S. Fish and Wildlife authorities do not allow visitors in pronghorn areas during fawning season. "They don't want us disturbing them if they're close by with their fawns," she says, "because then they won't have the milk that they're supposed to. The mortality of pronghorns is very, very high in the desert because of a shortage of resources." But, she adds, "It's futile. With all the illegals coming through, it probably doesn't do much good, but we're doing what we're supposed to do."

Although the effects of the flow of illegal immigrants have been almost all negative, there has been one unexpected positive for the small town of Ajo. "This town is flooded with law enforcement," Margot says, "and that's a big part of our economy now. Many, many people here are renting to Border Patrol. And you have temporary detailers that come in, and they pay the government price. . . . So there are many many-faceted economical considerations to this whole thing. . . . And where it's going to end is anybody's guess."

In the meantime, she is well aware of the economic damages others are suffering in the area. Margot reports that one of the biologists at another wildlife refuge nearby tells her that "they have had something like three vehicles stolen and others broken into many times. Their house has been ransacked eight times now; the people were looking for food. And one time she came home and they were in her house. Scared her to death. They weren't there to hurt her, they were just there to get food, and they ran away. So there are things like that. And the cattle ranchers talk about how the immigrants just cut the barbed wire to get through. That's not right. The cattle get out, and that's their livelihood, you know."

In his book *Illegals*, Jon Daugherty decries the trash, the violence, and the crime that he claims accompanies the immigrants. Ranchers have grown tired of the daily routine of repairing damage done by immigrants who have grown ever bolder—or more desperate. As Tucson writer Leo W. Banks says, landowners "find fences knocked down and water spigots left on, draining thousands of precious gallons. And then there's the trash: pill bottles, syringes, used needles, and pile after pile of human feces."[22]

It is in reaction to such abuses that a group of irate Arizona citizens recruited a "Minuteman" militia to take matters into their own hands, a move that met with the approval of 57 percent of the state's residents.[23] During the month of April 2005, the organization claimed to have mustered close to nine hundred volunteers to patrol the Arizona border, and to have apprehended 336 border crossers.[24] According to the group's founder, Jim Gilchrist, "The border has become a war zone. Until politicians find the will and the guts, the Minutemen Project will do the job the politicians are unwilling to do. It's dangerous and heart wrenching. Traffickers, gun runners and unfortunately potential terrorists are coming in. I've seen it all. They're exploiting society."[25] Jon Dougherty poses the question that if hundreds of people can cross our porous borders illegally, what's to prevent terrorists from doing the same thing? It's a question that has Condoleezza Rice worried, too, since al-Qaida "will do everything they can to cross borders," she says.[26] Columnist Kathleen Parker cites estimates that some 70,000 non-Mexican immigrants who have entered illegally are young Saudis.[27]

Arizona is the state that bears the brunt of the immigrant burden. As U.S. Immigration and Customs Enforcement (ICE), which replaced the INS, has cracked down on easier passages, more are tackling the rugged and remote paths of the southern Arizona desert.

Those individuals living on the border are not the only ones who suffer; the state's social services are stretched to the breaking point. Since hospitals must treat all emergency patients, some cross the border to obtain the medical care unavailable to them in Mexico, while many illegal residents also rely on treatment in local hospitals. According to an Arizona survey, thirty-eight medical centers had losses of $153 million on foreign patients, of which the U.S. government is expected to repay up to some $45 million a year.[28]

The vast majority of those who come to America by way of Mexico, however, do come for one purpose: to find work—and their destinations now span the country.

CHAPTER 2

Working Here

For some employers, having access to a vast pool of workers who have no recourse to legal protection must seem like a godsend, but it's more like a pact with the devil. It's unethical, as well as illegal; unfair to companies that would prefer to compete honestly; and unfair to American workers who deserve fair wages. Contractors, restaurants, megafarms, and factories—all are hiring hordes of workers who are often mistreated, underpaid, ill-housed, and placed at risk, afraid to complain for fear of deportation.

Those who get even the lowest pay here, however, may find themselves earning in one day what they would receive for a week's worth of work in Latin America, with the promise of a better future. The lure of a better income has led to the fact that, according to the Pew Hispanic Center, "illegal immigrants make up about a fourth of all drywall and ceiling-tile installers in the United States, about a fourth of all meat and poultry workers and a fourth of all dishwashers."[1] They—and we—pay a heavy price, however. Consider what José Silva has to say:

| José's Story

While other teens were coming home from school, José, who had left Ecuador at thirteen with a fifth-grade education, was headed for the Chinese restaurant where, unconcerned about child labor laws, he would work from 4:00 P.M. until 2:00 in the morning, cleaning and setting up the tables after the bar was closed. For this he was paid $350 every two weeks, which, he thinks, "was a lot for my age." He was grateful for the tips that the other servers gave him for cleaning up the tables. José and his brother, who had come some time before, shared one of the restaurant's apartments, which also housed Chinese immigrants.

After a brief stint at the Chinese restaurant and a fast-food place, the teenager was hired as a dishwasher at one of a chain of family restaurants. There he persuaded his boss to train him as a cook. By then his brother was working at a Mexican restaurant, so when José learned that they needed a cook, he took the job.

"When I went there," he says, "they didn't pay me what I thought they were going to pay me. They were paying me about $7–$7.50 an hour. The work was hard—it was hot, and the kitchen was very small. I worked there for about a year, and the raises were small, so one time I got mad and I said to my brother, 'I quit. I don't like this anymore.' My brother didn't want me to quit, so I went and talked to the owners. I said, 'We want more money.' They gave us a big raise, from $7.50 up to $12.00! It was a high-level restaurant and the food was expensive, but we weren't making that much before."

In the meantime, José was lucky. He had met the director of the local middle school, who spoke a little Spanish and who convinced him that he could, and should, attend high school. Having learned how important an education is in America, José enrolled toward the end of the school year and began a full year the following fall.

"High school was tough," he remembers, as he continued to work. He needed the money to send back home to his mother and to repay the loan from his brother to come to America. "The worst part," he says, "was that I couldn't understand one word of English." Jean Wagner, his English as a Second Language teacher, devoted a great deal of extra time to her struggling pupil. Exchange students from Uruguay, Colombia, and Spain were able to communicate with him and help him translate when the going got tough.

Slowly he learned, but it took its toll. "I would come home with these big headaches. I told Mrs. Wagner I didn't want to go back to school, and she'd say, 'Just come.' I don't know how I did it, but I did. The second year Mrs. Wagner said, 'Just come back one more year. Just come back next year.' So I went back the second year."

He managed to join a work-study program in which he received credit for work, going to school from 7:30 to 1:00, then starting work at about 3:30. "But," he says, "I almost didn't graduate. I had problems with the reading exam. It was tough for me."

He finally left the restaurant, he says, because "I had a problem with the owners, who were Colombian. I had to quit, I told them. They were rude sometimes and they were not treating the other people right in the kitchen. It was hard seeing those people getting yelled at and they didn't do anything. Most of them didn't have papers to work, so they were afraid of being kicked out." Not José. He was young and unmarried, with no family responsibilities. "You just have to take the risk and not worry about it," he thought.

"By that time I had a lot of friends from Ecuador living here working in construction, so I worked framing houses and building houses. There were a lot of hours and they were paying well, so I worked at that for about six months, then in a factory assembling truck parts for about a year."

The theme of how important it is to speak the language to make it in English-speaking America runs throughout everyone's narrative. For an ambitious young man like José, it has made all the difference in the world. The now twenty-five-year-old, who seems much more mature than his age, is living the American dream. He has a good job with a manufacturer of medical implants and a home of his own. Perhaps best of all, he recently became an American citizen. He knows how much he owes to his dedicated English teacher. When he married his lovely wife from Mexico, who also came here illegally, Jean Wagner was a witness at the ceremony. José and Gloria are the proud parents of Alexander, who will grow up learning English as well as Spanish.

It's no wonder José was Jean Wagner's prize pupil. "He must have been very smart," I tell her. "No, but he was very, very determined," she says.

LUIS, THE BURLY YOUNG MAN WHO ALMOST DIED OF THIRST IN THE DESERT, ALSO works in the kitchen of a Mexican restaurant, but a different one from the one that hired José. Life was better in Mexico, he says, but the money is better here. With his T-shirt, baggy jeans, earrings, tattoo, and backwards baseball cap, he might fit in in any blue-collar bar. In fact, it was in a bar that he met his American fiancée, who worked at a factory nearby. He comes from Michoacán, one of the Mexican states that has exported a large number of its population, where factory work from 9:00 A.M. to 8:00 P.M. Monday through Saturday earned him $60 per week, plus insurance and social security. Here he makes $225 for a 40-hour week, out of which he pays $150 a month for his room—with shared bath—above the restaurant. He's heard that the owners are going to raise the rent soon. In the meantime, he's learning some English from his American girlfriend and hopes to get a job that will allow him more time to learn the language.

Marta, a pretty woman in her thirties, made the trip with her teenage son and works at the same Mexican restaurant, back in the kitchen. She's glad she's here, because her son can go to school, but oh, how she misses her other children back home. Although she has met nothing but kindness among those in the area, it's a lonely life, especially when you can't speak English. She would like to learn the language, but there's neither the time nor the opportunity. Still, she is making more money than she would in Mexico: $175 for a 40-hour week, out of which she, too, pays $150 for the room she shares with her son, with the bath down the hall. With no car, it's hard to get around in the suburb where she lives, although there is a bus she can take to the shopping mall. She is surprised at the cost of everything, but somehow she manages to send money back home.

Stories of being overworked and underpaid are common among America's undocumented immigrants. "Among Janitors, Labor Violations Go with the Job," states the headline of a *New York Times* article. Steven Greenhouse describes "a large and largely unnoticed group of workers—the nation's 2.3 million janitors," who, according to the evidence from many interviews, lawsuits, and government reports, "are denied overtime pay, classified improperly as independent contractors, locked in the stores overnight and forced to work their first two weeks unpaid."[2]

JANITORS MAY BE WELL HIDDEN IN THEIR NOCTURNAL JOBS, BUT YOU HAVE ONLY to look up at almost any building site to see undocumented immigrants at work. While vacationing in Sanibel, Florida, I couldn't pass up the chance late one afternoon to speak to one of the construction workers on the block. A middle-aged man whom I'll call Jesús Perez, spattered with paint and carrying equipment, seemed friendly and eager to share his impressions. He had found plenty of work here, he said, and was able to send money to his mother, ill back home. He was obviously putting things away after a hard day's work, but he invited me to return the next morning to continue our conversation, pointing out the house where he would be working.

Early the next day, I appeared, tape recorder and notebook in hand, to be met not by Mr. Perez, but by the owner of the house, who was also the contractor for the construction projects in the neighborhood. No, he said, I could not speak with Mr. Perez. I was rudely told to leave his yard immediately and not come back, as he was tired of "you people" coming around. What people? Union organizers? Journalists? OSHA representatives?

It's good to know from the homeowner's reaction that someone besides employers must be looking out for the interests of those like Mr. Perez, for jobs in construction are known to be among the most dangerous for illegal immigrants.

Mr. Perez probably got his first job in the United States at one of the hundreds of sites where day laborers gather each morning; a survey reports that the first occupation of 60 percent of immigrant workers here is as a "*jornalero.*" At places like a Home Depot store in Atlanta; on Center Street in Jupiter, Florida; the 7-Eleven in Prince William County, Virginia; the one hundred-plus pickup spots in Los Angeles County; the more than sixty locations in the New York City area; or the hundreds of other locations throughout the country, you've probably seen those small but muscular men waving to indicate that they, too, are available for work not likely to pay more than $10 an hour. It's estimated that about 117,600 such *jornaleros* are working or looking for work every day.[3] They are undeterred by neighbors' complaints or by the jeers of passers-by. Or by the horrendous number of work-related injuries and deaths among their compatriots.

In 2002 "more Mexicans died in construction than any other industry—and more died from fatal falls than any other accident," Justin Prichard reports. Eighteen-year-old Carlos Huerta and sixteen-year-old Antonio García Reyes were among the number who plunged to their deaths; Rigouerto and Moses Xaca Sandoval, brothers only fifteen and sixteen years old, lost their lives when the walls of a trench they were digging collapsed. "In the mid-1990s, Mexicans were about 30 percent more likely to die than native-born workers; now they are about 80 percent more likely," with even higher rates in certain states, and "Mexicans are nearly twice as likely as the rest of the immigrant population to die at work," Prichard adds. Why is this happening? Part of the reason may be the fatalistic attitude toward safety found in the Third World. Or they could be overfatigued through working two or three jobs.[4]

Lack of familiarity with a more advanced technology may also play a part. Church worker Dick Korn tells the story of "the fellow who walked across the border in Laredo, Texas, and couldn't find a job. There had been a fight at a construction site and the section owner had just fired a guy, and he said to the man who had just crossed the border, 'Can you drive that tractor?' The man looks up at that big machine, and, even though he's never seen anything like it in his life, he says, 'Yes!'"

If they're here illegally, workers may hesitate to complain, especially if they can't speak English, and there are few OSHA inspectors or accident investigators who speak Spanish. Susan Feldman of the Centers for Disease Control and Prevention believes the high number of fatal accidents hinges on the fact that employers tend to give Mexicans the most dangerous tasks. "They're considered disposable," she says.[5]

AGRICULTURAL WORKERS, WELL OVER HALF OF WHOM ARE THOUGHT TO BE UN-documented immigrants, are also at risk.[6] In fact Josie Ellis, a North Carolina health worker, says that in 2005 "agri-business was ranked the most dangerous occupation," even surpassing mining.[7] Dairy workers have been overcome by fumes or drowned in liquid cow manure, and workers' families, as well as the workers themselves, have suffered the long-term effects of the improper handling of pesticides.

The Mexican television series *Sin Fronteras*, in a show called "Cosecha de Dolor" ("Harvest of Sorrow"), presented the tragic case of a baby born without extremities in Immolokee, Florida, where his parents picked tomatoes for the Ag-Mart Company.[8] In addition to the baby lacking arms and legs, another child was born with only a partially formed jaw, and another, who lived just a few days, was born without a nose or visible sex organs. An Associated Press article confirms that three deformed babies have been born to undocumented immigrant mothers who worked in the fields during their pregnancies—fields in which "more than two dozen pesticides and herbicides were used."[9]

One worker—his face splotched with lesions—described on the television show how he had suffered an accident when he was sprayed by a malfunctioning pump, inhaling the powder. Although women wore some protective clothing, the men were furnished with none. The worker stated that he was told that gloves were available, but he would have to pay for them. Yes, there was a safety video, but it was in English, and nobody understood it. The television show promises a follow-up, and we can hope that the attorney who has taken the case will be successful.

In Kentucky and North Carolina, those who work on tobacco farms run the risk of a serious condition called "green tobacco sickness": acute nicotine poisoning from absorbing the substance through the skin.

In Ohio, the Buckeye Egg Farm was finally closed down after years of complaints from neighbors, and conflict with state authorities over numerous abuses. In 2001 it was raided for having workers not authorized to be here; thirty-six were deported. Researchers Ann V. Millard and Jorge Chapa claim that many more continue to work at the megafarm, which had the worst conditions they encountered in their research. They describe a hellish workplace with a "sickening stench," where employees, many just arrived from Mexico, must keep their mouths shut all the time because of the clouds of flies. In 1997, says Ken Silverstein, "OSHA fined the company $1 million for miserable working conditions in its chicken houses and poor living quarters afforded its migrant workers. Inspectors found human sewage backing up in basements, inadequate heating and dangerous electrical wiring."[10] In 2002 the company once again made the news, this time charged with eighty-seven permit violations, including having caused a fish-killing manure spill in a creek, and piling up dead chickens, which attracted swarms of flies.[11]

In a class action brought by the Equal Justice Foundation and the Ohio Public Interest Research Group, workers claimed that "Buckeye subjected them to twelve-hour-plus shifts without paying hundreds of thousands of dollars in overtime"—and outdated eggs were passed off to the consumer as fresh.[12]

"In our study, the egg farm exemplifies an unfortunate Midwestern transition to megafarms and an associated widespread pattern of employing Latinos wherever working conditions are the most difficult and wages the lowest," said Millard and Chapa.[13] Buckeye Eggs was sold to Ohio Fresh Eggs LLC in May 2005. Let us hope that they can maintain better working conditions than Buckeye did, but it doesn't look promising. By June 2005, the state "had issued 11 enforcement actions against the company" and the company was facing a $212,000 fine for failure to control insects and rodents.[14] And in December 2006, Ohio Fresh Eggs was in the news again: its permits had been revoked because of falsified applications.[15]

Especially outrageous was the case in western New York, where grandmotherly Maria García, a labor contractor, was sentenced to forty-six months in prison for what the judge called a "despicable abuse of vulnerable people." García was accused of crowding workers into housing where as many as eleven people shared one bedroom. Some were virtual slaves, paid less than 13 cents an hour and threatened with violence if they tried to leave. At least forty-one employees were abused in 2001. It was claimed that García "deliberately recruited undocumented immigrants because they would be fearful of being deported and easy to control." Six men were finally able to escape and got in touch with the farm legal services agency. Daniel A. Werner, legal director of the Workers' Rights Law Center of New York said, "It was like one of the stories you hear of slaves escaping before the Civil War. . . . The heroes of this story are the workers who sneaked out in the middle of the night. They slept in a forest, near some railroad tracks, with people out looking for them."[16]

The farmers for whom the immigrants worked have not gone unnoticed, although they claim they knew nothing about the conditions at Mrs. García's camp. Although they are not charged with the same crimes of slavery and racketeering that the contractor is, they are charged with "labor law violations, failure to provide minimum wage and failure to provide working conditions required by federal law."[17]

Justice has been served in the García case, but when there may be 100,000 migrant workers every year in New York State alone, we wonder how many other abusers there are who are not apprehended.

If agribusiness is the worst occupation, meatpacking is the worst of the worst. An editorial in the *New York Times* explains "What Meat Means":

A large slaughterhouse is the truly industrial end of industrial farming. It is a factory for disassembly. Its high line speeds place enormous pressure on the workers hired to take apart the carcasses coming down the line. And because the basic job of the line is cutting flesh—hard, manual labor—the dangers are very high for meat workers, whose flesh is every bit as vulnerable as that of the pork or beef or chicken passing by.

The problem of worker safety is compounded by the fact that meatpackers, driven by the brutal economics of the industry, always try to hire the cheapest labor they can find. That increasingly means immigrants whose language difficulties compound the risks of the job. The result, according to a new report by Human Rights Watch, is "extraordinarily high rates of injury" in conditions that systematically violate human rights.

In fact, the report finds, some major players in the American meat industry prey upon a large population of immigrant workers who are either ignorant of their fundamental rights, or are undocumented aliens who are afraid of calling attention to themselves. As a result, those workers often receive little or no compensation for injuries, and any attempt to organize is met with hostility.[18]

The Smithfield Packing Company in North Carolina, where, says Bob Herbert, "serious injuries abound," is an example of such a "major player." A judge's investigation revealed that, among other things, the company "warned Latino workers that immigration authorities would be alerted if they voted for a union."[19]

Eric Schlosser, in his book *Fast Food Nation*, blames America's appetite for fast food for making meatpacking such a dangerous industry, as restaurant chains demand more and more meat that must be processed fast and uniformly. According to the Bureau of Labor Statistics, at least one-fourth of meatpacking workers suffer a serious injury every year, but the numbers are probably much higher. Since such workers can be summarily fired, they fear to complain about injuries or about unsafe practices.[20] Cleanup crews are especially vulnerable to injuries. Schlosser paints a graphic picture of amputated fingers, mutilated bodies, and decapitations.

Meat processed in such factories is dangerous for the health of the consumers as well, he adds, since "the overworked, often illiterate workers in the nation's slaughterhouses do not always understand the importance of good hygiene. They sometimes forget that this meat will eventually be eaten. They drop meat on the floor and then place it right back on the conveyor belt. They cook bite-sized pieces of meat in their sterilizers, as snacks, thereby rendering the sterilizers ineffective. They are directly exposed to a wide variety of pathogens in the meat, become infected, and inadvertently spread disease."[21]

Agriprocessor, the leading processor of kosher meat in the country, in 2008 was accused of employing almost four hundred illegal immigrants. Although the manager was later acquitted for lack of evidence that he knew their ages, thirty-two workers under the age of eighteen—seven younger than sixteen—were operating dangerous equipment and exposed to hazardous chemicals..[22]

John Pawelski is a former police officer and the founder of the Latino Connection, a group of representatives from many organizations who meet once a month to network over matters dealing with Hispanics. Completely bilingual, he grew up in Mexico as the son of missionary parents. He's heard many stories of workplace abuses. "A lot of companies," he says, "will not pay Bureau of Workmen's Comp, or they pay the employee in cash, or they'll subcontract when they're not supposed to, and they'll skirt around the Bureau of Workmen's Comp, especially industries that have a high rate of injuries. There are stories from Ohio and all over the country where people have gotten hurt, and what the companies have done is fire them. They say, 'If you can't come to work with a broken leg, then stay home, but if you turn any paperwork into Bureau of Workmen's Comp, you're going to get deported. We're going to have the INS sitting at your doorstep.'"

Some companies find other ways to exploit their employees' undocumented status. He tells me of the case of a meat-processing factory in our area. After hearing rumors that "you have to watch that company," John spoke with a supervisor, a woman who told him: "Look, let me tell you how it's done." As John explains:

What happens is that they bring somebody in and they say, "You come up here and we'll give you this job. It's a $9.50 an hour job. It pays well. It's a good, decent job. However, while you're learning the job, you need to start at $6.15 an hour. Once you learn the job and become proficient at it, then of course we can pay you what you deserve."

So they work and work and work several weeks, months, whatever. Then the worker says, "Hey, I'm good at the job now. I'm ready for my $9.50," and the company says, "We're going to give you a little raise, but you're not there yet." So finally the man says, "Look, I can't work for $6.15 an hour. It's time for me to make more than that. I've got to go somewhere else." Or, showing dissatisfaction, "Look, I've mastered this. I'm doing a $9.50 job, and the American sitting next to me is making $10.25 an hour doing the same thing. What's up with this?"

Then what happens, shortly thereafter, he's called into the office and he's told, "Mr. Lopez, we got a call yesterday from the immigration people, and they say your social security number doesn't match with your identifiers, therefore we can no longer employ you here, because it's come to our attention, and once it's come to our attention, we have to let you go."

Then what they say is, "However, if you come back with proper identification, meaning that you have a birth certificate and a social security card, then we can rehire you."

So what the person does, he goes out and pays $150, $200 to get a fake social security card and a fake birth certificate and comes back three days later to the same people that just fired him, and he says, "I'm now Mr. Rodriguez, and here's my social security card and my birth certificate."

"Oh, that's great."

"And since I already know the job, of course I'm going to get $9.50, right?"

"Well, it would look a little too obvious if the guy asks, of course, if we say we're paying you $9.50 right off the street. So just hang in there for a little bit and we'll fast-track you on up to where you were."

Now they've got him back down and there he sits. Three, four months go by and they repeat this cycle. Eventually somebody will threaten to report them, and of course that person is not rehired. They're simply let go and not rehired.

That's just one example, but I have had contact with numerous people who have told me that same exact scenario. They have American supervisors who are very, very rough on them—there have been a lot of times when they describe a situation that's almost like the sweatshop situation, where the supervisors are very controlling: "You're going to get fired. Not only are you going to get fired, you're going to get deported. Is that what you want? Now get back to work!"

John tells me that the immigration authorities know about the situation in the meatpacking company nearby, but they tell him, "We understand that there are a lot of violations, a lot of issues, a lot of problems. However, because we're so understaffed, we're dealing with the police arresting people for no license, taking them in for no seat belt, no ID, and sending us memos. When the police say there's somebody there, we have to respond to that. So we're running around in circles dealing with the petty stuff. We know that there are things that are going on, but we can't do anything about it."

It's not uncommon for an undocumented immigrant to be paid less than agreed upon, or not at all. A UCLA study reported that almost half of the laborers who had managed to find work had been cheated out of at least some of their pay during the two months of the study.[23] "This last year," says Carlos Martinez, a construction worker in Atlanta, "I did jobs for many people, and many of these people didn't pay me. Or people pay me later, three years later, two years later." But Carlos is learning—he has become selective about his customers. Others haven't had that opportunity. In the aftermath of Hurricane Katrina, many immigrants who rushed to help with the cleanup have gone unpaid, "stiffed" by the contractors who hired them.

THE PROBLEMS INVOLVED IN ENFORCING THE LAW ARE EVIDENT WHEN WE consider the case of Tyson Foods, the world's largest poultry producer, which has fifteen plants in nine states. In 2001, after two and a half years of investigation by the INS, the company was charged with a thirty-six-count indictment accusing the management of conspiring to smuggle illegal immigrants, a practice that was thought to have been going on since 1994. In 2003 Tyson Foods and its managers were acquitted of all charges, but not before the manager of their Shelbyville, Tennessee, plant committed suicide. Authorities must think long and hard before taking a powerful company to court for a time-consuming and expensive case that they may have a hard time proving. From 1993 to 2003, there were a mere 364 convictions against employers for hiring illegal immigrants; in 2004 only 46.

It's possible for employers to distance themselves from the hiring of illegal immigrants by using contractors as go-betweens, as local roofing companies did when a large windstorm created more work than they could handle. There are a number of such "storm chasers" who contact employers and offer to furnish roofers, who may or may not be here legally, when and where they are needed.

Migrant advocate Rob Williams describes how a contractor might order a van of workers up from the border. The coyote who has brought them here might appear at the job site on payday to collect what he is owed. Another common arrangement, however, is for the immigrant's debt to the coyote to be transferred to the contractor, who will then take money out of the worker's wages until it is paid off. Sometimes the contractor will not allow the worker to work elsewhere until the debt is clear.[24]

Those who borrow money in this way "unwittingly become trapped in a modern form of indentured servitude," say sociologists Richard Alba and Victor Nee—"working for ethnic entrepreneurs who exploit them as cheap labor."[25] Gina Stough, the Latino family advocate at Dayton's East End Community Services Corporation, has a client who is working hard to pay off the $12,000 debt to the coyote who brought her here from Ecuador. There is a lien on the family property back in Ecuador; she knows that the family will lose their home if she doesn't come up with the money.

WHEN COMPANIES LIKE THE ONES ABOVE DISREGARD THE LAW OF THE LAND, the field is not level for the other players. For this reason, local building contractors in Hamilton County, Ohio, "support [Sheriff Richard K. Jones] 125 percent" in his pursuit of those who hire undocumented immigrants. As Steve Hester of Benchmark Masonry Contractors said, "We who do things right, who have drug testing and check papers and have benefits, we can't compete with those who aren't."[26]

Some employers argue, however, that they can no longer find people to do the job. "It's hard to find good Americans to do the work," says the owner of a roofing company, whereas the Latino workers supplied by a contractor are "top-notch and conscientious, and do superior work." Landscapers in our area complain that they can no longer depend on high school or college help in the summer. In California, although Victor Davis Hanson laments the metamorphosis of his state into a Latino enclave, he admits that "young men and women from Mexico now take on tasks that whites, Asians, African-Americans and second-generation Mexican-Americans apparently will not." According to the U.S. Department of Labor statistics he cites, less than half of American teenagers look for summer jobs, evidently preferring to spend their idle days at shopping malls.[27]

The work ethic among Americans seems to be no longer what it was a decade or so ago. A plasterer tells me that in the late '80s and early '90s, he became aware that his workers were actually working only four or five hours in an eight-hour day. Then Hispanic workers began to arrive, and their work ethic was "phenomenal," he says. As for the plasterer, he's gone on to spend most of his time at another job and ceded the plastering profession to the newcomers.

With tighter security at the border and more opportunities for immigrant farm workers elsewhere, farmers in Georgia, California, and Washington complain that they can't find anyone to harvest their crops. When Georgia farmer Randy Scabor's usual fifteen immigrants left, he says, "I wound up hiring some locals that weren't worth hauling to the field. . . . It was the worst harvest labor in my life and I've been in the farming business 35 years."[28]

On the other hand, if American workers were paid more, perhaps they, too, would be willing to work at less desirable jobs, says economist George J. Borjas: "A more sensible inference may well be that immigrants take jobs that natives do not want *at the going wage.*"[29]

Matthew Philpott agrees. In a letter to the editor in the *New York Times* he writes, "There are many low-income citizens in my community who would welcome the opportunity to work at these jobs, but who are not being hired because the construction contractors hire undocumented workers at lower wages, pay them in cash and avoid paying Social Security and other taxes on a majority of their work force."[30] Bruce Wilcox of Texas, whose career in the drywall and carpenter trade spanned more than twenty years, complains that with the large influx of Mexicans, "wages dropped by half. All the benefits disappeared." He adds that "illegal immigrants took my job, and I still wanted it. All the jobs they do at such cheap costs got done before they arrived."[31]

Mexico's President Fox infuriated Americans of all colors when he said that Mexicans in our country take jobs that "not even blacks want to do."[32] It is not a question of wanting to do the job, Bob Herbert contends, but rather that "there are not enough jobs being created to accommodate the wide variety of demographic groups in need of work. With that being the case, and with some employers actively recruiting new immigrants, the inevitable result has been the displacement of previously employed workers, especially in the less skilled and lower-income categories," into which, unfortunately, many African-Americans fall.[33] David Holzman writes in another letter to the editor of the *New York Times*:

> One of the major causes of unemployment for black men, I believe, is that their jobs are being outsourced, figuratively speaking.
>
> Companies that cannot send jobs to other countries often encourage third-world workers to immigrate to the United States. These workers, used to earning as little as one-tenth the wages of American blue-collar workers, will work for wages that no American should have to accept.

There are millions of legal and illegal foreign workers in the United States. With that kind of competition, no wonder so many black men are out of work.[34]

Although some, like the *Wall Street Journal*'s Stephen Moore, say the figures don't show it,[35] the perception is indeed that a great many jobs are being taken away from poor African Americans. It's one that Rev. Jesse Jackson shares. Many immigrants "are hired to do work that blacks once had," he says.[36]

It's a situation that has created animosity between the immigrants and American blacks. As one African American shouted at a union demonstration near New York City, "My parents came over here in slave ships. They worked hard, according to the law. We got the legal system to free us. We didn't break the law. The jobs we used to have, they're taking now."[37]

Recent events in Stillmore, Georgia, seemed to lend some credence to African American complaints. When ICE raids netted 75 percent of the nine-hundred-member work force of the Crider chicken-processing company, African Americans eagerly replaced them at wages of more than a dollar an hour above what the company had been paying their immigrant workers. Americans, however, were apparently not willing to put up with the "long, arduous schedules, alleged health and safety hazards, and unrelenting supervisors" that some of the workers described. Turnover has been high—in a four-month period, the population of workers hired since the raids turned over three times—and management complains of low productivity.[38]

For the immigrants, the reason they are hired is simple. "We work harder," they say.

CHAPTER 3

Strangers in a Strange Land

WHAT ARE THEY LIKE, THESE NEWCOMERS WHO HAVE COME TO LIVE, ILLEGALLY, among us? Those who make the journey across our southern borders generally fall into two groups. In the first group are young men who seek adventure, as well as the chance to send money to their families and save some up for themselves. For them it's a rite of passage. The second group, smaller but growing fast, consists of older people, mostly men, who bring along their families or hope to send for them later. Whatever their category, the goal of essentially all of them is to find work here. To reach that goal, they need a good deal of determination, as well as courage, running the gauntlet of a border that is filled with danger.

More than half are Mexicans, and 80 to 85 percent of recent Mexican immigrants are undocumented. Although most are young adults, about one-sixth of those who come are children under eighteen years of age.[1] Their presence puts a strain on education and health services, but they are probably not on welfare. They have no intention of calling attention to themselves, for fear of deportation.

A surprising number of illegal immigrants pay taxes, and the numbers have increased with the prospect of immigration reforms. Their chances of becoming legal will be better, they believe, if they can provide such evidence of long-term, law-abiding residency.[2] Of course sales taxes are added to everyone's purchases where they apply. Although those who form part of the underground economy are not likely to pay income tax, according to researchers from the Urban Institute and the Migration Policy Institute, "the U.S. Social Security Administration has estimated that three quarters of undocumented immigrants pay payroll taxes, and that they contribute $6–7 billion in Social Security funds that they will be unable to claim."[3] When the IRS offered seminars at community centers focused on immigrants, they were overwhelmed by the numbers of those attending. Immigrant taxpayers know that they can get tax refunds by using tax ID numbers. The IRS has been offering tax ID numbers since 1996 for those without social security numbers and does not share information with ICE (the former INS).[4]

Those whose method of immigration has been to overstay a visa may be fairly well educated. But those who have walked across the border probably have no more than a grammar-school education. Only 2 percent of Mexico's citizens between the ages of 55 and 64 have the equivalent of a two-year college degree, while the figure for those between 25 and 34 is 5 percent. (Comparative figures are 26 percent of older Americans and 31 percent of the younger generation in the United States.)[5]

If sociologists Richard Alba and Victor Nee are correct, however, we may be acquiring the best and the brightest: "There can be little doubt," they say, "that immigration from Mexico is socially selective and generally includes individuals with above-average levels of education."[6] They are also hardworking, for those without money have learned that it is hard work that is the key to survival, not education, which is only for the rich.

The immigrant's employer probably thinks of him as docile and apparently happy to "work hard at an unpleasant job for low wages."[7] This submissive attitude in part is a reflection of history: Spanish conquistadores kept the Indians in their place by teaching that "individual initiative, achievement, self-reliance, ambition, [and] aggressiveness" were not to be tolerated.[8] The Catholic Church historically reinforced those teachings by stressing the values of subservience and the importance of accepting God's will. "Poverty is a virtue because it means that you will suffer, and those who suffer are more welcome in heaven," Lionel Sosa says, adding that "In Anglo Catholic churches I've never heard a 'poverty is virtue' sermon."[9]

Although the Catholic Church of today is an important part of many Hispanics' lives—and many parishes feature Masses in Spanish—it is not the only religion that appeals to the heartland's Hispanics. Only about 70 percent of American Hispanics would call themselves Catholic.[10] Protestant churches have long been gaining converts throughout Latin America, as well as the United States. According to Ken R. Crane and Ann V. Millard, it's not unusual for a Hispanic community to form its own church: "The decentralized and independent manner in which Protestants (particularly *evangélicos* and Pentecostals) have operated has worked to their advantage in creating Latino churches. They can organize themselves quickly into tight-knit, semiautonomous units and recruit their own leaders."[11]

Thomas Moss of Minnesota, who served on former governor Jesse Ventura's staff and whose wife is an Episcopal priest, spoke about the Episcopal Hispanic congregation he is involved with. Due to a divorce in the family or another situation of which the Catholic hierarchy disapproves, he says:

> Most of the members of this church are disaffected Catholics. Some of the people had run across priests who were pretty strict. The way our church got started was that there were two married people who had been divorced and they felt shunned by the church. Their eight-year-old daughter died, and when they went to the Catholic church, the priest wouldn't bury her. There was an Episcopal priest who spoke Spanish and who had a great affinity for Latin culture. He met the family and he said, "I'll do it." The family was quite well known and there were about 250 people at the service. The priest did a high church Episcopal funeral which felt Catholic, plenty Catholic to these folks. These were Mexican people, and there were so many people who came who hadn't been in church for such a long time that they just decided, "Let's start doing this on Saturday nights." Unlike a church where the diocese or somebody says, "We're going to start a church here," this one came up out of human need. Because of this little girl, the name of this church is 'El Santo Niño,' which of course refers to the baby Christ, but they wanted something about a child.

Cultural misunderstandings can occur in every aspect of the newcomers' lives, and church is no exception. Tom Moss, who acts as the head of the finance committee of the church, has encountered such differences. He notes that

> In Mexico the government owns and maintains all the church buildings, since the revolution in the 1920s. . . . During the revolution they said the church had been so much part of the problem and was so hooked up with the establishment and it owned so much land, so much property, that they nationalized all of it. The result was that in most of the communities you've got this old church, somebody from Rome subsidizes the priest's salary, and there are five or six wealthy families in town who also put money in, because there has to be a church and they can afford it. The people show up and all they are really expected to do is reach in their pocket on Sunday and if they feel grateful, throw a few bucks in.
>
> So now we've got this church up in Minnesota and this is how parishioners operate, so we're getting heavily subsidized by the diocese. I think we actually get about 30 percent of what it takes to run this church from the members. I'm trying to say, "You've got to start acting like Americans here. There's no government help; you're in the Episcopal

church now, not the Catholic. We don't have these deep pockets, and there are no patrons, no wealthy families. Now the individual members have to face up to this." Our priest is from the Dominican Republic and I'm saying, "All we're going to do is send a letter telling them that they need to make a pledge." He frowns on this: "It's too pushy." It's a cultural deal. They say, "Oh, don't talk about money in church because that's defiling Christ. That's making religion just about money." I'm saying, "When are we going to talk about it? Because we're running out, we're not going to be allowed a church." The point here is that there are some pretty important cultural things besides the language.

While church is important, family is the institution that plays the greatest role in Latino society. It's interesting to note that while eating dinner as a family is declining in the United States, "Latino families have the highest rate of sharing a meal."[12] Daniel Vargas of Vargas & Co., which specializes in marketing to Hispanics, advises his Anglo clients not to jump right into business with Hispanic customers. Warm up the conversation first with questions about the family, since family is so important. Unlike in some cultures, it's a welcome topic.

So important are family ties that sending money home has become an important part of the culture. "If you don't send remittances, you're viewed as selfish," says Roberto Suro of the Pew Hispanic Center.[13] It is members of the family who have probably scraped up the money to allow the immigrant to pay his way to America. If others have paved the way before him, he can rely on them to help him find a job and a place to live. In fact, for the undocumented, a network of friends and family is essential, since they can't depend on other resources and are probably not eligible for most social services. It is family, rather than the government, that people know they can count on. In fact, as Leo R. Chavez says, "They are not accustomed to governmental assistance and view dependency on the government very negatively."[14]

If they don't depend on their government, however, their government does depend on them. Money sent back to Mexico is the second largest source of foreign exchange: $9.6 billion was sent back to family members in 2004, representing a 150 percent increase since 2000. Some say the figure is much higher—$16.6 billion in 2004—while Juan Cervantes of the Bank of Mexico estimates a figure of $20.6 billion for 2005 and a whopping $24 billion for 2006.[15] While some decline is expected in the recession period beginning in 2008, the Multilateral Investment Fund put the figure for Latin America and the Caribbean at $69.2 billion in 2008.[16]

Being far from family is hard enough, but it's especially devastating when a loved one dies, as when Carmen lost her beloved *abuelito*, or when the twelve-year-old daughter of a local man died in Mexico. Manuel Gomez from Ecuador has not been home in sixteen years and was unable to attend his father's recent funeral. He misses his mother. "It hurts on my heart," he says.[17] Separation from the family is always hard on the man who comes alone. In Kentucky, notes health worker Susan Fister, "isolation and depression are problems."[18] Throughout the country, writes sociologist Marta Tienda in a government report, "there are two ominous trends for Hispanics—worsening health status and increased risk of family disruption."[19] When federal agents conduct periodic crackdowns on illegal immigration, the whole community lives in fear, staying indoors and putting off things like shopping or taking the children to the park. Alcoholism and high blood pressure, perhaps from the stress of living a life in hiding, present problems. Without his family, a single man may find there's not much to do when he's not working. As Rev. Stan Puryear, who has a Hispanic ministry in Owensboro, Kentucky, says, "The young men . . . have never been away from home before. They are socially isolated and lonely, and they begin drinking, some heavily."[20] Sister Maria Stacy in Dayton agrees that lonely men turn to alcohol, because they "don't have any kind of outlet for healthy diversion; drinking is cheap and it's a palliative." Sexually transmitted diseases acquired from prostitutes are also a health concern. Richard Korn, a bilingual former Catholic priest who now runs the Episcopal Hispanic Ministry in Southern Ohio, is another who sees the lack of recreation as a big problem. "They don't think about entertainment other than having excessive drinking at the end of the week." Alcoholism among the immigrants is a problem with which Dick is familiar, since he also works as a counselor at the Maryhaven Rehabilitation Center. There he deals with those who have been arrested for drunk driving, among other things. "The problems arise," says Dick, "when they drive the way they shouldn't. That could happen to anybody, but they don't know the consequences. There you buy justice, but here you have to pay the piper."

Dick is very proud of the soccer league at which he referees, which was started by Pedro Reyes, an immigrant himself from Oaxaca, and which fills an important recreation need. Today the league has seventy teams and is the largest in Columbus.

The formation of the league has been instrumental in creating, or perhaps is reflective of, a new kind of Latino culture, Dick Korn believes. Rather than think of themselves as Mexican or Guatemalan, Salvadoran or Argentinian, the members think of themselves as one nationality and members of one team.

Dick sees this reflected in musical tastes, too. "There are several radio stations here, some with Tex-Mex type of language that is often part of the music that young people listen to, but because the Latino community is changing by the hour, you never know what a given person might be listening to. Some like jazz, some like rock, some like certain music from Mexico, and finally, traditional Mexican music is less and less something they feel comfortable with. It's something that apparently they get second hand from their parents." He thinks the very fact that the festival we are attending is "the Latino festival," where people are from all over but think of themselves as Latinos, is an indication of this new hybrid Hispanic culture.

We tend to lump Latinos together, but there are definitely differences, a fact of which Daniel Vargas is very much aware. An approach suitable for marketing to Mexicans in California may not be the same for Cubans in Florida or Puerto Ricans in New York. When he produces a commercial, he has to make sure the actors are appropriate to potential customers, both physically and linguistically, since otherwise the audience will think, "They're not talking to me." If it's a nationwide ad, he strives for a generic Spanish accent, the equivalent of a Latino Walter Cronkite, he says.

Officer Minerva Virola in Louisville, Kentucky, who is from Puerto Rico says, "If you ask me if I'm Cuban, I won't be offended. You ask a Cuban, 'Are you a Puerto Rican?' and they won't get offended. You can ask either one of us if we're Mexican, and watch us immediately say, 'We're Cuban' or 'We're Puerto Rican.'" Nor do they want to be Dominican, since they may have a reputation for crime, but, Officer Virola explains:

> That's not the whole picture. It's a matter of geography. Cuba and Puerto Rico are so close in our cultures, in our language, in our history. The same Indians that were there in Puerto Rico were in Cuba. Same conquistadores that were in Cuba were in Puerto Rico, but they were different in Haiti and all the other islands. The Indians in Mexico were different, their conquistadores were different. I have a lot of Cuban friends, and they ask, "Is she Cubana?" "No, she's not Cubana," not with an attitude. I'll be around Mexicans, and a Mexican will ask, "Is she Mexican?" And they'll answer, "No, she's Puerto Rican," with an attitude. I don't know why, but it happens. But the Cubans and Puerto Ricans are basically almost the same, the accent's the same, religion's the same, the same Indians over in Cuba were in Puerto Rico, same conquistadores. When Christopher Columbus came with that crew, the same crew visited Cuba and some of them stayed. Some of the same Africans and Spaniards were left in Cuba and in Puerto Rico. So we're close, so close.

Father Benjamin Santana is an Episcopal priest from Puerto Rico who ministers to the Spanish-speaking community in Chautauqua County, New York, which includes city-dwelling Puerto Ricans and Mexican migrant workers, most of the latter here illegally. He remembers that when he first moved to the United States, he was assigned to a Cuban congregation and found that he was not as warmly welcomed as he had expected. "You see," he says, "for the Puerto Rico community, the Puerto Rico church, to be assigned a Cuban pastor is no problem. But for a Cuban congregation to be assigned a Puerto Rican pastor, there is a problem, and I will tell you why it took me a year to gain their trust. Back in their mind, in their consciousness, is a historical problem. At the Spanish-American War, the U.S. invaded both countries, that's how they got Guantanamo. Then in 1917 the U.S. gave citizenship to the Puerto Ricans, but not to the Cubans. . . . Finally I learned what was going on, and I told the Cubans,

'I wasn't even born then. I didn't ask for that. I didn't ask for citizenship. I was given that. When a kid is born he isn't asked whether he wants to be a U.S. citizen, he is one. So I had nothing to do with that." On the other hand, Cubans have been given a lot of benefits that he feels have not been given to Puerto Ricans.

Ana is a Mexican American who works at a community center in Jamestown, New York, that serves mostly Puerto Rican residents. While Officer Virola thinks there may be some indication that Puerto Ricans look down on Mexicans, she has a different attitude. The Puerto Ricans are very different from Mexicans, she claims, "starting with their food, how they talk, how they treat people," and they are not as willing to work as Mexicans. She and her boss, Dr. Carmen Lydell from Colombia, agree that the Puerto Ricans won't do farm work. "They don't like it when the weather turns cold, and unlike the Mexicans, they'd rather accept welfare."

ALTHOUGH LATINOS MAY DIFFER WIDELY, THEY DO SHARE SOME CULTURAL mores that we in the host country do not, and ignorance of our ways can lead to unexpected difficulties. Americans may question the honesty of someone who doesn't make eye contact, whereas that's respectful behavior in Mexican culture, says John Pawelski, the retired bilingual police officer. Respectful behavior might also mean not always speaking your mind, he adds. Citing sociologist Boye DeMente, the North Carolina Children's Services newsletter cautions its readers that "to avoid disappointing people, Latinos may say what they think the other party wants to hear or give ambiguous responses."[21] A carpenter speaks of a coworker who, he thought, had assured him that he would lock up after the work was done, but he hadn't understood a word the carpenter said. His "yes" was just a way to be agreeable. In one case of what could be a cultural misunderstanding, a vegetable vendor at a Tennessee Farmer's Market resents "immigrant customers who often want to pay below the asking price for the fruits and vegetables he has been selling there for 20 years."[22] The Mexican custom of bargaining is not welcome here. Mexicans, like some other cultural groups, may stand closer to us than we're comfortable with; we feel our personal space is being invaded.

Although he probably won't be deported if he's arrested for a minor charge, our newcomer may find that police procedures can differ from those in the home country, as John Pawelski explains. Ignorance on both sides can exacerbate a problem:

> As an example, if you get pulled over by the police, just by being an American for a long time, you know that your job is not to jump out of the car, fishing through your pockets. You wait until the officer comes up. A normal traffic stop. Very simple.
>
> However, in Mexico and in many Latino countries, if you sit there and wait in your car, with your hands on the steering wheel, making no effort to get your papers, making no

effort to get your license, making no effort to come back to the *federales*, you're probably going to go to jail, because you're the one who violated the law, you're the one who ran through the red light, but yet the federal agent would think, "You're going to make *me*, the federal agent, come out of *my* car, and I'm going to straighten up all my clothes and my hat, and I'm going to walk all the way up to *you*, because you're so arrogant you can't come up to *me*?' It's an absolute no-no.

What's interesting is when I tell the officers here, "Of course this is how we do a traffic stop," everybody says, "Oh, yeah, sure, that makes sense." Then I say in Mexico, your job is to hop out of that car, fish for your papers, and in many cases—now the federals, the actual state police, they're trying to get off the bribing system—but the other case is that in the other hand you get what you think is the appropriate fine for that ticket. And that's how it's done. To this day, you can go to Cancun, and if you get pulled over for speeding, they're going to tell you it's $100. If you go into court you're going to pay $100, but you can pay the fine in $20 cash right now. But in the United States one of the worst insults you can give a police officer is that he was bribed. If you give me a $20 bill when I'm getting ready to give you a ticket, you're going to go to jail. We're going to give you the maximum, because you have so challenged my integrity, that you're going to suggest that by giving me $20 or $100 that I would violate what I stand for and risk my life for every day? That's an absolute insult.

In June this year we went down to Mexico to the town where I grew up. The police chief—a former classmate of mine—said, "Look, we would like to have you folks share with us a little bit what you're doing in the United States. We understand there are a lot of things going on." So I had the privilege of sharing about twenty minutes with the federal agents, and the agricultural specialists, the whole government building came and sat in a conference room. . . .

When I shared with them this point about the traffic stop, I said, "You know how it is. When you get stopped, you're supposed to get out of the car, you're supposed to bring your paper work back." And they're like,

"Yeah. Well, sure, of course."

"Now, in the United States, what you have to do, you have to sit in that car, don't move, keep your hands on there, don't look for your papers, don't do anything until that police officer gets out of his car and walks over to you."

They said, "What?!?" They were amazed. "You sit in the car and you have the police come up?"

Now, here I am, I come up to the United States, I get stopped for some minor violation, the first thing I do is jump out of the car and dig in my pockets. Well, number one, the adrenaline goes up on that officer. He pulls his gun out and says, "Get back in the car." I don't understand him, so I continue walking back toward the officer, wondering what the deal is, and what happens? Nothing good can come of that scenario, right?

John sees that his mission is to try to educate people on both sides. But, he insists, "We're not going to compromise safety at the risk of offending somebody, so there may be a citizen that gets taken to the ground pretty rough, totally innocent, and that's OK as long as it keeps officers from getting killed. Those things we don't give on."

Given the distrust that native Mexicans harbor toward those in authority, American police need all the help they can get. It's an attitude that works against the very people who are especially vulnerable. The Southern Poverty Law Center, which tracks hate crimes across the country, notes that there has been an increase in such crimes that they believe is due to the recent focus on immigration. A spokesman for the center says that it "has seen increasing signs that groups that have encouraged a particularly aggressive response to illegal immigration are working with neo-Nazi organizations to try to intimidate illegal immigrants. Groups like Border Guardians and American Border Patrol have been accused of abusing those here without documents.[23]

In New Orleans, where many came to repair the damage from Katrina, day laborers are known as "walking ATMs," the *New York Times* reports—"easy prey" for common criminals.[24]

Many who listened to Spanish-language radio shows in several cities were victims of bogus investment schemes promoted on the stations; because such listeners "typically are immigrants who speak little English, know little about their rights and aren't likely to complain," they were easy marks.[25]

Fraudulent "immigration consultants" also take advantage of those eager to rectify their illegal status, sometimes absconding with their clients' life savings. One legitimate consultant, Nelly Reyes in San Francisco, thinks that "more than half her counterparts should be put out of business, because they are either scam artists or incompetents selling skills they do not possess."[26]

The newcomers are also prey to other criminals, like the gangs that have followed the move of immigrants into areas that once were considered relatively crime-free. Isabel, a chambermaid in North Carolina, left California for a place she thought would be safer, but she found that her new community had its share of criminals. She laments that not all Mexicans come to America to work. Some, who prey on their fellow immigrants, "drink, take drugs—cocaine—and they go crazy. And they steal." She's sorry that people like that give all Mexicans a bad name.

Ezra Escudero, the executive director of the Ohio Commission on Hispanic/Latino Affairs, notes that the immigrants "get targeted by the criminal element, because they feel that the police and other safety officials are out to get them. When they hear sirens, they don't realize the sirens are there to help them, too."

Officer Minerva Virola is working with the Latino community in Kentucky to change this attitude:

The police are responding to a lot of domestic violence, and the police are responding to a lot of public intoxication, because the Latinos say, "This is my property. I can drink if I want," because nobody's educating them. So here we are, we're working as a unit now to educate them.

There was a group of Mexicans who moved into our community, in a building with a drainage ditch behind the property. Outside was a big receptacle for all the trash. The Mexicans never paid for that receptacle, so guess what? They were throwing their trash in the ditch. And management would go and clean it all up and put a note on their door, in English, "Put the trash in the receptacle." One day management got really mad about it, because now there are rodents out there. So at their request we went and knocked on the door and said, "What seems to be the problem?" They said, "We know there's a receptacle out there and people put their trash in it. But we never paid for it. No one ever told me I could throw my trash there, so I throw it out here. This is where we throw the trash." They had just come in from Mexico, so we had to teach them: "This is free. It's part of the rent. You did pay for that, so put your trash in there." They used to hang their clothes outside their window. You don't do that. They had a free dryer downstairs. They wash their clothes in the bathtub, they hang their clothes outside in the front, so we said, "You can wash your clothes in the bathtub if you want to, but you have a free washer and dryer downstairs." . . . It's a matter of education.

We try to create a relationship. My job now is community relations. I work with the Latino community and try to teach them our procedures, so when they do need help, they know exactly who to call: "I can call homicide, I can call robbery, I can call canine. If my light is out in the street, I know who to call, because Officer Virola told me who to call."

This question of trash has been a problem for Victor Hanson on his California ranch, where he thinks perhaps the notion of property rights is one the immigrants don't accept. There are garbage dumps near his property, he says, "Yet for some reason—perhaps it is an atavism from the old country where trash is everywhere dumped outside city limits?—illegal aliens still go out to the country to dump their refuse, furniture, cars, and pets on farmland."[27]

Wherever they live, be it in the country or the city, the newcomers are likely to find that their new home is not up to the standards most Americans would expect.

PART 2

"Bienvenidos" in the Heartland

CHAPTER 4

Living Here

WHEN LABOR CONTRACTOR MARIA GARCÍA AND HER FAMILY BROUGHT MEXICAN workers from Arizona to rural western New York State, they did more than enslave them. They also forced more than thirty of them to live in a single farmhouse, where eleven workers shared three beds in one room. Perhaps the García story is an extreme case, but there are other accounts of similar substandard housing. David K. Shipler describes a migrant camp in North Carolina: "There, in a weedy lot less than twenty feet from where Thanksgiving yams were grown stood the building, as dismal as a neglected barn. Long and narrow with a peaked roof, its single story had many doors, each opening into an unpainted cinder-block room resembling a cell. Each cell smelled of mold, was lit by a bare bulb on the ceiling, and contained two or three bunks, not enough for the laborers who crowded in there." The mattresses were moldy, "sticky" and "disgusting," so foul that the residents preferred to sleep on the floor for fear of getting a disease. "The farm owners usually provide housing for the migrants—either barracks like this one, run-down trailers, or dilapidated wooden farmhouses that look like shipwrecks on a horizon of tilled earth."[1]

The author and his guide, Episcopal priest Father Tony Rojas, drove by a subdivision of brick homes to "a pair of decaying houses that seemed abandoned. Screens were torn, doors were half off their hinges, the paint looked decades old; the inside was bare, dirty, gray, and dark. So many workers lived here, Father Tony said, that they slept in the hallways." At another camp, "the men's bathroom had one sink, four toilets in full view, and four showerheads in a stall too cramped for four people to shower at once. The women's bathroom had the same arrangement, with two toilets and two showerheads. It looked as if nothing had ever been cleaned or repaired. There was no privacy, no comfort, not even the quiet sense of sparse simplicity that could be found in a primitive village."

Throughout the country, immigrants are living in makeshift shelters or run-down trailers. In Colorado, workers at the Perdue Sandstone Quarry were housed in broken-down school buses, and used water from a hose for drinking and bathing, while in Siler City, North Carolina, writer Paul Cuadros reports, "a family of six was paying $450 a month for a house where the toilet constantly overflowed, the floors were soft, and there was no heat or hot water in the winter." Living conditions in such places pose health and safety issues for children, especially. A pediatrician reports that one child received a bad shock when his metal bed was on top of a live wire, and a trailer park was recently closed because of the presence of open sewage. In Rose Hill, North Carolina, four men live in an old gas station that has been converted into living space with a bare cement floor and no kitchen. The former restrooms of the station serve as bathrooms. The rent? $240 a month.[2] Residents don't often complain, however, because like employees that put up with abuse in the workplace, they're too afraid of deportation.

It's not just in the countryside that living conditions are bad. A recent *New York Times* article described the situation in one Long Island town: "Farmingville has been torn for several years as thousands of Mexicans, many of them illegal aliens, flooded into its mostly white working-class neighborhoods. Longtime residents often complain about throngs of men congregating on sidewalks, waiting to be hired for the day, and about blight they say is caused by overcrowded flophouses." In another community, with the help of the police, officials succeeded in "arresting a landlord and closing a 900-square-foot single-family house for safety violations. Inspectors said they found 44 beds and that up to 64 men had stayed there."[3] Marilyn Rosenblum of Katonah, New York, complains that in her area, landlords take advantage of immigrants, who "pay top dollar" for apartments in which twelve or fifteen people might live, "sharing dangerous spaces with poor or no heat and dreadful or nonexistent sanitary facilities."[4]

The need for adequate housing is critical throughout the country, but it is the immigrant population, especially Hispanics, who suffer the most. Statistics show that immigrant working families are almost 70 percent more likely than comparable native-born Americans to spend over half their income on housing, and Hispanics make up almost 60 percent of such families, spending "more than half their income on housing" and/or living in "severely dilapidated conditions."[5]

According to Ezra Escudero, executive director of the Ohio Commission on Hispanic/Latino Affairs, some companies will take deductions out of the immigrants' pay for company housing, even though "in some cases the company housing consists of ten single guys in a two-bedroom apartment. They'll 'hot bunk'—different shifts will come in and they'll take turns sleeping in the beds."

Because of the closeness of families, often new arrivals can move in with relatives. They're the lucky ones, like Gabriel Ruiz. He and his two brothers share an apartment in Columbus, Ohio, which is "very comfortable." But other families have been known to crowd more people into houses than the houses were ever intended for. It's a common practice in many areas.

In the fall of 2004, in what was called the deadliest residential fire in Ohio's capital city in eighty-five years, ten members of one immigrant family, including three small children, lost their lives. An eleventh person had also moved into the two-bedroom apartment but was away that night.

Escudero stresses the need for following the occupancy law. "We can't have ten people in a two-bedroom apartment. You can't overcrowd," he says. "It's not healthy, it's not safe, and it's not legal. Unfortunately we lost ten people in the fire. If you want to be grim about it, at least if they had been following the law on occupancy, maybe we would have only lost five—five additional lives would have been saved."

As in so many situations, the lack of communication made things worse. "One of the problems that came out of the fire here," he adds, "was because there was a communication breakdown between the firefighters and the victims. There have been just all kinds of awful allegations, that 'the firefighters were racist, they weren't trying to save lives, because we were pulled away from the buildings. We weren't allowed to go in and save our relatives.' The firefighters couldn't tell them, 'Look, unfortunately it's too late. There are no survivors in the building, and if you go in there, we're going to have another casualty.' That basic communication could not take place. So if there was a lack of trust before, there is now distrust between the immigrant neighborhoods and our safety officials."

Moving Inland

Communication is but one of many problems that newcomers and old-timers must address as Hispanic immigrants move inland in unprecedented numbers and populations approach exponential expansion. In 1990, roughly 88 percent of illegal immigrants lived in the "settlement states": California, New York, Texas, Illinois,

Florida, and New Jersey; but by 2004, only 61 percent lived in those six states.[6] Today Mexicans, especially, are leaving the traditional areas to head for new destinations, like the Midwest and the South. Although other areas of the country have seen more and more immigrants, too, the American South has been an unexpected beneficiary of the Mexican diaspora, due to its economic growth: "For Hispanics migrating in search of work in the 1990s, the new settlement areas of the South were particularly attractive destinations. Not only was the region's economy one of the most robust in the country, but its evolution and diversification created job opportunities that Hispanics were eager and willing to fill. Many new settlement counties in the South were adding manufacturing jobs at a time when such jobs were on the decline in most other areas, and these became a magnet for Hispanics," says a Pew Hispanic Center report.[7]

According to another report by that organization, "the rapid growth of the undocumented population has been the principal driver of growth in the foreign-born populations in new settlement states such as Arizona, North Carolina, Georgia, and Tennessee. . . . In 17 new settlement states stretching from the northwest through the mountain states to the southeast, the undocumented make up 40% or more of the total foreign-born population."[8] The 2000 Census confirmed that Latinos, whatever their legal status may be, are moving into such nontraditional destinations, eighteen of which "can be categorized as locations with 'hypergrowth' because between 1980 and 2000, the Latino population grew by more than 300 percent." Raleigh, North Carolina, for example, "experienced a jaw-dropping 1180% increase; Atlanta, Georgia, saw a 995% growth; Greensboro, North Carolina, experienced a 962% jump; and Charlotte, North Carolina, had a 932% increase in its Latino population," says Nicolas Vaca.[9] From 1990 to 2000, six southern states saw their Hispanic populations grow by, respectively, 394 percent in North Carolina; 337 percent in Arkansas, 300 percent in Georgia, 278 percent in Tennessee, 211 percent in South Carolina, and 208 percent in Alabama. Other states were not far behind: Kentucky, 173 percent; Minnesota, 166 percent; and Nebraska, 155 percent. Some counties found their Latino population increased by an incredible 1,000 percent, and many others experienced a 500 percent growth.[10] The Southeast continues to see its illegal population grow; the number of Georgia's undocumented doubled between January 2000 and January 2009.[11] With an estimated 400,000 people crossing the border every year, it has been hard to keep pace with the figures.

While it's true that we have seen unprecedented numbers of newcomers heading for the heartland, there have been some immigrants living far from the border for many years. The Immigration and Reform and Control Act of 1986 was partly responsible for adding to their numbers, as Ann Millard and Jorge Chapa discovered. Faced with stricter controls called for by the IRCA, farm workers without documentation headed for other areas, including the Midwest, in order to escape detection. "In addition," say the researchers, in another unexpected consequence of the reform bill, "the density of Mexican immigrants and other Latinos in the Southwest resulting from widespread legalization under IRCA saturated the labor market and drove down wages. This drop in wages also encouraged migration of Latinos to the Midwest."[12]

There were other reasons for the arrival of Latinos in the Midwest in the 1980s, as agricultural employers sought seasonal workers by "aggressively" recruiting in Texas and the South. A Michigan survey in 1989 revealed that at that time most migrant farm workers in the state were Mexican. Millard and Chapa note that "the 1990s saw additional changes in the landscape of the Midwest. Most significantly, employment opportunities in the meatpacking industry expanded dramatically in the rural Midwest as part of the industry's rural industrialization strategy."[13] Land was cheaper in the countryside, wages were lower where there was less of a union presence, and mechanization reduced the need for skilled employees. Rural communities often offered tax incentives in order to attract industry and improve local economies. With technological improvements for meat storage, companies no longer had to be close to their urban markets, and could benefit from locating near where food for the animals is raised. Employers found, however, that they would have to look for new sources of labor when they experienced high turnover among native-born rural workers who found their jobs too demanding, dangerous, and inadequately compensated.

As job opportunities grew, employers stepped up recruiting efforts in Mexico in order to acquire cheaper labor. One example, says Eric Schlosser, has been Iowa Beef Packers (IBP), which "maintains a labor office in Mexico City, runs ads on Mexican radio stations offering jobs in the United States, and operates a bus service from rural Mexico to the heartland of America." At least a fourth of the meatpacking workers in Iowa and Nebraska are illegal immigrants, he claims, a figure that has undoubtedly increased since his research in the first few years of this century.[14]

If opportunities for work have pulled immigrants inland, other factors have tended to push them away from the border. As competition for jobs close to the border has intensified, more hostility against the newcomers has arisen among native-born Americans, including those of Hispanic descent. "Most Mexican-Americans along the frontier support strong border enforcement," says Gregory Rodriguez. "In El Paso, for instance, a predominantly Mexican-American electorate sent Silvestre Reyes, a former high-ranking INS official, to Congress in 1996. Reyes had gained recognition as the architect of Operation Hold the Line, the labor-intensive INS strategy to prevent illegal immigration along the El Paso border. In a 1994 *El Paso Times* poll, 78 percent of local Latino respondents said they were generally in favor of Operation Hold the Line, while 17 percent opposed it."[15]

When Reyes went to El Paso as the top border agent, he found that it was difficult to apprehend illegal immigrants once they had blended in with the community. Trying to apprehend them led to harassment of people who were here legally, but who were indistinguishable from the newcomers, and so "the Border Patrol's mistakes—stopping U.S. citizens or legal immigrants and demanding that they prove their immigration status—inevitably led to complaints and lawsuits," Roberto Suro explains. People were being stopped just because of their Hispanic appearance. "'One of my major concerns in planning the operation,' Reyes said, 'was to get my agents out of the neighborhoods, out of those situations that had created so much tension with the community. My idea was that if we put our people right up on the line, they weren't going to have contact with anybody but aliens, and that turned out to be right.'" He surmised that "El Paso's Latinos would not object to a crackdown on illegal immigration as long as they did not get caught up in it." There was a decrease in crime as well as a reduction in complaints from Mexican Americans about being harassed by the Border Patrol. At the same time, says Suro, "the idea of a hard, cold barrier between the U.S. and Mexico became not only acceptable but desirable."[16]

In Arizona, the state most affected by illegal immigration, it was not only Anglo voters who were in favor of a bill to deny certain public services to illegal aliens. In November 2004, some 47 percent of Latino voters cast their ballots for Proposition 200, which passed with a 56 percent majority. Later it was overturned by a federal judge.[17]

According to a survey conducted by the Pew Hispanic Center, "a majority of Latinos born in the United States would support measures that would discourage illegal immigration by denying driver's licenses to people who are in the country illegally."[18] The survey revealed that "a majority of Latino voters—52.4%—support initiatives that would not allow the naturalization of foreigners who enter the United States illegally."[19]

Other illegals who have preceded the newcomers probably won't welcome them either, since "*the principal adverse impact is on already-resident migrants from Mexico or elsewhere,*" as researchers stressed in the binational study *Migration between Mexico and the United States.* They noted that "a simulated 20 percent increase in the number of foreign-born, low-skill Mexican workers lowered the average wage of this labor group by 3 percent, but left the wages of other labor categories almost unchanged."[20] Perhaps this is why two chambermaids in North

Carolina told me that it was not the Anglos who were hostile, but rather other Mexicans who had come before them.

Ironically, it was the government crackdowns at El Paso and at San Diego in the early '90s that increased the number of immigrants who chose to stay, since going back and forth proved too difficult. Now, says Douglas S. Massey, "migrants simply hunkered down and stayed longer once they had successfully run the gauntlet of the border." It also led to the spread of immigrants beyond the usual destinations. As they chose more risky, isolated places to cross, he adds, "the net effect of [the] billions spent on border enforcement was not to stop undocumented migration from Mexico, however, but to reduce the odds of apprehension to a 40-year low, deflect migratory flows away from California, Texas and Illinois and redirect them to 47 other states."[21]

SOME NEWCOMERS MIGHT WISH TO HEAD INLAND IN ORDER TO ESCAPE THE crime and drug problems in the border cities like Los Angeles or Houston, where the second generation, eager to assimilate, might be drawn into one of the vicious street gangs. But urban gangs have "followed the beef and chicken workers across the United States" and are "spreading the culture of alienated youth" in places like Dodge City, Kansas, and Shenandoah Valley, Virginia.[22]

The notorious and extremely vicious Salvadoran gang "Mara Salvatrucha," or "MS-13," has some 10,000 members in thirty states—1,500 members in northern Virginia alone. "They're recruiting everywhere. They're looking for people who don't belong," said Sheriff Ed Boober of West Virginia's Virginia County. "The bad thing is, once you join, you can't unjoin."[23]

Virtually no place is free of the criminal element for vulnerable newcomers, especially when they are young men without their families. Like Willie Sutton—who robbed banks because, he said, "That's where the money is"—in the Midwest communities in which meatpacking companies have set up business, "drug dealers prey on recent immigrants, and the large, transient population usually brings more crime," says Eric Schlosser.[24] As Matthew Brzezinski explains, "Alienated and isolated in what are effectively rural ghettos, many immigrant workers find solace in alcohol and are easy prey for drug dealers."[25]

Choosing a Location

Having family and friends in an area is a prime incentive for moving there. It comes as no surprise to learn that people do a lot better when they have the civilizing influence of families and a social support system to help them "learn the ropes." Hispanic churches can also help. As Leo R. Chavez found in his research, "the individuals with the fewest friends and relatives to help them find jobs and explain American culture to them were the most susceptible to having [work-related abuses.]"[26]

Once what Samuel P. Huntington calls a "beachhead" is established, more Latin Americans arrive in a community, following the first pioneers. When Southern California was no longer a "welcoming Eden," the word was spread that the Midwest, the Great Plains, and the Deep South were the places to go, says Hector Tobar. "The first pioneers arrived in these towns alone, disoriented by the strange surroundings. . . . But those who were resettled Californians and Texans brought a deeper Latino way of living with them, a strain of Latinoness toughened by time spent in those teeming Spanish-speaking places." Then they called their families in Mexico, El Salvador, and California to say, "Come, and be quick about it, because God knows how long this is going to last."[27]

Tobar tells the story of Socorro Ibarra, who arrived in Los Angeles at the age of fifteen, "but after a few disappointing and exhausting years in California—'what we found there was lies and abuse'—she joined her family in an eastward exodus. Socorro ended up in Ashland, Alabama, pioneering the route followed later by her brother Martín, who came directly from Jalisco, Mexico."[28]

Dalton, Georgia, became a popular destination among disaffected Hispanic immigrants in the border states. "Word of Dalton's good teachers and the carpeted hallways at the schoolhouse had quickly spread through the Mexican community, reaching by international mail and long-distance telephone to Zacatecas and also to San Luis Potosí and Oaxaca." In contrast, in 1996, "in California, the majority of the electorate had just voted to keep illegal immigrants out of schools. But here in Georgia, the locals' honeymoon with all things Latin American was just beginning."[29]

In rural places like Dalton, Georgia, people find they feel more at home, says Hector Tabor: "The *mexicanos* fit in because at heart they were country people like the locals, puttering around North Georgia in beat-up pickups . . . same down-home outlook. Flocelo Aguirre saw Dalton as a Dixified version of that small pueblo in rural Guerrero, Mexico, he had left many years earlier. Life was slower here, you took time for the little courtesies," and people wave from their cars as they pass by, just like in Mexico. Oldtimers in Dalton have made them welcome and are facing up to the challenges of the new arrivals.[30]

Newcomers find the reception they receive varies from place to place, however, even within the same state, but it still may be better than the treatment of those who have left rural Mexico for its cities. There they are looked down upon even more than in the United States, especially since many do not speak good Spanish. When Leo R. Chavez researched the situation of illegal Hispanic immigrants, he says, regarding one interviewee, "I had many occasions to interact with Jorge and the only time I saw him agitated was when he spoke of the treatment laborers receive from well-off Mexicans. In his view, laborers in the United States, regardless of race, receive more respect than those in Mexico.[31]

Those who expect a warm reception throughout the Midwest might be disappointed, though. Researchers Millard and Chapa found widespread "subtle and covert racism and institutional discrimination" in the communities they studied. They noted that "rural Michigan and Indiana are particularly well known for militia groups and Ku Klux Klan organizations," adding that "many Latinos in our study see racism (*racismo*) as an everyday fact of Midwestern life."[32]

The word spreads quickly about less desirable destinations. You might want to steer clear of New Ipswich, New Hampshire, a city in the news when the police "took the highly unusual step of charging Mr. [Jorge Mora] Ramirez with criminal trespassing, and held him overnight. . . . 'I wanted the federal government to understand that I was going to take some type of action,' said the New Ipswich police chief, W. Garrett Chamberlain. 'If I can discourage illegal aliens from coming to or passing through my community, then I think I've succeeded.'"[33]

Hazleton, Pennsylvania, enacted a law, later ruled unconstitutional, that would have punished landlords renting to illegal immigrants, a law that other communities—like Avon Park, Florida, and Carpentersville, Illinois—hoped to emulate. As Tom Macklin, the mayor of the Florida city said, "If we can address the housing issue—make it as difficult as possible for illegals to find a safe haven in Avon Park—then they are going to have to find someplace else to go."[34]

In some areas, day laborers are "jeered by suburbanites, harassed by Minuteman vigilantes and hounded by communities with police crack-downs, anti-loitering statutes, and mass evictions," says Lawrence Downes. "Contractors cheat them. People beat them up and fire-bomb their homes."[35] So you don't want to spend much time in places like Farmingville, New York, where immigrant laborers have been beaten, one Mexican family barely escaped when their house was set on fire, and officials evicted sixty-four men from a 900-square-foot single-family home.[36] Or in Morristown, Tennessee, where, inspired by the border Minutemen vigilante group, the Tennessee Volunteer Minutemen organization has sprung up. It is one of at least forty similar groups that were begun in emulation of the original Minuteman Project. The organization vows "to guard the United States from a wave of illegal immigration, . . . exposing those who employ illegal immigrants."[37]

The *Tennessean* newspaper in Nashville reports that "a new poll shows that negative feelings about Hispanic immigrants in Middle Tennessee are increasing."[38] Residents complain that immigrants are taking jobs away from Americans and that they are receiving government assistance. "The negative feelings about immigrants in the poll may reflect the newness of the immigrant population to Middle Tennessee rather than just poor opinions about Hispanics and other immigrants," according to Robert Wyatt, a professor at Middle Tennessee State University, who conducted the poll. "In Davidson County the Hispanic population grew more than fourfold in the past 10 years to about 26,000"; such large increases must seem threatening in themselves. The more numbers of any group there may be, the more threatening they may appear to the community: Roberto Suro notes that "resentment against the newcomers has developed only where Latinos have become a conspicuously large presence,"[39] as has been the case in Tennessee. The state's Hispanic population has tripled in the last ten years.

And yet many immigrants have been flocking to Tennessee for one reason: to get a special easy-to-obtain driver's certificate available for undocumented immigrants. Although the certificate is not valid for identification, "people are paying hundreds of dollars on the black market and traveling hundreds of miles to get one," says the *Washington Post.*[40]

Undocumented immigrants won't get a warm reception in Butler County, Ohio, where Sheriff Richard Jones has made national news with his get-tough practices and for billing the federal government for housing illegal immigrants. The bill so far amounts to $125,000. A large yellow sign near his office says, "Illegal Aliens This Way," with an arrow pointing to the jail. Unhappy about the burden on schools, social services, and law enforcement, he maintains a hot line for citizens to report those who they suspect are here illegally. When illegal drivers don't have insurance, he says, "you and I have to pay for it, so it's costing us every single day we do nothing, and the numbers continue to increase. We have to do something, and I agree they either have to go to prison, they have to go to jail. If you ship them back to the country where they came from and they come back again, they're going to go to prison. Let them go to some other country, or some other state. I don't care where they go."

Yet in the Columbus, Ohio, area, less than a two-hour drive away, undocumented resident Pedro Cortés says that it is people who make a place livable. He likes everything about his community except the weather; it never got this cold where he lived in Mexico.

In Atlanta, with its estimated Hispanic population of some 100,000, people are "very nice," says Carlos Martinez, but in some areas of Georgia, he says,

the people are really bad. For example, over there in Gainesville—the Ku Klux Klan is still there—less than one hour from here, they are really terrible people. They are the most terrible people. One day my brother was driving over there, and the police stopped him. They asked him for his license. He showed the license, but he showed a North Carolina license, and the policeman said, "This license is not good. Go to jail!" They put my brother in jail! We went to the court, and I talked to the judge. I said, "For what reason did the police put him in jail? Because he has a license," and he said, "But that license is not good." And I said, "It's good, because it is from the United States and it's from North Carolina." "Yes, but it's not good here. Do you want to go to jail or do you want to leave right now?" The judge said, "You are free to go, or do you want to stay in jail?" We left. We don't want to be in trouble, because the people in Gainesville are bad people, very scary. They really abuse everyone, not only Latinos. They abuse other cultures, too.

With all the reports of hostility, it's refreshing to read about events in Marshall, Missouri, where a civic volunteer and church leader known as Manuel "Poco" Lopez offered to help the police with interrogating a Spanish-speaking murder suspect. When it was revealed that Poco was actually an illegal immigrant named Francisco Xavier Inzunza, the whole town, including the mayor, police chief, school superintendent, and prosecutor, rallied around him to keep him in Marshall.

One of the main considerations for choosing a location is the cost of living. Here's where the South comes into its own, especially Arkansas, even if newcomers may not always feel welcome. As a worker named Alejandro says, "Outside, we are Mexicans, but it is different. We're still screwed, but in a different way. We are foreigners. We don't belong. At least here in the plant, we belong, even if we are exploited. Outside, we live better than in Mexico; but we do not belong, we are not from here and keep to ourselves."[41] And as "Tyson Foods pays $8 an hour, offers insurance, and consistently offers forty hours of work a week," one can live with the "overwhelming sounds, sights and smells" of their production line.[42]

Meanwhile, America must deal with the immigrants and the stresses they put on social services. Even though many come without their families, with a higher birthrate among Hispanics than among other population groups, it was projected that by 2007 the "Latino school enrollment in the six Southern states [would] increase by 210 percent while the number of all non-Hispanic students [would increase] by a mere 2 percent."[43] The next chapter looks at how many communities are facing the challenges presented by the vast influx of Hispanics.

CHAPTER 5

Community Reaction

WHILE SOME STATES ARE LOOKING FOR WAYS TO REDUCE THE NUMBERS OF THOSE arriving illegally, at the same time virtually all of them have offices dedicated to dealing with the newcomers already here, as do many communities. In North Carolina, for example, its Children's Services Division works to educate social workers about "the growing number of Latinos [who] are calling North Carolina home." It urges child welfare workers, rather than adding to the pressure of adaptation, to learn about their culture and "find out how they have traditionally solved problems."[1]

Although many communities are striving to face the challenges, there is still more to be done, say leaders like Charles Short of the Catholic Archdiocese of Washington, DC. He hopes that a planned—and long overdue—community center in Langley Park, Maryland, 65 percent of whose residents are Latino, will serve as a model for the rest of the country. A report issued by the National Conference for Community and Justice in the Lexington, Kentucky, area notes that "our businesses, government, faith communities and social service agencies have responded at first with denial, secondly with benign neglect and most recently by making small individual attempts to address the issues that confront us. In our opinion, we have been putting band-aids on a heart attack." The report describes the abuses that immigrant workers have suffered, and calls out for more financial and legal support for a vulnerable workforce. "One very disturbing example was the story of the construction worker who died recently. We did not even know his name; *we did not even know his name!* The last time we exploited people for their labor, without knowing their names, we called it slavery," say the authors.[2]

According to a report by a University of Tennessee researcher, the "volunteer state" has been slower to recognize its problems and how to confront them than have its neighboring states of Georgia and North Carolina, but "in the last several years, private institutions, local governments, and practitioners in the fields of health care, social work, and legal services have begun to take stock of the state's changing demographics."[3]

In my own city of Dayton, Ohio, information is available in Spanish on every conceivable topic. The division of housing inspection asks, "Are you infringing?" in its pamphlet on the twelve regulations concerning yards; the garbage collection department gives details on its services; the Ohio Consumers' Counsel covers public utilities; Children's Services offers information for its clients; the Red Cross lists equipment to have in case of a disaster; the State of Ohio's Paternity Enhancement Program explains how to establish paternity; the IRS has notices in Spanish on how to claim reimbursement for Earned Income Credit; and there is information on how to get Medicare and other medical services. Such materials are available through churches, community centers, and at Mexican restaurants. It's easy to obtain a Spanish language newspaper, like *Midwest Latino*, which is distributed in Ohio, Kentucky, Indiana, Pennsylvania, and Michigan; *La Voz* and *El Mundo* in Kentucky; *Mundo Hispánico* in Georgia; *Mundo Hispano* in Tennessee; *La Noticia* in the Carolinas; and many others.

Dayton's Latino Connection must have been one of the first on the scene to recognize and respond to the challenge. John Pawelski, a major force behind its establishment, describes how it came about:

In March of 2001, I was working fulltime at the Dayton Police Department. We had a lot of contact with Latinos, and we realized that there was no place for anybody to go with problems. If a Latino came in and had proper documentation, visa, or whatever and said, "I went down to pay my water bill and nobody speaks Spanish there. What do I do?" there was no place to turn. If you called the Dayton Police Department, there was no organized system to get a translator. If they'd called and said, "I don't speak any English, but I need the police," generally you would send it out as domestic violence. You hear a bunch of stuff going on in the background, so I'm going to send two crews out and see what's going on. But there was no system, there was no group in place. There were a lot of individuals who cared, but there was nothing—I couldn't send anybody anywhere. Somebody needs a job, somebody needs translation, whatever, I had no place to go with that.

John contacted his major, who agreed that something had to be done. After receiving encouragement from the major, he turned to his sergeant, who, saying that John was the one with the tools that were needed—the knowledge of the language and culture—offered to help in any way. John relates what happened next:

> So that's when we started the Latino Connection, in March of 2001. I went to fifteen different leaders. I specifically targeted people who had reputations of getting things done. I didn't go to organizations, I went to individuals, and I said, "Would you be interested in being part of a group where we would meet once a month and just discuss what the issues are, how we can help, rely on each other, bounce things off each other, help each other out?" And I picked out somebody from the schools, somebody from the priority board, somebody from the city, a couple of city representatives . . .

At a typical meeting today, about fifty people might attend, representing organizations like the Family Services Association; Community Health Services' health centers for children; Vectren, the power company; the public library, which offers information on materials in Spanish and for learning English; Artemis, which works against domestic violence; CARE, a group that combats child abuse; a community college teacher who is touting the school's program for skilled trades; a sociology professor who wants to make an announcement on predatory lending; the Hispanic Chamber of Commerce, which promotes Latino-owned businesses; Protestant and Catholic churches, which make available food and clothing; as well as a Hispanic AA group. The city's Division of Housing Inspection, the homeless shelter, the free clinic, the medical school, and several attorneys are also represented.

One attorney brought up the case of schools that are demanding social security numbers before students can be registered. Officer Pawelski agreed to call and set them straight. The latter problem is something with which John has had experience:

> We had a court case where a Latino gentleman was given a jail sentence, which was later suspended, because he would not make his son go to school. It was truancy, he was warned. They said, "It's suspended as long as you make sure he shows up for school." So somebody brought it to my attention that it's hard to get registered. I called up the school, and I talked with a Mexican accent, and I said, "I need to put my son in school. I not have all documentation, but I leeve here in Dayton. What do I do?"
>
> "I'm sorry, Sir, we can't help you with that. If you don't have a social security number, your child can't go to school."

"Well, they tell me sometheeng about the federal law . . ." I went into this kind of thing.

They said, "No, if you don't have a social security number, can't do it."

So I said, "OK, can I have your name? And then I need to speak with your supervisor." Then when they got the supervisor on the phone, I spoke regular English. I said, "I'm John Pawelski, president of the Latino Connection. I'm with the Police Department, and we have a situation here. Our judges are telling people they'll go to jail if they don't send their kids to school, and you're telling them they can't put them in school. Something's got to give here." . . . She said, "Let me check into this," and to her credit, she got back with me, and she said, "I don't know what that person was thinking. Yes, we'd love to do whatever we have to do to get him registered. If we need some translators, we'll get that taken care of." Once they realized, you see. Up until then, though, you have a Latino family that comes up with three kids and they try to get registered, and they're told, "No! Can't do it. Don't do it here. If you don't have a social security number, can't go to school." And the parents say, "OK" and walk away. You see, they don't know.

People began to realize, "You know what? We've been wrong here." And they've changed and now, every year the School Board has at least two or three places where they have Spanish-speaking folks to register the people who come in.

With the increase in the Latino population in Jackson, Wyoming, a similar forum was established in the spring of 2007 to meet the challenge, inspired in part by such groups in Michigan, Minnesota, and Colorado, and aided by a conflict-resolution organization. James Wolfe, a management consultant and member of the task force, describes what a challenge it has been, as schools and health services have become overburdened with the surge in the new population. Wyoming as a whole saw its Hispanic population increase by 12.8 percent from the 2000 Census to July 1, 2006, and nearby eastern Idaho went from a total of 309 foreign workers in 1997 to almost 90,000 in 2006. Jim is concerned about the long-term effects of such changes. Will the third generation truly assimilate, as has been true of immigrants in the past, when they live in an all-Hispanic community, as is the case in Jackson? The task force's research so far indicates that many of the strengths that families arrive with—good health, a strong work ethic, ambition for the future, close family ties—erode over time. Although those in the tourist industry in this resort town welcome the workers, what will be the long-term effects when 70 percent come with less than a high school education, and at least half don't speak English? And who will pay for the services they require? Jim notes that in the United States "you've got the preponderance of the tax paid by a relatively few people. The bottom half of the population pays a very small portion of the total taxes." One report indicates that while immigrants do pay taxes, those taxes are likely to go to the federal treasury, while the cost for education, criminal justice, and emergency medical care for illegal immigrants comes from state and local coffers. Jim is also concerned about how we can motivate non-Hispanic young people to work. He, too, sees a lack of work ethic among today's American youth. These are the kinds of questions that the forum will be considering as they work toward practical solutions that are best for the whole community. Jim would welcome a national referendum to see just how Americans as a whole feel about the subject.

Schools

In Dalton, Georgia, Hector Tobar reports, Latinos make up over half the school-age population; in the school that Tobar visited, 80 percent of the student body were Hispanic.[4] Since the town was unable to recruit bilingual teachers from the big cities, they now send their staff down to Mexico to learn Spanish. It's expensive, says Dr. Frankie Beard, the principal at Roan Elementary School, "but the people here think it's important."[5] The teachers use a mixture of English and Spanish. In Dalton, which spends more than $7,400 per student, schools are funded by the one hundred-plus carpet factories where the parents work. Erwin Mitchell, who is cofounder of the "Georgia Project," which helps new arrivals assimilate, believes that "the factories need the workers, and the workers come with families. . . . Without good schools for the workers' children, the county would leave itself wide open to a whole host of social problems down the road. Giving Dalton's Mexican kids a decent education was the sensible thing to do, 'pure self-interest.'"[6]

The jury is still out on how best to integrate children labeled with "limited English proficiency" (ELP) into the school system. It's become an important question as nationally the population of Hispanic children has increased so dramatically, between 1993 and 2003—by some 1.6 million in public elementary schools.[7] It is up to the states to decide which method they will use, and there is a patchwork of programs. While some states mandate bilingual education, others forbid it. Some states have chosen—or been forced by legal decisions to choose—an English immersion approach. Funding for such programs varies, too.

Since November 2000, when voters approved "the most restrictive English-only education law in the country,"[8] in Arizona public schools non-English-speakers have been part of an English-only program. This means everything—textbooks and all materials, including bulletin boards, as well as instruction—must be in English. Due to lack of progress in the language, students in that state "start behind and stay behind," claim their teachers. They assert that the best way for them to learn would be if they were taught in both English and their native language, but that would be against the law.[9]

Bilingual education, in which children receive instruction in their native language, is also controversial. Those who oppose it say that children taught that way are distanced from their new culture and fail to learn its language, making it more difficult to assimilate. Those who support bilingual education claim that students are better able to progress in "content" courses, like science and math, if they are taught in their native language, leading to more self-confidence and pride in their heritage.[10]

Since I live in what's been called the quintessentially typical American city, I wanted to see what was happening in my own backyard.

Lourdes de Pilar Otero Lambert is the Cuban-born head of Dayton's East End Community School, whose student body of 180 is 20 percent Hispanic. The method that has worked for the school in its four years of existence has been total immersion, but with help in Spanish as needed. As Lourdes says, "We plunge them in. We let them sit in the English class throughout the day. We try to have bilingual programs available. If they have questions on what to do, we then give them directions in Spanish. And we have Spanish classes for the whole school, so that means other kids can learn to communicate with the Spanish-speaking children as well. One of our teacher's aides is bilingual—she used to live in Chile—but she can't be in every class. We do all carry around walkie-talkies, and either she or I will go and help. It has worked out just fine."

I asked what happens when an older child enters the school not speaking English, but it is a problem that has not yet arisen. "Most of our children have come in through kindergarten," Lourdes says, "and by the end of kindergarten, they've been bilingual."

One advantage in having a bilingual director, says Lourdes, is that all of the school's newsletters are bilingual. "I think it's nice for the parents so they don't feel so intimidated by school, especially if we're talking about parents who may be illegal. It's already frightening to be in a country where you may be deported, and then you don't want to get involved in your child's school, because you don't know what's going on, because you can't understand the paperwork. So we've tried to make it more friendly for the parents to be a part of their child's education, because you know, without the parents, we can't be successful with the child."

Lourdes favors their English-only program, because, she says, "A lot of the desire to learn has to come from a need, and if you need to communicate—and I think that's a good point for our immersion program—the children feel an urgency because they feel a need to communicate. I think sometimes if you make them feel comfortable, they don't have that urgency and they don't want to learn."

Nolan Graham, the principal of a large elementary school in the same city, has a different system for the 17 percent of its students who lack English proficiency. "We have two ESL teachers," he says, "and an ESL interpreter, and in this building we actually have four teachers who speak Spanish. One of the ESL teachers, Mr. Keene, works with the kindergarten, first-, second-grade children. He pulls them out for forty-five minutes a day, and in his class he teaches them math, he teaches them language arts. Then they go back into the regular setting. At kindergarten we have a teacher who speaks Spanish fluently, and all the Spanish kids who come into kindergarten are in her classroom, so she understands them, they understand her, and she teaches English and math, in Spanish and English. Mr. Todd, a first-grade teacher, speaks Spanish fluently. There it's the same thing. All the ESL children are in his class. Most of them are Hispanic."

Most, but not all classes can boast a teacher who speaks Spanish. Now Graham is interviewing and hiring more teachers who can speak Spanish, as the number of Latino children has been increasing. His goal is to have a Spanish-speaking teacher at each grade level, for, he thinks, "that is the only way you can truly, truly overcome the barrier, the best way to overcome the barrier—probably there is no ideal way.

"In the seventh grade they're compartmentalized—those kids have a math teacher, a science teacher, an art teacher, gym teachers. If at that grade level you have one teacher who's fluent, then that teacher can help with any kind of issues, but in this building, ironically, most of the kids who speak Spanish in the 7th grade by now speak English, because they've grown up here—we've had the program here now for four years. The main ones that have difficulties here are the ones in K-one, two, and three. But once they've been here three or four years, they're picking up English on the playground and in art classes, in gym classes, in the classroom and so forth."

"What happens if a child comes in in the seventh grade not speaking English?"

"We have them. We place the student in that Spanish teacher's homeroom, and she's assigned to that teacher, although she does go from class to class, usually every hour she has to move to a class. Now we give them a buddy system, where the one Latino child who speaks good English is assigned to that new child that does not speak English. You'd be surprised. Within a month—a month! The thing is most of those parents don't speak English, and then the children become the interpreters for the parents."

"And that's not always good."

"They tell the parents what they want to hear."

Mr. Graham is proud of the Spanish class at the school:

We're one of only two elementary schools in Dayton that have a foreign language class. It's for everybody, for English-speaking children, as well as Latinos. When the Spanish-speaking children go to Spanish class, they're there with white and African

American children who speak English, and the Spanish teacher teaches the Latinos English at the same time that she's teaching children Spanish, and to be honest with you, as the Latino children are becoming friends with the African Americans, with the white Appalachians, they're learning their language, and that's really helping them out, much faster. . . . Ironically, we have a number of English-speaking parents, African Americans and Appalachians, who bring their children here because they want them to learn Spanish.

Mr. Graham anticipates greater and greater numbers of Hispanic students, but he says, "I don't see a problem. I think it's a blessing. I really do. If you really want to raise your children in a multiethnic environment, Patterson-Kennedy School is the place to do it, because we have probably about ten different nationalities attending here."

Among the three choices available—bilingual education in which classes are taught in Spanish, total immersion in English, or a transition from one to the other—Jean Wagner would opt for the third. Jean has twenty years experience teaching English as a Second Language in a large suburban school in Centerville, Ohio. She explains that every school system has a choice. "They can do it on a professional basis where they hire professional teachers or they can do it on a volunteer basis. . . . In Centerville we're very lucky," she says, "because we do have the money to spend on them. And in the elementary and middle schools and high schools they have a group of teachers who are all certified."

Its ESL program has such a good reputation that families have been known to lie about their residency in order to get children enrolled in the school. "These folks will come in and say, 'This is my nephew so-and-so, and he's living with us,' and they enroll him in school. Then such students get put into the ESL program and they get a lot of extra help and support, and then you begin to realize that they're not related at all to the people they're living with. . . . It gets very involved, and it is not our job as educators to try to sort that out."

Instead, she focuses on her job:

What we do is first of all, we identify the kids that need help and then, depending on what age level they are or what school they're in, we set them up with a program and they are put in the regular classrooms and they're taken out for specialized time alone, one-on-one or two-on-two or whatever, with an ESL tutor. . . . Maybe it's just an hour a day, but that tutor will work with the child's homeroom teacher or math teacher or English teacher or second-grade teacher or whatever it is, and work with that teacher to set up some kind of an educational plan for that child and then make sure that they're in the gym class, or the music class, or the art class with the other kids. When those other kids are learning English may be the time that that child is taken out of the classroom and given specialized, individualized help in learning English. At the high school level, we try to get them in some of the more basic classes if we can, although we don't like to take that specialized help away from the American kids that need it. . . . I think that when a child starts school in the U.S., whether they're starting in third grade or fifth grade or ninth grade, they need to be in totally English-speaking classrooms, and then they need to have support and they need to have help learning English. I think when you isolate them in ESL programs, the English that they learn is second class.

If the language skills of Jean's student José are any indication, Centerville must be doing something right. He is quite fluent in almost accentless English, in spite of the fact that he knew not a word when he arrived after his harrowing journey from Ecuador.

I wondered about the possibility of expanding such a program throughout the country. It would be possible, says Jean, but expensive. And there's the rub. Can we justify spending taxpayers' money on special treatment for immigrants, especially illegal ones—or the children of illegal immigrants? In Arizona, where then governor Janet Napolitano proposed spending $45 million a year to expand English-language instruction in public schools, some taxpayers balked at the cost. Others feared that enhancing public services would attract more immigrants.[11]

In the meantime there is a lot of interest in Spanish classes for native English speakers. As one mother of a kindergartener in Oregon says, "The way that society is now, it's almost imperative that you speak Spanish," and she hopes that her daughter will later pick up a third language.

It is the question of the English language that looms most important as new-comers adjust to American society, for a knowledge of English is one of the few things that unite us, as well as an important rung on the ladder to success. For this reason, parents are generally against bilingual education, which too often is closer to monolingual—in Spanish. As one New York mother said through an interpreter, "I'm very angry. . . . The school is supposed to do what's best for the kids. The school puts my kids' education in danger because everything is in English here,"[12] which the children are not learning when everything is taught in Spanish.

On the other hand, some parents would prefer bilingual classes in order to be more involved with their children's education. Parental involvement is "a huge issue," says Dr. Pedro A. Noguera, director of the Metropolitan Center for Urban Education at New York University, and one that educators recommend as a "cure for dropout rates, poor test scores and almost everything else that ails schoolchildren."[13]

As for the parents themselves, English language classes at no charge are easily available—if you're not working two or more jobs and if you can arrange transportation, that is. YMCAs and community centers, as well as a number of churches, have stepped up to meet the need.

Churches

Gone are the days when the American Catholic church saw its fellow Christians from south of the border as "less than fully Catholic," and when Mexicans themselves "felt considerable distrust" toward the U.S. Church as an elite organization.[14] Today's Catholic churches have taken the lead in assisting the newcomers, most of whom are Catholic.

Stephanie Tristan of Catholic Social Services is very knowledgeable about the kinds of work permits for which immigrants might be eligible, and different ways to obtain documentation. "There are a number of people out there that are undocumented who could get documentation," she says. "They just don't know"—as in the case of a Mexican gentleman who has been married to an American woman for several years. "They have never filed paperwork, either because they didn't know they could, somebody told them they couldn't, or they just couldn't afford an attorney. . . . Part of my job here is that I write a little blurb, like a one-paragraph thing, once a month that I send to a number of churches in the area that have Spanish Masses. They put it in their bulletin, just as a way to educate and say, 'Hey, you might have a way to become legal. Why don't you come on in and we'll talk about it.'" She explains also that even though you may be here illegally, you still have rights, as in the case of domestic violence or abuse in the workplace.

In 2005 Catholic bishops in the United States joined with twenty Roman Catholic organizations—encompassing health-care providers, universities, and charities—to initiate "Justice for Immigrants: A Journey of Hope. The Catholic Campaign for Immigration Reform." In addition to advocating for just immigration laws, the campaign stressed the positive aspects of immigration and sought to make immigrants aware of their legal rights.[15] More recently, the U.S. Conference of Catholic Bishops called for a stop to massive federal raids of workplaces employing immigrants, going so far as to ask immigration agents "who oppose the raids on moral grounds to sidestep their duties."[16]

In Kentucky, "churches have seen Hispanics breathe new life into congregations that were dying," the *Louisville Courier-Journal* claims. According to Rev. Tom Smith, who directs the Hispanic ministries program at St. Rita Catholic Church in Louisville, Kentucky, churches have become more than centers of worship. They now fill a social need for the Hispanic community, helping with such things as housing, employment, medical care, and translations.[17]

Sister Maria Stacy heads the Hispanic Ministry in Dayton. With twenty years of experience as a Spanish teacher, she is called to help in many ways, as when she accompanied a man who had been driving without a license to help him pay his fine.

She bristles over the inequities. "The woman at the desk who took his money said, 'Boy, we're really robbing these people, aren't we?' In the sense that we're getting all this money from their not having driver's licenses, but we don't allow them to even have the possibility of getting one."

Sister Maria handles a variety of tasks. When I spoke with her, she was involved with arranging for a man, here illegally, to return to Mexico for the funeral of his twelve-year-old daughter and be able to return to his job.

She dreams of the day when borders will have no need to exist, reciting one of her favorite quotations, from T. H. White's *The Once and Future King*. King Arthur envisions a better world in which there would be no borders: "The imaginary lines on the earth's surface only needed to be unimagined."

Sister Maria refers me to the joint pastoral letter concerning migrants issued by the Catholic bishops of Mexico and the United States. With many biblical references on welcoming the stranger, they call for the presidents of both countries to "achieve a system of migration" that will be "more generous, just, and humane." Pope John Paul II's 1999 *Ecclesia in America*, say the bishops, "reiterates the rights of migrants and their families and the respect for human dignity 'even in cases of non-legal immigration.'" Immigrants, no matter what their legal status may be, should not be treated as criminals, they assert.[18]

"Never again!" cried Rev. Gerald F. Kicanas, the Roman Catholic bishop who visited a Mexican staging point for would-be border crossers, where he compared the barracks to Germany's concentration camps. "It is one thing to develop homeland security to deter terrorists. It is quite another to treat innocent people as less than human," he wrote in a Catholic publication.[19]

Catholics are not the only ones concerned about conditions for migrants. Articles in the *Mennonite Review* and *Episcopal Life* are among those that call attention to the problems migrants encounter. Rev. Thomas Buechele and Rev. M. Lucie Thomas are Episcopal priests in Arizona who have accompanied groups of their denomination to witness firsthand what immigrants must go through, and to pay their respects at a monument to the more than 2,500 people who have lost their lives in the desert. An interfaith mission composed of 150 Roman Catholic, Protestant, Jewish, and Muslim leaders of Arizona is also addressing the problem. As Maggie Burnett reports, "The faith leaders stressed that engaging in dialogue with legislators does not mean acting against the law. Rather, they said, they want to assist those responsible for the law, as well as provide humanitarian aid and general understanding to migrants in need."[20]

Rick Uffort-Chase, head of the U.S. Presbyterian Church, is another activist for the cause of improving conditions for those who would cross the border. He, too, is seeking a solution to the problem. "Our immigration policy stinks to high heaven," he says."[21] He is founder of BorderLinks, which works to improve the economic relationship between the United States and Latin America, as well as help people who want to cross the border. He is also an active member of Humane Borders, a volunteer organization that puts water in the desert for travelers, and of Samaritan, a search-and-rescue group.

Once arrived in the community, the newcomers find that there are churches eager to welcome them. A listing of congregations in the Columbus, Ohio, area contains over a dozen places of worship where services are held in Spanish—four of which are Catholic. Many would be described as Pentecostal.

A phenomenon new to the heartland is the G-12 or "cell" church. It's a system that has come to America from South Korea by way of Colombia, where Rev. Cesar Castellanos adapted the movement with great success. Members of the organization meet in small groups in private homes. Such "cells" are headed by "leaders" trained in Christian beliefs and leadership skills. G-12 churches have been highly successful in the Hispanic community especially, since "smaller groups that allow for one-to-one interaction appeal to the Hispanic sense of family. . . . They also help new immigrants to feel a sense of belonging in a strange land," reports the *Wall Street Journal*'s Andrea Tunarosa.[22]

According to Richard Korn, who is head of the Southern Ohio Episcopal Ministry, about 85 percent of the 50,000 Latinos in the Columbus area have no church connections. "We are reaching out to the unchurched," he says—"to those who are not particularly going into any particular community, but searching. And it's amazing how they admit they're searching. They recognize that their lives are not full and complete. And God is found here even before they get here, God is ahead of them, God invites them, God draws them here." Dick, a former Roman Catholic priest, works with an Episcopal church to offer computer classes, as well as English lessons. Although no services have been held in Spanish yet, his wife copies the plan of service from English to Spanish so that Spanish-speaking participants can follow along. Fluent in Spanish and Portuguese, he spends about fifty to eighty hours a month interpreting, and anticipates that he will soon be interpreting the church services.

Medical Care

Schools, social-service organizations, and health-care providers for the most part follow a "don't ask, don't tell" policy when it comes to those they serve. When a patient comes to the emergency room, says Bill Thornton of the Miami Valley Hospital, they're not asked for their green card. "If you're sitting there bleeding or have a major condition that needs treatment, we're not going to throw you out. We're not going to send you to Immigration and tell them, 'You take care of it.'" And he feels sure that "even if it's not illegal not to treat illegal immigrants, most hospitals and most physicians, when a person comes to your door in need of care, are not going to say, 'I can't do it. The door's closed.'"

Although patient representatives Chris Green and Paula Burton do not ask to know their patients' legal status, they say,

> Our sense is that the vast majority of them are illegal, just because they provide names that are incorrect, they provide addresses that are not correct, they lie about social security numbers. . . . We've actually had people who have gone to agencies that advocate for them and said, "If I go to the hospital and seek treatment, are they going to turn me in?" And of course that's not what we're here to do. We're here to care for them, and we have to get that message out: "Don't not come because you're afraid we'll turn you in."
>
> A patient safety issue is the sharing of social security numbers or making them up, because when they use someone else's social security number, they come and they say, "Here's my number." We pull it up and we get Maria Gonzalez instead of Elena García, and they say, "Yeah, that's me." Now if you're treating me with Maria Gonzalez's records and I'm allergic to penicillin and Maria isn't, you think I'm not allergic to penicillin because her records say I'm not. Now all my information's on her, so if she comes, not only have you put her health care in jeopardy, you've also put my health care in jeopardy.

Chris and Paula see their job in many ways as that of education, informing immigrants of the dangers in such fake ID and directing them to the medical services they might need, as at free clinics. They agree that their business is to help people. "Very rarely do we turn people away," although they do have to draw the line sometimes when they feel that people are taking advantage of the system.

"Barbara" is a postpartum nurse at a satellite hospital who resents the fact that there is an increasing number of patients who don't speak English. In such cases it takes time to get an interpreter and communicate when there is a possibility of after-birth complications, or to explain post-circumcision care. "If you are spending so much time in that room," she says, "you have to be negligent in your care of the other patients." Her "pet peeve," she admits, is people who come to this country and don't speak English. She also resents the high cost of interpreter services for which the hospital is not reimbursed. She finds some customs irritating, too, like the fact that so many family members want to be with the expectant mother at the hospital.

Growing numbers of Hispanic immigrants have meant an added expense for interpreter services at Miami Valley Hospital, too. It is now in the process of setting up an on-site interpreter service, which they hope will reduce costs that have run from $300,000 to $400,000 annually. This expense is what is called an "unfunded mandate"; the federal government requires that the hospital make available interpreter services for its non-English-speaking patients, expenses for which they are not reimbursed.

The *Courier-Journal* reports that in Kentucky, the medical needs of Hispanic immigrants "are especially daunting." Susan Fister, director of the Bluegrass Farmworker Health Center, which operates clinics in Lexington and Richmond funded primarily by grants, says that with their limited resources "there is not enough money to do much more than primary care and some prevention programs."[23]

So far, hospitals in the heartland seem to be managing to keep from going under. Doctors Michael Arnold Glueck and Robert J. Cihak, however, quote an "old axiom" that "what happens in California is a precursor to what happens in the rest of nation." If that's the case, we may be heading for trouble, because, they say, "a study by the Federation for American Immigration Reform estimated that in 2004 the annual uncompensated cost of medical care for illegal immigrants in California was $1.4 billion, and total uncompensated educational, health care, and incarceration costs were estimated to be 10.5 billion."[24] As it is, some border hospitals have been forced to curtail services.[25]

In Los Angeles County, it's estimated that $349 million is spent each year to treat illegal immigrants; "the county is considering hospital closures to deal with a budget shortfall."[26] Texas has struggled with the cost of medical care for its undocumented residents as well. In Harris County, in which Houston is located, about one-fifth of those seeking treatment were illegal immigrants, costing the county $97.3 million in 2005.[27]

At the present time, $250 million a year in federal funds is available to reimburse states for emergency health care for undocumented patients.[28] A $1 billion program is planned to offer more compensation for those who treat illegal immigrants. In order to receive the money, however, hospitals will have to ask patients about their immigration status. It's a move that medical service providers fear will deter those who need it from seeking emergency care, which could lead to "serious public health problems, including the spread of communicable diseases."[29] A new concern is diseases that immigrants bring across the border and that American doctors are no longer familiar with: tuberculosis, for one. Or Chagas' disease, and who has ever heard of that? And yet as many as 100,000 Hispanic immigrants may have brought with them this potentially fatal parasite, which affects up to 11 million people in Latin America.[30]

Another unexpected problem for Americans: When new federal regulations for Medicaid aimed at keeping illegal immigrants off the rolls went into effect in 2007 requiring stricter proof of citizenship, "tens of thousands" of citizens, including many young children, were unable to get the prompt treatment they needed. The search for proof of citizenship in the form of birth certificates or other documents, a backlog of applications, and even the cost of the required documents created obstacles to delay their care.[31]

Police

Those who handle law enforcement have been in the forefront in recognizing the need to communicate with the rising number of Spanish-speaking persons. John Pawelski has offered an eight-hour course to over four hundred officers in Ohio: "We do some culture and we do a little bit of just phonetics so that they're able to read. One of the things we've found across the board—and we've taught correction officers, judges, and bailiffs—is that their heart is in the right place. They don't want to do these people wrong. They want to do what's right. They just don't know the situation."

Sometimes problems with the police arise from simple misunderstandings. John speaks of the common mistake of seeing "exp" on a Mexican driver's license and assuming it stands for "expired," when actually it means *expedido*, "issued." (The word for expired in Spanish is *vencido*.) "We had a situation," he says, "where they put a gentleman in jail because they said his license had been expired for five months. They called us and we talked to them and said, 'No, it hasn't. It was actually issued five months ago; it expires five years down the road.' And actually you do have to honor Mexican licenses. The United States does not require an international driver's license.

Officer Pawelski gives another example of how the police might need to use a different approach with the Hispanic community:

> The Latino countries look at domestic violence totally different from how we do. When we go to a house, our natural tendency as police officers is to side with the victim, "Where's the lady?" And the guy comes up, "Well, you don't need to talk with her."
>
> "Let me tell you something, Buddy. I'm not your wife. I'll hit you back. Now sit down and shut up." Because they've called big brother now. Big brother's here to protect her—usually it's the female that's the victim—so we make it a point to say, "Look, we're in control here. You no longer run the show."
>
> But in a Latino family, if I walk in and just ask for the wife immediately, I have insulted not only the man who did the striking, I have insulted their entire culture, because I have not respected that home enough to talk to the man of the house. We tell people, "Now look, if they're laying there bleeding, you don't sit there and go through. . . . Offend them. Do what you've got to do. But if we're not talking about a situation like that, maybe talk to the man and have one of the officers say to him, "We're here on a

domestic violence call. We need to speak with your wife. The law requires us to do that, but is there anything that you want to tell us, or is there any information . . . ?" And if he gets belligerent from there, then that's fine, but even then, even if he ends up having to go to jail, he will be much more respectful to those officers. And see, the bottom line is we know it takes seven times for somebody to press charges, so chances are that's not going to go anywhere, but that person's still in our neighborhood, that family still lives in our neighborhood, and now when we go down to ask about a homicide that occurred down the road, what does the Martinez family do? Well, they know the police system. They don't want to talk to the police. "You come out and disrespect me every time we have a problem, you come out and disrespect our whole culture, but now you want information, stuff I know? No, don't know anything, haven't seen anything, have a nice day."

Whereas the other officer who walks up and says, "Mr. Martinez, here's what we're going to have to do. We've got to talk to your wife . . . those are our rules." OK, talk to him: "Mr. Martinez, I've got to take you down to jail. If she doesn't press charges, that's up to her, but here's what we have to do to proceed." You know what? Two months later, when there's a homicide, "Mr. Pawelski, you nice to me. Come here, I tell you information."

"Those are things that we try to educate our police officers on," he continues. "Don't just do it the way you were brought up. Adapt to those things, and those are things you're not giving up safety to do, but you can respect that so much more and get so much more out of those interactions there. That's one of the things that through the Latino Connection we've been able to do." And through his three-day courses in Spanish language and culture that can give students a working knowledge in order to communicate in emergency situations. In the classes, students learn that cultural misunderstandings can arise from such simple things as Mexican ideas of politeness, according to which you look down rather than look someone in the eye, and you say "yes, yes, yes" whether you mean it or not, he explains.

Officer Minerva Virola in Kentucky is conducting much the same kind of programs. As the first Spanish-speaking female in the whole department, she proposed an officer-safety lesson plan. "We're teaching them about our religion, our communication, how to communicate, our gestures, how to approach the Latino, how to defuse the situation vs. escalating. When I started eleven years ago this technique was new. Now it's expanded, it's everywhere. So my stuff has been all over the place, we have made copies of it, and that's OK with me, because my main message was to make sure that the message was out there for the officers, for their safety, and of course with their experience they expanded it even more." Their course has included a two- to five-week stay in Mexico to learn even more about the Mexican culture and language.

Officer Virola agrees that it's important to remember that the man in the family is the head of the house. "I don't expect an officer to go into someone's house and start talking to a child," she says, "just because the child is bilingual. You'd better address the father, because he's the head of the house, even though he only speaks Spanish. Now if he's the one who caused the problem, as officers we know how to defuse the situation. So you try to save face for the head of the house. So we don't put handcuffs on him in front of the house, we don't have him walk out of the house without his shoes."

In Tennessee, too, where the Hispanic population has tripled in the last decade, police officers are learning about the culture of the newcomers, since, in both urban and rural areas, law enforcement officers "increasingly find the need to speak Spanish." Recognizing this need, in 2003 the Governor's Highway Safety Office awarded a $180,000 grant to start the Tennessee Criminal Justice Language Academy.[32]

Kory Hammond is a Tucson police officer who teaches a class through a program created by Partners in Training Consultants, an Arizona company that offers language and culture training throughout the country. It boasts that its courses have been held in thirty-three states, and that it graduates over 2,100 students a year. Officers learn not only basic Spanish, but certain aspects of Hispanic culture. Hammond also teaches that a failure to make eye contact or to speak up is "more than likely a sign of respect, not an attempt to mask guilt." Nor should officers feel threatened when they think Hispanics come too close, interpreting this as "a sign of aggression." To make his point, he'll sit very close to a couple of students, "explaining to them that the personal space Americans like is not part of Hispanic culture."[33]

Thanks to the efforts of those like John Pawelski, Minerva Virola, Kory Hammond, and others, communication today is much better. No longer will an incident occur like the one that Officer Pawelski recalls from a few years ago—one that illustrates what can happen when there is misunderstanding on both sides:

When a 911 call went to the local emergency number, the person answering the call could not make sense out of what the woman, Spanish-speaking, was trying to say, but he could hear her crying and a man's voice in the background. "Domestic violence" was the immediate assumption, and so police officers were dispatched to the home. They, too, couldn't understand what was going on, but everyone was obviously upset. When the husband stood up from his chair, the officer insisted that he sit back down. But after a while the restless man stood up and walked toward the door. The officer chased him, tackled him to the ground, and handcuffed him. When an interpreter finally arrived on the scene, it turned out that the young son of the family was missing, and the father, anxious to find his child, had gotten up to go look for him.

As COMMUNITIES WORK TO MEET THE CHALLENGE OF THE NEW WAVE OF IM-
migrants, some, like those who must foot the bill for expensive English-learner
programs, balk at the expense of services, especially when there's a good chance
that the newcomers are not here legally. They are also concerned that too warm a
welcome will attract even more immigrants. On the other hand, others argue that
it is better for us all to have a healthy, educated population, documented or not.
Many of the children are, after all, American citizens, and like all our children they
are the future of the country.

CHAPTER 6

Law and Disorder

AMERICANS, SAYS GARY ALTHEN IN HIS BOOK *AMERICAN WAYS*, "BELIEVE FIRMLY in what they call 'the rule of law.'"[1] But to which law do they refer? Federal, state, city? Immigration has added a new dimension to the usual conflicts. Enforcement of immigration laws has always been considered almost exclusively a federal prerogative, but now, given what they see as the lack of response from Washington, communities throughout the country have sought their own solutions to what polls indicate is a major concern. The immigration problem has created a new "civil war," and although this conflict doesn't pit brother against brother,[2] it has led to battles between conservatives and liberals, Democrats against Republicans, Republicans against Republicans, law enforcement agencies against other law enforcement agencies, and almost everybody against the federal government. As the numbers of new arrivals continue to increase, laws at the state, federal, and local level are also in a state of flux. Numerous lawsuits are filed as those who are pro-immigrant, anti-immigrant, and in the middle disagree over how the immigration problem should be addressed. Without immigration reform at the federal level, warned former Homeland Security Secretary Michael Chertoff, there would be "a patchwork of laws across the country" as state and local governments would step in to take control of the issue.[3]

States' Rights

Every state in the union debated immigration issues in 2007. A total of 1,404 measures were considered, and an unprecedented 170 were enacted in forty-one states, reports the *New York Times*.[4] Many states have stepped up enforcement of employer verification of status. Arizona's primarily Republican legislature introduced the most stringent bill, calling for English to be the official language, denying certain state benefits such as in-state tuition to undocumented aliens, limiting health care to emergency services only, and prohibiting illegal immigrants from receiving punitive damages in civil lawsuits. When the bill was vetoed by Democratic governor Janet Napolitano, a citizen's initiative called "Protect Our City" vowed an attempt to change the Phoenix City Charter to allow more local law-enforcement authority. And when Governor Napolitano was succeeded by Republican Jan Brewer, she signed an even more stringent bill, making it a crime for immigrants not to carry documents and allowing police to stop anyone suspected of being an illegal alien, among other things. It remains to be seen if the law will stay on the books.

Colorado, too, has been working to revamp legislation on illegal immigration. One measure under consideration would allow the state's attorney general to sue the federal government if it fails to enforce current federal immigration laws.[5] Georgia has passed a far-reaching law that demands that employers verify their workers' legality through a federal database. Employees who cannot furnish a social security number or taxpayer identification will be subject to a 6 percent state withholding tax. Recipients of state benefits must prove that they are here legally. "And a new criminal offense, human trafficking, has been added to the books to crack down on those who bring in large groups of immigrants." Law enforcement officers are also authorized to seek training "to enforce federal immigration laws."[6]

In Ohio, legislators have worked on measures that would require verification of the legal status of those seeking government benefits and set up a state investigative office that would liaise with federal immigration officials, impose a $50,000 fine for counterfeiting identification documents, and prohibit state agencies and local governments from contracting with employers who knowingly hire undocumented immigrants. In addition, a proposal was considered that would allow local law enforcement officers to arrest illegal immigrants.[7] State Rep. Courtney Combs introduced a bill that would make it a crime to trespass in the United States, to be enforced by local law enforcement.

As states looked to legislation to address the immigration problem, Washington's Governor Chris Gregoire tried another tactic to get the federal government's attention: sending it a $50 million bill to cover the cost to the state of housing illegal immigrants convicted of a crime. In 2005 the state of Arizona also sent an invoice to the U.S. attorney general "requesting $118 million to house illegal alien criminals" whom the government failed to deport.[8]

Throughout the country, says the National Conference of State Legislators, more than five hundred state bills on immigration were introduced by July 2006, and fifty-seven have been enacted.[9] The State of Arizona considered a "felony trespass proposal" before backing off in the face of consistent court rulings that immigration is a concern of the federal government, not state authorities.

Enforcing the Law at the Local Level

Phoenix isn't the only city that has sought its own solution. "More than 50 municipalities nationwide have considered, passed or rejected laws banning landlords from leasing to illegal immigrants, penalizing businesses that employ undocumented workers and making English the local official language," Anabelle Garay reports.[10] Until it was ruled unconstitutional, Hazleton, Pennsylvania, denied permits to businesses that employed illegals, and fined landlords renting to them—as did Riverside, New Jersey; Avon Park, Florida; Valley Park, Missouri; and Escondido, California. New Ipswich, New Hampshire, turned to laws against trespassing to have a group of immigrants arrested. Although law enforcement officials throughout the country praised the New Ipswich initiative, the judge dismissed the case, calling it unconstitutional.[11] Sheriff's deputies in Maricopa County, Arizona, invoked anti-smuggling laws in order to arrest dozens of illegal immigrants.[12] Robert Vasquez, a county commissioner in Caldwell, Idaho, even tried to get his county declared a disaster area because of the "invasion" from south of the border—sending a $2 million bill to the Mexican government to pay for economic damages.

According to the Center for New Community, some 211 "grassroots" organizations have sprung up across the country to prevent illegal immigrants from receiving in-state tuition at colleges, deny them state benefits, prevent the hiring of undocumented aliens, and allow local enforcement of immigration laws.[13]

Other groups have also joined the conflict, including dissatisfied workers at Dalton, Georgia's Mohawk Industries. They have won the right to sue the company under racketeering laws over the lower wages they claim they receive due to the low pay allotted the company's illegal employees.

Backed by businesses that would like to see the law enforced, more and more communities are cracking down on employers who hire illegal immigrants. In California, companies have turned to federal anti-racketeering laws in their efforts to redress the situation. A bill presented in Suffolk County, New York, by Steve Levy, a cofounder of a national coalition called Mayors and Executives for Immigration Reform, "will level the playing field." Levy adds that "if you want a contract with Suffolk County, you have to play by the rules."[14] Local building contractors in Hamilton, Ohio, support Sheriff Richard K. Jones "125 percent" in his pursuit of those who hire undocumented immigrants, because, says one executive, "Competitors hiring illegal immigrants is hurting our business badly. . . . It's to the point that doing business legally isn't worth it."[15]

Sheriff Jones of Butler County, Ohio, is one of the more vocal proponents of the enforcement of immigration laws. Together with county commissioner Michael Fox and state representative Courtney Combs, he has proposed a program that would require "a declaration of citizenship from all inmates booked into the county jail."[16]

Jones has made national news with his campaign to rid his community of those not legally here, and for charging the federal government for the expense of jailing them. He thinks the presence of illegal immigrants is unfair to American citizens, like the eighty-two-year-old woman he knows who works at McDonald's. He says:

> She works probably for minimum wage, and she mops the floor, and she has to pay taxes on what she makes. But yet the illegal immigrants, no matter what country you come from, you come here, you don't have to pay any taxes, you end up actually making more than the lady who's been a U.S. citizen her whole life—I don't know much about her but she's probably worked her whole life, but she pays her taxes and has to mop the floor. And a lot of illegals have no driver's license but they still drive, they don't pay any taxes whatever. Those that are here get false social security cards, and they use those fake cards to claim they're married and have six or eight children. Because they don't have any plans on paying any taxes at the end of the year anyway. It's just ripping off the U.S. government.
>
> As the head law enforcement official in the county, my job is to enforce the law, and if you're here illegally, that means you have broken the law.
>
> When the local law enforcement catch somebody for speeding or a small crash, they don't know what to do. [The drivers] are not here legally. They don't have insurance . . .
>
> I'll tell you what else. I feel that Mexico should have to pay all the damages to the victims of these crimes of these illegals that are over here. They should have to pay for the security on our borders, and if they are not willing to pay, we should confiscate anything that they have here in the United States, banks, bank rolls, investments, property, whatever it takes. If they don't want to enforce it, we should enforce it. Now that's a very controversial approach, but that's my approach.
>
> When we don't respect our criminal enforcement system, the basic rule of law breaks down, and it's the only thing that unites us and keeps us safe. If you're here illegally, get legal or go back to whatever country you come from, I care not what it is, but go back. I don't care if you want to stay here or not, don't care if these things I talk about hurt

your feelings and make you angry. If you're illegal, that's my job. That means that you're violating the law. If you sneak in at dark and hidden, that means that you're sneaking in because you won't go through the normal checkpoints, and it's thumbing your nose at all the people that came here legally and went through the whole process. If you're not going to do that, do away with all of it. Do away with the system. You can't be half pregnant, and right now that's kind of where we are.

The sheriff thinks that stricter penalties for those who hire illegal immigrants might go a long way to resolving the problem, but he has no faith in reform proposals in Congress. "I like those *ideas*," he says, "but I've not seen anything. Show me the meat. You know the old Wendy's commercial: Where's the beef? I don't see any beef. I see a lot of talk, I've not seen any beef at all. Local law enforcement sees no beef. The federal government moves extremely slow." In the meantime, Sheriff Jones will continue to bill the federal government $70 a day for each illegal immigrant housed in his jail. And he'll maintain the big yellow sign near his office that says, "Illegal Aliens: This Way," with an arrow pointing toward the jail.

Sheriff Jones also believes that undocumented immigrants should not be allowed to have driver's licenses: "They can't take the test, they can't read stop signs, traffic signs. Why do we want somebody on the road who can't read our signs and the lines on the road? . . . When you lie and you forge those documents, you've committed another crime, and you should go to jail for that."

The question of driver's licenses is one on which the states haven't always agreed. Ten states—Maryland, Michigan, Montana, New Mexico, North Carolina, Hawaii, Oregon, Washington, and Wisconsin—have allowed noncitizens without visas to obtain permits, while Tennessee began issuing a "certificate for driving" for those ineligible for a regular driver's license. Utah, which previously did allow driver's licenses to those who could not prove legal residency, in 2005 approved the issuing of a driving "privilege" card instead, since illegal immigrants were using Utah driver's licenses as identification for other privileges.[17] The federal "Real ID" Act, however, aims at uniformity. It will require states to verify that applicants for a driver's license are citizens or legal residents. The law is now scheduled to be put into effect in all states in the year 2014. Some oppose the act on privacy grounds, and at least seventeen states oppose it because of its cost, estimated at $11 billion.[18]

Even the officials are often at odds when it comes to the enforcement of immigration law. Outspoken Sheriff Richard Jones was recently accused of overstepping the bounds when he detained nineteen suspected illegal aliens. Attorneys from the American Civil Liberties Union and the American Immigration Lawyers Association argued that enforcement of immigration law is, with few exceptions, a federal prerogative. (Several months later, Jones did obtain special federal authority to arrest and detain suspected illegal aliens.)[19] When two police agencies in Southern California developed plans to have their officers trained in immigration law enforcement, it brought interest from other police departments throughout the country, protest from human rights groups, and—surprisingly—disagreement among the police officers themselves.

Sanctuaries

The sanctuary movement began as a way to grant asylum to refugees from El Salvador and Guatemala in the turbulent 1980s. Although sanctuary laws were criticized by the executive branch of the government, they were never challenged in court. In 1996 Guatemalan and Salvadoran illegal immigrants became eligible for special refugee consideration, rendering such laws no longer necessary insofar as their original intention was concerned.

Now, says the anti-immigration firebrand Rep. Tom Tancredo, Takoma Park, Maryland, and large cities like Houston, Los Angeles, San Francisco, Denver, Chicago, and Salt Lake City, plus the state of Maine, have instituted "policies prohibiting police officers from arresting anyone solely based on immigration status." He adds that "in some cases, law-enforcement personnel are forbidden from checking the immigration status of persons encountered in the course of routine police work." He calls such an attitude "a slippery slope" that can lead to lax law enforcement and a disrespect for federal laws.[20]

The city council of Maywood, California, where almost all residents are Latino and over half are non-natives, "passed a resolution opposing a proposed federal law that would criminalize illegal immigration and make local police departments enforce immigration law."[21] Because the police were allegedly targeting illegal immigrants at sobriety checkpoints, the laws were changed to make it more difficult for the police to tow cars whose owners don't have driver's licenses, which is the case with many here without documents.

Until December 2002, New York City maintained a sanctuary ordinance, under which police were not allowed to question the status of those they arrested for minor offenses. Then a brutal attack and rape was committed by four illegal aliens who had been released from police custody—indeed, the police had not been allowed to inform immigration officials. That sanctuary law was repealed, but later, after pressure from immigrant rights groups, a slightly modified version was passed.

James H. Walsh, a former associate general counsel of the United States Immigration and Naturalization Service, asserts that "with cities and states choosing to defy U.S. immigration laws, the result is anarchy at the borders—immigration anarchy." He includes California and Oregon, as well as Maine, in the list of such sanctuary states, and the cities of Anchorage, Baltimore, Durham (NC), Madison (WI), Boston, Houston, Los Angeles, and New York City. (He also puts the number of illegal aliens in the United States at 30 million, much more than the usual more conservative estimate of 12 million.)[22]

Political-science professor Edward J. Erler of the Claremont Institute equates the creation of sanctuary cities with "a new civil war," since sanctuary cities are illegal and in clear violation of two laws that Congress passed in 1996: "Under both statutes state and local governments could no longer prohibit employees from inquiring about immigration status or tipping off immigration authorities." And both were upheld in the Court of Appeals in 1999. He claims that such policies "actively abet and protect criminal activity by handcuffing the powers of the police." He notes that there are almost 100,000 convicted criminals who have been ordered deported, but who have failed to show up for deportation—and yet the police in sanctuary cities are not allowed to apprehend them until they have committed another crime. Almost one-fourth of California's prison population consists of illegal aliens, he says. He attributes the proliferation of the notorious Mara Salvatrucha gang to the limiting of police officers to enforce the law.[23]

A number of bills pending in Congress would grant state and local police more authority to enforce federal immigration laws; proponents claim they would address the kinds of problems Erler describes, but there are many who oppose the measure.

The Case against Local Enforcement

Sanctuary laws are more complex than Rep. Tom Tancredo would suggest, says Professor Huyen Pham of the Texas Wesleyan University School of Law, who refers me to her publications on the subject. There are good and valid reasons for rejecting local law enforcement of immigration law, including the question of sovereignty. The U.S. Constitution "requires uniform enforcement in immigration laws because the immigration power is an exclusively federal power that must be exercised uniformly." She argues that "allowing local authorities to choose whether to enforce immigration laws will result in patchwork enforcement, even within the same state." She also points out that immigration policy and foreign policy are closely linked. "Because it is a sovereign nation," she adds, "the United States must necessarily have the exclusive power to control entry and exit from its borders; otherwise, it would be subject to the control of other nations."[24]

Because of constitutional restraints, "the federal government cannot force local governments to enforce federal immigration laws (e.g., to arrest those who are illegally present). Therefore, short of exercising its Spending Clause powers to entice that joint enforcement, the federal government is limited to seeking local governments' voluntary cooperation."[25]

If some fifty municipalities are seeking ways to limit their immigration population, as Anabelle Garay reports, an almost equal number are at the opposite end of the spectrum. Pham tells us that "forty-nine cities and towns and three states have non-cooperation laws limiting or prohibiting their police and other authorities from cooperating in immigration law enforcement." They have "various reasons" for taking these measures:

> concern for immigrants who may shun essential government services (police protection, schools, and hospitals) for fear of being deported; concern for public safety as immigrants may not report crimes or cooperate in criminal investigations; concern about racial profiling and civil liberties generally; and concern for overburdened police departments in times of strained local budgets.[26]

Police officers often hesitate to detain someone over the illegality of his civil status, especially if that person is a longstanding, law-abiding resident. It's expensive to incarcerate, bring to trial, and possibly deport someone who apparently is doing no harm. So it's often left up to the individual officer to decide what to do, says Chautauqua County, New York's Sheriff Joseph Gerace. "Someone might be here for years and years and years, and we didn't know that they were undocumented or illegal, so I don't think that every illegal alien is going to be turned into the INS," he says.

Federal magistrate Judge Michael Merz in Dayton explains that because it is "such a tremendous strain on resources," those who are here illegally are prosecuted only after numerous reentries, which happens often in Texas and other border states. "I don't think we're at the stage where we need to do a lot of dragnetting and try to send a lot of people home," he adds.

For Ohio's Montgomery County Prosecutor Matthias Heck, it's a question of fairness; his policy of not asking questions about nationality ensures that justice is blind. "Our concern is that we treat people just the same," he says.

It's important to keep the immigrant community on the side of law enforcement for their own protection, as well as for that of others. "According to police officials across the country," says Huyen Pham, "growing distrust between their departments and immigrant communities would be a public safety disaster, affecting both the documented and undocumented communities."[27] Those who won't report crimes for fear of deportation are especially vulnerable. Amelia Berry, project coordinator of the Alliance for Immigrant Women in Cincinnati, Ohio, deals with this vulnerability among her clients:

So often what happens in a domestic violence situation where one partner has legal status and the other doesn't is that it is used as part of the abuse: "I'm not going to submit this paperwork if you leave me. I'm going to withdraw the papers that I already filed if you don't do a, b, and c. Either you stay in this house or—," you know. They use it to their advantage because domestic violence is all about power and control, and it's a wonderful way for people to have control. And going along with that, they say things like, "If you call the police, you'll be deported. No one will help you because you don't speak English. "

Amelia's organization works hard to get the message out to clients about what resources are available and what measures they can take; clients are encouraged to call the police. Because of this, she says, "We were so very concerned about what's going on in Butler County," where Sheriff Jones has established his "get-tough" policy.

The International Association of Chiefs of Police does not want local police to be in the business of enforcing immigration law. They, too, like John Pawelski and Officer Minerva Virola and many others, want the immigrants on their side. Given the complexity of immigration law, they're also concerned about protection from civil suits and accusations of profiling, as well as more pressure being placed on already overburdened forces. In Los Angeles, Sheriff Lee Baca and Police Chief William J. Bratton also oppose local enforcement, fearing that "it would damage hard-earned efforts to build trust in immigrant communities," and immigrants would be less likely to report crimes, they say.[28]

High on the list of opponents of local enforcement are Ohio's Roman Catholic bishops. "We're saying let the enforcement be a federal issue," Archbishop Pilarczyk says. Critics fear, too, that it will lead to the racial profiling of all Hispanics. Misael Mayorga, director of the Office of Hispanic Ministry in Ohio, thinks the proposal is having an effect already: "People are afraid to go to church," he says.[29]

Individual Rights

As I learned on jury duty, immigrants, even those here illegally, have many of the rights of citizens, even though many would not have the courage to assert those rights. According to immigration attorney Rosalba Piña, illegal immigrants can join or organize unions, receive compensation for injuries, and demand payment while they are recuperating. Since immigrants, like all workers, are covered by the National Labor Relations Act (NLRA), "all workers (no matter their migratory status) are protected by the overtime and federal minimum wage law," she says, "as well as the state wage and number of hours per day established by law. In addition to having the right to recover every penny of the salary which unscrupulous employers may have refused to pay them."[30] In fact, in 2004 the Mexican government, through its consulate in San Diego, encouraged janitors, many of whom were here illegally, to join a class action suit against several large supermarket chains in California. The companies had treated the janitors as contractors in order to avoid paying benefits and overtime wages.[31]

Two illegal immigrants were even awarded an Arizona ranch when they sued its owners, claiming they were mistreated when the ranch owners apprehended them. They accused one rancher of threatening them and of hitting one of the men with a pistol, although they did admit that they were given cookies, water, and a blanket and released after about an hour. It should be noted that the ranchers had long been in the sights of immigrant rights advocates, and it was not the first time they had been accused of abuse.[32] Still, that's not bad compensation for an hour of detention.

The Arizona immigrants then applied for visas for crime victims who cooperate with authorities—visas that are also available for witnesses who come forth to testify to crimes.

We'll recall that undocumented immigrants under federal law also have the right to public education and emergency medical care, which, as critics have noted, come at the expense of local taxpayers.

Carlos Martinez, of Atlanta and Mexico, boasts that he has all the rights of a citizen except for the right to vote, but even that is available in some communities where noncitizens can vote in local elections. Initiatives to enfranchise noncitizens have been introduced in Washington, DC, as well as New York, Connecticut, and other states. Noncitizens can also vote in municipal or school elections in several cities, including Chicago and Tacoma Park, Maryland. In 2004 voters in San Francisco narrowly defeated a proposition that would have granted the ballot to all immigrants—legal and illegal—in school elections. FAIR, the Federation for American Immigration Reform, declares that their investigations have revealed numerous incidents of election fraud, stating that driver's licenses are easy to counterfeit, and that such fake documents are often used as identification at the voting booth. Georgia's Governor Sonny Perdue says, "It's simply unacceptable for people to sneak into the country illegally on Thursday, obtain a government-issued ID on Friday, head for the welfare office on Monday and go to vote on Tuesday."[33] But when the state election board told voters they would need photo ID in order to exercise voting rights, the court ruled that such a requirement violated the state constitution. A similar law was overturned in Missouri. Arizona's photo ID requirement, however, still stands, thanks to a decision made by the Supreme Court. Opponents of such laws argue that they disenfranchise many voters, especially the elderly, who may not have driver's licenses.

Those in favor of noncitizen voting rights counter with the argument that such rights are not new; they were "widespread in 40 states and federal territories until the demise of the practice in the 1920s."[34]

Even those immigrants who can't vote have had a strong effect on American elections, since the U.S. Census counts everybody in the country, not just those here legally. It was because of the number of illegal immigrants who were counted that California gained six seats in the House of Representatives and North Carolina gained one, as did Florida, New York, and Texas—while Indiana, Michigan, and Mississippi each lost a seat, and "Montana failed to gain a seat it otherwise would have."[35]

"Catch-22s"

As if all of the legal ramifications were not discouraging enough, the federal government sometimes seems to be its own worst enemy. In North Carolina, efforts by the state and federal labor departments to cut down on the extraordinarily high number of injuries among Hispanic workers were thwarted recently by the Bureau of Immigration and Customs Enforcement. Rather than undergoing mandatory safety training for government jobs, as they expected, forty-eight immigrants were met instead by ICE officers masquerading as OSHA officials. The action caused labor and safety representatives to speak out against what they called a "scam" that would undermine the trust that they had worked hard to build.

Angry, too, was Cecilia Muñoz, an officer of the National Council of La Raza advocacy group, who called the sting operation "an absolute outrage." "Our labor law system is completely complaint-driven," she said, "and our ability to keep the work force safe depends on workers being able to complain, and by masquerading as OSHA officials, immigration authorities will clearly discourage immigrant workers from coming forward. This won't affect just immigrant workers, it will affect the safety of all workers."[36]

According to Joe Hansen, president of the United Food and Commercial Workers Union, "The word being brought back to worksites after a scam like this is that OSHA can't be trusted. That kind of perception diminishes OSHA's ability to do the critical work of protecting America's labor force."[37]

In another clash of priorities, the Census Bureau would like for immigration agents to suspend raids during the 2010 Census in order to encourage cooperation from those here illegally. It's unlikely to happen, however, with the current increase in enforcement efforts.[38]

In 1996 the IRS created a controversial taxpayer identification number, "designed for anyone who doesn't have a social security number," i.e., undocumented immigrants. The agency holds frequent seminars to assist such taxpayers, who, for their part, are eager to get the refunds they are due. The IRS claims it's not their business to determine who's documented or not; their job is to collect taxes, and to do that job, "they needed to find a way to cut down on fraud." Critics, however, argue that "one federal agency is accommodating lawbreakers that another agency is trying to ferret out."[39]

Father Benjamin Santana, an Episcopal priest in rural Western New York who conducts services in Spanish, is also angry with the federal government. "Three or four years ago," he relates, "there was a big celebration of first communion and confirmation for Mexican kids. They all crowded to the church in Buffalo, a Catholic church—very neatly dressed, very clean, with all the rites and ceremonies. There were over two hundred of them being confirmed. When the service ended and they started walking out, Immigration was outside. So from then on it has been uphill to get their trust." Echoing the comments of Ohio's director of the Catholic Office of Hispanic Ministry, he says, "Now they even suspect the churches!"

For Father Santana, as well as for Sister Maria Stacy and other immigrants-rights advocates, God's law comes before any law of the land. Many see the issue as primarily one of human rights, like John Pawelski, who says, "If you say to me a new federal law goes into effect September 1 that children under the age of fifteen are not allowed to eat, do you think I would follow that law? I would do whatever it took to make sure my children could eat. . . . A lot of undocumented immigrants see it as their family is going to starve and their only choice is to come to the United States to work. You cannot put somebody in that kind of decision-making process and expect them to follow your rules vs. nature's rules that say I'm going to provide for myself and my family."

The House of Representatives passed a bill that would have made it a felony to render assistance to illegal immigrants, which incurred the wrath of church and social-service workers throughout the country. It brought forth a call for civil disobedience from many Catholic clergy, including Cardinal Roger Mahony of Los Angeles, who "instructed priests in his archdiocese to disobey any law that would prevent them from helping illegal immigrants."[40] Fortunately it was defeated in the Senate.

Such a law would present more than one "Catch-22." By law, states must furnish public education, and hospitals must accept all emergency room patients. Yet teachers, nurses, pastors and volunteers—even those who put water in the desert for thirsty travelers—would all be subject to arrest as felons, as well as the immigrants themselves. And what would we do with more than 12 million additional felons in the country?

PART 3

The Bigger Picture

CHAPTER 7

Looking Back

According to Carlos Martinez, who left Mexico ten years ago for a better life in the States, immigration is part of nature's plan. "People are always looking for something better," he says, beginning with the first humans to leave their African homeland. It is a good and natural thing, he thinks, because we can learn from one another. As Jared Diamond so compellingly argues in his book *Guns, Germs, and Steel*, for better or worse, we would not have the life we know today if our forebears had not strayed from home, since "the history of interactions among disparate peoples is what shaped the modern world."[1]

But let's fast-forward many millennia to look at the history of our own country, when the original inhabitants—who themselves had migrated from Asia—encountered new groups of people who intended to stay. After a turbulent century, by 1800 the Spanish had established settlements in today's American West. In the eastern colonies there lived not only the mainstream English, but, among others, slaves and "free persons of color" from Africa, Dutch, Scotch-Irish, French, Swiss, and Jews—the first synagogue in America dates from 1695. A popular legend has it that there were so many Germans that German came close to being an official language. Even though historians disclaim it, they were here in great numbers: some 277,000 in 1790, about half of whom lived in Pennsylvania, where they constituted one-third of the population.

The Great Wave

It is the first Great Wave of Immigration, however, that created the image of America today as a multicultural land. Between 1790 and 1840, less than a million immigrants had arrived, a situation that would soon change as better transportation, Ireland's potato famines, and unrest in Europe sent hordes of poor, tired, "huddled masses yearning to breathe free," or at least yearning to eat. Between 1841 and 1860, 4,311,000 came to stay.[2]

Germans came in great numbers—more than 5 million in the nineteenth century—as the word spread that life was good for farmers in America. Many communities boasted German schools and German newspapers, until World War I made it unpopular to be known as German. The centenarian Evangeline Lindsley vividly recalled that then there was a "great hatred of anything German. There were many schoolteachers of German extraction in Dayton, and there was quite a protest against them teaching because of their German parentage." She remembered the "shocking" burning of German books, the closing of German schools, and the harassing of even highly respected German Americans.[3]

The Irish made up a good part of that first wave, most making the dangerous journey in "coffin ships." They were called that for good reason: Due to a lack of food, water, and sanitation, "in the most disastrous year of all," Thomas Sowell reports, "about 20 percent of the huge famine immigration died en route to America or upon landing," more than on slave ships from Africa in the nineteenth century.[4] Many who proudly acclaim their Irish roots today, however, would have been ashamed to admit kinship with their immigrant ancestors, if contemporary accounts are reliable. Martin Scorsese's film *Gangs of New York*, although fictionalized and made with some poetic license, sticks closely to the nonfiction book that inspired it. In Herbert Asbury's *The Gangs of New York*, written in 1927, the same gangs are described: the Dead Rabbits, the Pug Uglies, the Roach Guards, the Bowery Boys . . . And the same kinds of colorful characters were real, those with names like Hell-Cat Maggie, Sadie the Goat, Gallus Mag, Mush Riley, and Boiled Oysters Malloy. The Daniel Day-Lewis character was based on a Native American gang leader called "Bill the Butcher" Poole. The Old Brewery, the locale for much of the action, once housed more than one thousand men, women, and children. It's said that for fifteen years there was an average of a murder a night in the building. Dickens described a tenement in the notorious Five Points neighborhood when he wrote: "Where dogs would howl to lie, men and women and boys slink off to sleep, forcing the dislodged rats to move away in quest of better lodgings." He spoke of "hideous tenements which take their names from robbery and murder; all that is loathsome, drooping and decayed is here."[5]

If anything, life for the immigrant Irish was even more brutal and bloody than depicted in the movie. Women were just as violent, if not more so. And yet today, who can imagine a time when ads for jobs said, "NO IRISH NEED APPLY," or bars posted prominently, "NO MICKS ALLOWED HERE"? Through political action, beginning with the corrupt Tammany Hall organization, the Irish eventually gained a place for themselves in America. Referring to both the Irish and Italians, write Richard Alba and Victor Nee, "Roman Catholics so dominated the political structure of some major cities that they were able in the late nineteenth and early twentieth centuries to convert municipal employment into an ethnic preserve."[6]

Desperately poor like the Irish, those who came from southern Italy, unlike the Irish, depended on strong family ties to endure. Even the Mafia was "centered on the family," says Thomas Sowell.[7] As in the case of the Mexicans who come today, it was the family—not any outside authority—that could be trusted, and like today's Mexican newcomers, they dutifully sent large sums back to the home country. Also, as with the Mexicans, education didn't count for much, especially when it came to educating the women in the family. Education, they feared, might cause a breach between young scholars and their kin.

On the other hand, to the Jews who came from eastern Europe, it was education, as well as family, that mattered. Nevertheless they were looked down upon by the earlier Jewish arrivals from Western Europe. "It was the German Jews," says Sowell, "who coined the epithet 'kike' to apply to eastern European Jews."[8] Although we think of ourselves as a nation of immigrants, that doesn't mean that we ever welcomed newcomers, even when we shared their cultural roots. "When Eastern European Jews moved into German Jewish neighborhoods in Chicago," Sowell tells us, "the German Jews moved out."[9]

In other cities, too, each group would leave with a "there goes the neighborhood" attitude when another moved in: "When the nineteenth-century Irish immigrants flooded into New York and Boston, the native Americans fled. . . . Blacks fled a whole series of neighborhoods in nineteenth-century New York, 'pursued' by new Italian immigrants who moved in. In nineteenth-century Detroit, blacks moved out of neighborhoods as Polish immigrants moved in. The first blacks in Harlem were fleeing from the tough Irish neighborhoods in mid-Manhattan."[10]

As early as the 1830s, some states were reacting to the perceived threat of so many newcomers by passing laws on immigration, but in 1876 the Supreme Court decreed that immigration control was a federal prerogative.

In the antebellum period, the Know-Nothing Party gave voice to rising anti-immigrant attitudes. Organized in 1852, it joined together various nativist parties already in existence. Within three years, the party was established in thirty-five states and territories, spreading its message that Catholics, and especially those from Ireland, were anti-American, since they owed allegiance to a foreign power—namely, the pope. In 1854, forty Know-Nothing candidates for Congress were elected, as was the governor of Massachusetts, also of the party. In 1855 three more states, New Hampshire, Connecticut, and Rhode Island, elected Know-Nothing governors. Nine different states were carried by the party in that year's elections. By 1860 Know-Nothingism had lost its appeal, however, as the country turned to more pressing matters presaging the Civil War, and when members in the North and South were split by their views. But not before riots and anti-Catholic demonstrations inspired by the Know-Nothings had erupted throughout the East and at least as far west as Texas.[11] On "Bloody Monday," August 6, 1855, in Louisville, Kentucky, spurred on by the editor of the *Louisville Journal*, mobs attacked residents of the Irish and German neighborhoods of the city, burning down numerous buildings and killing at least twenty-two, and perhaps even more than one hundred. No one was ever punished for the massacre.[12]

AS THE NINETEENTH CENTURY PROGRESSED, OTHER GROUPS, INCLUDING SLOVAKS, Poles, and Scandinavians, arrived from Europe and quickly spread west, building the railroads, working in the burgeoning industries, and farming the fields of the heartland. Between 1880 and 1924, some 26 million immigrants landed on our shores. Among them: "one-third of all the Jews in eastern Europe," 2 million people fleeing persecution that had worsened in 1881 when Russia's new czar issued even more anti-Jewish laws.[13]

Whatever their ethnic classification, all were encouraged to lose their old ways, learn English, and become American. Henry Ford was one who worked hard to "Americanize his foreign-born workers." Becoming American, to his mind, was "all-encompassing—to the point that it meant, among other things, giving up garlic," while Theodore Roosevelt thought all foreign-born Americans should Anglicize their names.[14] Hostility toward the outsiders continued: "Immigrants were occasionally lynched or gunned down by the forces of putative 'law and order,' especially when they became economic competitors of native-born white men or joined in labor unrest," say Richard Alba and Victor Nee.[15] In one notorious incident, eleven Italians were lynched in New Orleans in 1891.

Meanwhile, on the West Coast, thousands of Chinese and fewer numbers of Japanese had arrived to work on the railroads and farms and in the mines of California and the other western states. They, too, were met with hostility from the natives, who felt they were losing jobs to the Asians. However bad things were for European immigrants, they were worse for the Chinese, who were often beaten and sometimes murdered by white Americans.[16]

Restrictions

Under pressure from the unions over unfair competition, Congress enacted the Chinese Exclusion Act in 1882. The first to restrict immigration in any way, the law also excluded those of all races who were criminals, insane, or likely to end up as public charges. A "gentleman's agreement" with Japan in 1907 curtailed immigration from that country.

It was not until 1918 that the United States required passports. Back then, "new arrivals were required only to prove their identity and find a relative or friend who could vouch for them."[17] In the face of the great influx of unskilled workers and a decrease in the demand for labor, however, more restrictions were enacted in the 1920s. After the Russian Revolution in 1917, a "Red Scare" resulted when Americans feared that Communism might spread across the Atlantic. Quota laws were passed to limit the numbers of immigrants, especially those not from Western Europe; all immigration from Japan was prohibited. It was not until 1952, with the McCarran-Walter Act, that racial restrictions on naturalization were completely eliminated, which meant that Korean and Japanese spouses of American citizens were now eligible for citizenship.[18]

Quotas based on nationality came to an end in 1965—although immigration was limited, in theory, to 170,000 from the Western Hemisphere each year, and 120,000 from the Eastern. Later, in 1976, the numbers for both hemispheres were made equal. In practice, however, family members were exempt from such restrictions. From 1965 on, "family ties to persons already living in the United States [has been] the key factor that determines whether a visa applicant is admitted into the country."[19] Numerous refugees have also been admitted beyond the immigration limitations—more than 400,000 Europeans entered under the Displaced Persons Acts following World War II.

The Mexicans

While the potato blight in Ireland was causing thousands of starving Irish to head for America's shores, most of today's Southwest still belonged to Mexico. An influx of Anglo settlers and the opening of the Santa Fe Trail made for closer commercial ties with the United States than with the far-away government of Mexico City, or the closest trading center of Chihuahua.

In the spirit of Manifest Destiny, America declared war against Mexico over boundary disputes and claims of debts to American citizens. When the war ended in 1848, roughly 500,000 square miles—California, Nevada, New Mexico, Utah, most of Arizona, and parts of Colorado and Wyoming—were ceded to the United States by the Treaty of Guadalupe Hidalgo. When militant Hispanic immigration advocates speak of the *Reconquista*, this is the land they wish to reclaim and to which they feel they have a historical right.

The area equaled one-half of Mexico's territory, and not all of its inhabitants were happy about the change. Estimates of the population at that time range from 75,000 to 116,000.[20] Only about 10,000 people lived in California,[21] but in New Mexico, where 60,000 people spoke Spanish, "cultural conflict developed because most Spanish-speaking New Mexicans found it difficult to accept concepts of government, taxation, and land tenure based on Anglo-Saxon legal norms."[22] Other sections were later purchased from Mexico. Texas, with many more Anglo residents, was another story. Having won its independence from Mexico in 1836, it was annexed to the Union in 1845.

In California, the discovery of gold in 1849 drew some 100,000 people, most of them Anglos. Soon after the "Forty-niners," the Anglo farmers arrived; squatters claimed land that Hispanic residents also claimed, leading to lawsuits and violence that went on for years.

Mexicans continued to come north—some to California, and others to work in the mines of Nevada, Arizona, and, later, Colorado. The 1900 Census recorded that 8,086 Mexicans were living in California, 14,172 in Arizona, and 274 in Colorado. The greatest number—71,060—were in Texas. Some researchers, however, believe the figures were much higher, perhaps 350,000 or more Hispanics in the United States at the turn of the century.[23]

It was an easy matter to cross the border at that time, and many went back and forth at will. The first border controls were established early in the twentieth century—for the main purpose of apprehending illegal Chinese immigrants. Because officials felt that "Mexican labor was needed in the Southwest," says Nicolas C. Vaca, "they turned a blind eye to the stream of Mexicans crossing the border."[24] It was not until 1924 that the U.S. Border Patrol was established, with a staff of 450 men to patrol the 2,000-mile border. "Besides," Meier and Ribera confirm, "undocumented entrance was not prohibited until 1929, and even then it was a misdemeanor with no legal penalty."[25]

The coming of the railroad to both Mexico and the United States influenced the numbers of Mexican immigrants in two ways: Now it was much easier to travel to the Southwest and even into the interior, plus the railroads offered plenty of work. The nativist antipathy toward Asians that culminated in the Chinese Exclusion Act of 1882 offered more opportunities for Mexican workers, who were actively recruited in El Paso by the railroad companies. "Most Mexican immigrants in the early twentieth century," says Thomas Sowell, "worked for the railroad at some time or other—as construction workers, as watchmen, or as laborers maintaining the tracks."[26]

Events in Mexico sent people streaming north, too. The Mexican Revolution in 1910 created bloody chaos throughout the country, sending thousands fleeing to America. It had, ironically, perhaps been influenced by those returning to Mexico from the United States "with new social and political ideals engendered by American labor union experience."[27] Fortunately the influx of Mexicans coincided with a need for their labor as the Southwest prospered, especially in agriculture. The newcomers were happy to supply it when they could earn two or three times, or more, what they could make in the home country. The Northeast, and especially the Midwest, also drew Mexican workers during the labor shortages of World War I. A government program to bring in contract workers, the forerunner of the *bracero* programs of the 1940s, was instituted at this time.

When the Great Depression brought an end to the booming '20s, "as many as a million Mexicans, and even Mexican-Americans, were ousted, along with their American-born children, to spare relief costs or discourage efforts to unionize," says Nina Bernstein.[28] Some of the deportations were brutal enough to cause lawmakers today to call for an apology to those so shabbily treated. Ignacio Piña recalls what happened to his family in 1931, when he was six years old: "They came in with guns and told us to get out. . . . They didn't let us take anything"—including the trunk that held the birth certificates that proved that the six children were U.S. citizens. The family spent ten days in jail before being put on a train for Mexico, where, says Piña, he spent sixteen years of "pure hell."[29] In the racist climate of the times, George Clements of the Los Angeles Chamber of Commerce urged that no Mexican be employed while a white man was out of work, writing that "the Mexicans' legal status was not a factor: 'It is a question of pigment, not a question of citizenship or right.'"[30]

America has waxed and waned in its reception of those coming from Mexico, welcoming immigrants when we need them, harshly rejecting them when we do not. As one rancher told his Mexican worker, according to immigration scholar Aristide R. Zolberg, "When we want you, we'll call you; when we don't—git."[31]

Soon we needed them again, when American workers left the farm to fight or work in defense industries in World War II and later in the Korean War. In 1942 an agreement was reached between Mexico and the United States that would lead to the employment of more than 5 million *braceros*, or guest workers, over the next twenty-two years. Those workers returned to their villages and spoke of the great opportunities waiting for others in the North, enticing them to come too, one way or another. The *bracero* program, while bringing workers in legally, says Vaca, "developed a shadowy twin brother not anticipated by the federal authorities—illegal immigration." In one of those decisions that makes one wonder, "What were they thinking?"—in a later extension to the agreement, the Mexican government included a clause "that illegal immigrants already in the United States should be given preference over newly imported Mexicans for *bracero* status." Naturally, "word spread among Mexicans that a surefire way to get a *bracero* contract was to cross the border illegally." Coming without documentation offered other advantages, too: no need to wait for bureaucratic red tape, pay the bribes that were frequently required, or bear other *bracero*-related expenses.[32]

In the postwar years, more and more Mexicans came north without legal permission, encouraged by "the absence of legal penalties, insufficient border control, a heavily mexicano rural Southwest, the increase in border and transborder recruiters, and widespread lack of public concern." By now, many villages had established ties with certain labor markets in the States, which needed them just as much as they needed the work.[33]

The '60s—bell bottoms, hippies, antiwar protests, "do your own thing." These years were a "watershed period," according to Richard Alba and Victor Nee, in which the ideal of "assimilation" was replaced by more politically correct goals like "transnationalism," "pluralism," or "multiculturism."[34] We would pay a price later for such rebellion against the old, established ways. Hanson contends that multiculturism led to a "new race industry" in California and to a "society that rejects any unifying core." It is one in which ethnic pride has been substituted for pride in intellectual achievement.[35] The Civil Rights movements of the 1960s played a role in the passage of the Immigration and Nationality Act of 1965, which did away with quotas based on national origins. An additional factor dating from the '60s that Thomas Sowell credits in part for increased immigration from Mexico has been "the growth of American legal and social agencies to protect and defend illegal aliens."[36]

The 1980s, a time of economic crisis in Mexico, coincided with a boom period in the States, drawing more immigrants northward. Then, in another of those "What were they thinking?" decisions, the Immigration Reform and Control Act (IRCA), passed in 1986, granted amnesty to some 3 million undocumented immigrants, allowing them to leap ahead of those who had been waiting for legal residency for years. Due to the provisions of 1965's legislation, they were able to bring in their family members, too. The granting of amnesty led others to hope that if they managed to get to the United States, they, too, eventually would be granted legal residency. Which is why politicians who speak of immigration reform are very sensitive about anything that smacks of the "A" word.

Perhaps the worst of the unintended consequences of IRCA were the results of the provisions on employer sanctions, which proved unenforceable. According to Alba and Nee, the "provisions, intended to undermine the labor market footholds of the undocumented, have turned out to be largely ineffective and, if anything, have spawned an underground industry processing fraudulent identity documents."[37] They also led, as some predicted they would, to ethnic profiling by employers in their attempts to obey the law. "The chickens came home to roost," says Nicolas Vaca, when a government report in 1990 revealed that there had been extensive discrimination against eligible workers who appeared or sounded foreign.[38] In addition, the "control" part of the measure led many undocumented aliens to leave the border states for other regions where they would be less likely to be detected.

Since Mexicans continue to represent the bulk of our undocumented population, in the next chapter we'll look at Mexico's take on the situation.

CHAPTER 8

Mexico

THE HONORABLE REMEDIOS GÓMEZ-ARNAU IS CONSUL GENERAL FOR THE STATES of Georgia, Tennessee, Alabama, and Mississippi, all of which have seen their Hispanic populations at least quadruple in the last decade. If federal immigration agents are correct in their estimates, Mississippi has gone from an estimated 2,000 illegal immigrants in 1990 to between 90,000 and 100,000 today.[1] With her light brown hair, slender and stylishly dressed in a camel skirt, black sweater set, and tan boots, the consul bears little physical resemblance to the smaller, darker people gathered outside her offices in Atlanta. The parking lot is full of the older model cars and pickup trucks of her clients, who come to register births, obtain Mexican identity cards, consult the civil registration department, seek legal advice, or avail themselves of the many other services that the consulate offers.

Although Ms. Gómez-Arnau may not look like many of her clients, she takes her responsibilities for their welfare very seriously. In fact, she is the author of a book on the protection of such immigrants, published while she was a researcher at Mexico's Centro de Investigaciones sobre el América del Norte.[2] The main task of the consulate, she says, "is to protect the interests and rights of our nationals," as any other consulate would do. For this reason, it maintains a hotline for workers who are concerned about health or safety hazards or other abuses at work. Her office's responsibilities also include informing the Mexican expatriates of their rights should they be detained, including the right to communicate with the consulate. It's a right that has sometimes been ignored, when legal authorities fail to notify her offices. And "if nobody calls us, how can we know when somebody is detained?" The problem becomes especially important when parents are separated from their children.

Education is an essential part of the consulate's services because, she says, it is important for people to learn English "in order better to defend their rights." This is why the Mexican government offers free English lessons, along with classes for immigrants to complete the education they started in the home country.

Ms. Gómez-Arnau, like many of her countrymen, is incensed by America's construction of a wall along the Mexican-U.S. border, which Atlanta's Hispanic newspaper *Mundo Hispánico* says will be seen as "a symbol of arrogance, arbitrariness, and injustice."[3] It's a move that Vicente Fox calls "a disgrace for the United States," as well as "useless," while Felipe Calderón finds the decision "deplorable." The twenty-seven countries of the Organization of American States have joined in expressing their "profound concern."[4] Mexico's official stance is one of "outright rejection of the construction of fences or other similar structures" along the border.[5] Does the consul feel, as the *Mundo Hispánico* editors do, that such a wall is an insult? "Yes," she replies, "because we are neighbors. And there are many contributions from the Mexican people, to economy, to the culture." What's more, the wall will only encourage people to cross at more dangerous places and take greater risks.

"It doesn't address the real problem," she continues. "The real problem is that the people are being demanded by the American economy, by the American labor market. . . . [The wall] won't stop the migration, because that depends on the demand. It's supply and demand. It's very important the people understand that we are living in a new globalized world. That means that not only is trade globalized, but the labor market is too."

When I asked about the status of the Mexican economy and its relation to the immigration situation, I had obviously brought up a subject she felt very strongly about. She replied that

> it's important that we improve the size of our economy—and the government is working on that—but that's only one side of the story. The other side of the story is that the U.S. labor market requires the input by now of almost 900,000 immigrants from all over the world to fill up the jobs that the American people cannot do. And there are studies, even by the U.S. Congress, telling this truth. Even though Mexico improves its economy, that has nothing to do with the need of the U.S. labor market of importing workers from all over the world, because it's estimated that about 400,000 Mexicans are coming annually

to the United States, and you don't see the people begging in the streets. They are working. If they are working, that means that there is a demand for their labor force. And that's true! Estimates from the U.S. Labor Department are that by 2010 there will be 10 million jobs in the United States that won't be able to be filled all by American citizens. That means that they will have to import that labor force. They estimate that by 2014 there will be 14 million jobs, and so on. Why is that happening? Very simple. It's a matter of demographics. People are not having kids here. People are retiring. . . . So you have places in the labor market that are not filled up. People need to understand that, because they say that it is a very simple solution: "Improve your economy and the people will come back." No, no, no, no, no! That's not the only part of the story. We need to improve our economy, and it is not easy to get to the level of the more prosperous economies of the world like the United States, but it's also important to understand that the industries now are competing in a more globalized world. They are looking for the place where the productivity is highest, and that includes many things, among them the salaries that are being paid. The world is much more complicated than just saying, "Improve your economy and we won't have any immigrants." Nobody is looking at the need, the real need that there is for all these workers. Now you can see what's happening in California, where many growers are complaining that there's no one to harvest their crops. These workers are being required by the U.S. economy, the U.S. labor force, the U.S. labor market, and then the solution for the people that are here illegally is to make them legal.

The Mexican journalist Sergio Sarmiento also asserts that the United States needs Mexican workers. He claims that if American legislators pass laws to crack down on those who hire illegal workers, it would provoke an economic collapse, adding that it's a fact the senators are well aware of, and one that deters action on their part.[6] Rafael Fernández de Castro, who heads the International Studies department of Mexico's Instituto Tecnológico Autónomo University, is another who believes that America's businesses have not declared themselves because it is "they who will keep the valve open because they need immigrants."[7]

Everyone concurs, however, that the presence of large numbers of those here without permission creates an unhealthy situation. How to remedy the problem? Provide them with visas, says the consul general. "We are not interested in having people here illegally because that promotes many abuses." It would also be better for the United States, too, to know just who is coming in. "Otherwise you get all kinds of people," she says.

Ms. Gómez-Arnau is not the only government spokesperson to foster the promotion of visas. In a document issued by the Congress of Mexico, the legislators agreed upon eight major points to be considered in immigration reform: After conceding that a country has the right to regulate the entry and stay of foreigners in its territories, the government supports a wide-ranging guest worker program, which would also take into account the undocumented immigrants already in the United States. Its position is that any immigration action should be taken with the cooperation of both countries; Mexico wants an active part in seeing that "all those who decide to leave national territory do it through legal channels." The document assures us that "Mexico does not promote undocumented migration, and wishes to contribute to finding solutions which will allow confronting the migratory phenomenon in the best way."[8] As Demetrios G. Papademetriou of the Migration Policy Institute points out, Mexico would have much to offer in the administration of large-scale immigration programs, since it would have access to public records to check on the backgrounds of applicants.[9]

Although the government's proposals to ensure a legal, safe, and orderly flow of emigrants are good ones, writes Francesc Relea in *El Pais*, they come up against the brick wall of hard facts that makes this goal very difficult.[10] As we might say, How are you going to keep them back on the farm after they've been north—or even heard about life in the North? Especially as networks of their countrymen make it easier to adjust to life in the new land.

Statistics show that those who leave the country are not among the poorest, and may be better educated—and certainly more ambitious—than those who stay behind.[11] As a Binational Study on Migration reported, "It is common for the young people with the most initiative to leave, with the result that communities lose their current and potential leaders as well as have a weakened capacity for interaction with the exterior."[12]

Such an exodus is not only taking away the unskilled, but as researcher Rodolfo Tuirán says, will adversely affect the country's future in other ways, since "one of every three Mexican professionals who enter the labor market choose to do so in the United States."[13]

If so many people are leaving Mexico to head north, we may ask what is happening back home. A Mexican government report states that 96.2 percent of Mexican towns have some type of contact with the United States, "expressed through migration toward our neighbor to the north and/or through return to Mexico, as well as by means of money transfers from that country."[14] While some towns are benefiting financially from money sent by individuals or by increasingly active "home town associations" throughout the United States, they are paying a price.

Nathan Thornburgh in a *Time* magazine article writes, "Roberto Suro, director of the Pew Hispanic Center in Washington, says the great irony of Mexican migration is that it often feeds the same problems that sent people north in the first place. 'Many towns have lost the best of their labor force. There's money coming in [from the U.S.]

but no job creation back home," he says. 'It just shows that migration does not solve migration.'" Thornburgh describes how "there is a palpable lack of vitality on the streets" with so many young people gone. "In the summer working season," he says of one such town, "Tuxpan feels as if there's some great war on: all the fighting-age men have gone to battle the hedgerows up north. Only women, children and the elderly remain." He adds that "the northern migration has taken its toll on nuclear family life in towns like Tuxpan. Countless men have girlfriends in the north, while their wives and children remain in the south. And the women left behind in Mexico are faced with the same temptations."[15] Or the women left behind are left with no husbands at all, like thirty-three-year-old Victoria in El Paxtle, a community where "almost no young men are left," many having sought greener pastures in Ohio.[16] A devastating consequence when some men do return home is the AIDS virus that they bring with them, now spreading quickly in those rural areas that furnish the greatest number of emigrants.[17]

A report from Ecuador, a country that has also lost a large part of its population to emigration, describes the psychological damage that occurs when children are raised without one, or in many cases both parents. Like many villages in Mexico, towns in Ecuador pay a price. The estimated $2 billion a year in remittances cannot compensate for the social cost for its youth: a high rate of suicides, teen pregnancy, and alcoholism.[18]

I asked the Mexican consul general, "Don't you worry about losing the 'best and the brightest' of the population?"

"Of course!" she replied. "We don't want to lose them, because they are our people. And we have a social cost, because we now have local communities that are completely deserted. Senior citizens live there, but the young labor force is elsewhere, and it's very difficult to promote investment in those places. So yes, of course, we are very concerned about that, and we don't like it."

Of particular concern are the areas that export most of Mexico's emigrants: the "west-central core states" of Guanajuato, Michoacán, Jalisco, and Colima, although the northern border states and the states located between those two regions are also troublesome.[19] The Mexican government, well aware of the problem, has instituted small loan programs to put to better use the remittances that family members send home from abroad. In an example of cooperation between Mexico and the United States, the U.S.-Mexico Partnership for Prosperity has made it possible to send such money home at reduced rates. A project of the Inter-American Development Bank, through loans and grants to Mexico's Hipotecaria Su Casita (Su Casita Mortgage Company) will also provide a way for Mexican workers to finance houses in Mexico.

Should a guest worker program be put in place, officials would be wary of repeating the mistakes of the *bracero* programs, which encouraged workers to stay in the United States after their contracts ended. For this reason, certain incentives to ensure "circularity" have been proposed, such as contributions to voluntary savings accounts, to be collected when the worker returns home. Workers might also take advantage of special government-sponsored mortgages "with special tax-saving provisions" for returnees. The Bush administration agreed to work with Mexico on plans to guarantee that guest workers would receive credit for their time abroad when they enter Mexico's pension plan, and they would not be taxed for social security in both countries.[20] Jorge Castañeda, former foreign minister of Mexico who lectures frequently on foreign policy, suggests other incentives that the government might offer. It "could, for example, double welfare payments to households whose male heads stay home, [or] threaten to revoke land reform rights after years of absence in rural communities."[21]

Like many others, Castañeda calls for the legalization of undocumented Mexican immigrants in order to alleviate the problem, at least in the short run, but he believes that "this is not necessarily a good thing for Mexico in the long term." He also favors dual citizenship—Mexico passed a dual nationality law in the 1990s—so that Mexican expatriates can maintain their ties with the home country. He envisions, as did his former boss Vicente Fox, that someday NAFTA will become a North American Economic Community similar to the European Union. In the meantime, it is important that Mexicans in the United States not become a permanent underclass. This is one reason why the Mexican government has fostered education programs for its expatriates that will allow them to function in American society, whether they intend to stay or not. As Castañeda puts it, "We have to move forward in fostering the integration of Mexican immigrants into the United States. . . . We want Mexicans who move to the United States to retain their Mexican citizenship, to retain their roots, to retain their culture but to become full-fledged Americans. If they become a permanent underclass in the United States, it would be terrible for Mexico, in the first place, and also, at the end of the day, for the United States."[22]

VICTOR DAVIS HANSON, AUTHOR OF *MEXIFORNIA*, BLAMES MEXICO FOR MUCH OF today's immigration problem. The country "both deliberately exports its unwanted and, once they safely reach American soil, suddenly becomes their champion and absent parent, as much out of resentment toward the United States as in real concern for people whom they apparently are so gladly free of." He claims that over the decades, we have provided a convenient escape valve. "Simply put," he continues, "Mexican elites rely on immigration northward as a means of avoiding domestic reform. Market capitalism, constitutional government, the creation of a middle-class ethic or an independent judiciary will never fully come to Mexico as long as its potential critics go north instead of marching for a redress of grievances on the suited bureaucrats in Mexico City."[23]

This has not always been the case. In the early part of the twentieth century, "federal and state authorities ordered the municipal governments in . . . towns across the sending regions to crack down on emigration." Not only were officials angry about the poor treatment of Mexicans in the United States, they also felt that "peasants made poor ambassadors for Mexico's national image. . . . They were embarrassed by the Mexican migrants themselves for being poor and badly treated," says David Fitzgerald, adding that "the humiliations of emigrants in the United States were interpreted not only as the humiliations of individuals, but also of the Mexican nation and state they represented."[24]

The journalist Ruben Navarrette notes that unlike today's Mexico, "the old and proud Mexico ignored or condemned those who abandoned it in favor of greater opportunity on 'the other side.'"[25]

Samuel Huntington recalls that "for most of the twentieth century, Mexicans, including government officials . . . looked down on their countrymen who had migrated to the United States. They were disparaged as *pochos*, or, in the term used by Octavio Paz, *pachucos*, who had lost their 'whole inheritance: language, religion, customs, beliefs.' Mexican officials rejected them as traitors to their country."[26] Of course, there was little they could do when the Mexican Revolution of 1910–1920 "sent hundreds of thousands fleeing north."[27]

There were other times when, even though the federal government wished to curtail emigration, local authorities were eager to rid their areas of troublemakers, as during the "Cristero" civil wars. From 1926 to 1929, Catholic rebels fought with the federal government over its efforts to limit the power of the Church. According to David Fitzgerald, the conflict created "explosive social conditions":

> At three different periods during the war, the federal army forcibly concentrated peasants and residents of villages throughout the Los Altos area into larger towns or deported them to the neighboring state of Guanajuato. . . . Tens of thousands of peasants were forced to leave their crops and cattle behind. In some cases, they practiced their own scorched earth policy to deny the federal troops food. Cristero and federal troops destroyed much of what was left.[28]

Smallpox, crowded conditions, and food shortages led to a volatile situation. "The easiest way to ameliorate the crisis was simply to encourage people to leave," says Fitzgerald. While the Interior Ministry was working to decrease emigration, "in war-torn areas, local governments, economic elites, and the army eagerly opened the economic and political escape valve. The imperative to remove large masses of hungry, angry people easily trumped directives from Mexico City to restrict emigration."[29]

Fitzgerald concedes that at times, as when Sinarquista right-wing opposition in the '30s and '40s posed a threat, the federal government has indeed used emigration as an escape valve, in this case within the framework of the *bracero* programs. Following this period, the government "distinguished between labor emigrants and political exiles, trying to keep the former in and the latter out." "Restricting *bracero* eligibility in theory allowed the government to exchange a pool of unemployed laborers for a source of remittances and modernizing influences, while preventing a skills drain and reassuring the corporatist pillars of the ruling Institutional Revolutionary Party." There have also been times when Mexico has used emigration as a negotiating tool, as in the 1950s when "Mexico promoted bracero emigration and then suddenly tried to stop *all* emigration" while guest worker negotiations were being conducted with Washington. But there have also been times when American immigration policy has "turned a blind eye when convenient" and undercut Mexico's stance on emigration. For most of the twentieth century, Fitzgerald claims, "the record shows a consistent effort on the part of the Mexican federal government to control what *types* of people left, *where* they came from, *when* they left, and the *conditions* of their exit and return."[30]

The situation is not as simple as some critics imagine, as when Hanson speaks of Mexico's "leaders' deliberate export of their own citizenry in staggering numbers."[31] Or when Jon E. Dougherty complains that "the government of Mexico is quite content to export its poverty, rather than face the difficult task of providing its citizens with the opportunity to stay at home and earn their way out of destitution."[32] When the Mexican government published a "Guide for the Mexican Migrant," Americans who were against immigration called it "a how-to manual for illegal aliens, which blatantly encourages people to break United States law."[33] The booklet, in comic book form, warns of the dangers of attempting to cross the border and gives instructions of what to do in the case of apprehension, spelling out the rights of the migrants. Mexico's National Human Rights Commission has also distributed 70,000 maps of the Arizona desert to those intending to enter; these, too, contain warnings and indicate just how dangerous such an attempt would be.

The publication of such materials for the protection of its citizens abroad is in line with Mexico's long-held position of at least defending "the rights of the immigrants through a weak consular protection," according to researcher Federico Novelo Uradanivía.[34] Basically it was "a policy of no policy," as many describe it. Or, in those days before Vicente Fox became president, Mexican policy was characterized by "the tendency to 'buck' the United States to demonstrate its independence," says

Robert Leiken.[35] This passive approach, according to the authors of the binational study "Migration between Mexico and the United States, "was believed to suit the principle of mutual respect and recognition of both national sovereignties."[36]

The election of Vicente Fox as president in July 2000 gave rise to a new spirit of cooperation on the border, quite different from Mexico's attitude in the past. "In the June 22, 2001 'Joint Communiqué' of the U.S.-Mexico Migration Talks *both* governments agreed to 'strengthen public safety campaigns to alert potential migrants of the dangers of crossing the border in high-risk areas.'" American Border Patrol officials and the INS credited the "new cooperative attitude of Mexican state and federal governments" with helping reduce the number of subsequent deaths.[37] Mexico's foreign minister Jorge Castañeda "hoped to change the reactive—sometimes even passive—character of Mexico's traditional foreign policy for a more proactive approach, where Mexico would take the initiative vis-à-vis the U.S."[38] His time in office, says Robert Leiken, was "marked by turning away from the traditional line of emphasizing Mexican sovereignty 'at all costs' in favor of a more accommodationist approach."[39] The stage seemed set for real progress in negotiations over illegal immigration between the two countries when the talks were derailed by the terrorist attacks of September 11, 2001; America's primary interests turned to security.

Even before September 11, there had not been as much progress as expected. Some blamed Castañeda's inflexible attitude, expressed in his insistence that Mexico's proposals be accepted in their entirety—that is, the "whole enchilada." Leiken sums up the five "ingredients" in the "enchilada":

> Mexico proposes to make the border safe, to increase the quota of Mexican resident visas, to revise the status of unauthorized Mexican migrants currently in the United States, to establish a guest worker program for Mexicans and to encourage international investment to flow into Mexico so as to provide jobs in Mexico as an alternative to migration."[40]

In 2002 Castañeda was optimistic that any programs involving Mexican emigrants would be merely temporary, estimating that given the decreasing birth rate, Mexican migration would "'peter out' over the next decade or so."[41] There had been great hopes that NAFTA would bring prosperity, leading to a reduction in the number of migrants seeking a better life elsewhere. But results did not live up to expectations when China, with its low wages, became a strong competitor in the world market. Nevertheless, there is no going back to pre-NAFTA thinking; Mexico is "firmly committed to economic liberalization," said Luis Ernesto Derbez, secretary of the economy, reporting that in 2001 "Mexico's foreign trade surpassed $326 billion."[42]

Castañeda resigned in January 2003—in part, it was said, "out of frustration with the lack of progress in negotiating a migration accord with the United States."[43] As

Global Distinguished Professor of Politics and Latin American Studies at New York University, he continues to lecture and write on foreign affairs. On the ever-present threat of China, he says, "We now know in Mexico that we cannot compete with countries like India and China simply through low wages. What we need to do is to build skills that can make us competitive in other areas, or perhaps in the same areas. Issues such as fair trade, respecting basic labour standards, basic human rights standards, basic environmental standards, and basic rule of law are absolutely indispensable for making Mexico a modern, democratic and more prosperous country. I think that there is great awareness of this in Mexico today."[44]

Castañeda was replaced by Según Derbez, who stressed the importance of resolving the migrant problem—and who said he looked at China as a strategic partner. Having signed a series of agreements with the Asian country, Mexico began to work on programs that would take advantage of its large market in the long term.

Felipe Calderón, who succeeded Vicente Fox as president in July 2006, stated, after meeting with President Bush in November of that year, that unlike Fox, "who had made immigration practically the only subject of the bilateral relationship" with the United States, he would "insist on the subject, but without converting it into the sole priority of our bilateral relationship."

In addition to joining with the United States to fight against drugs and crime, he stressed the need "to promote investments in Mexico [and] to improve the infrastructure in the zones which send out more migrants in the southern region of the country."[45] It's a message that Calderón continues to emphasize, calling for renewed American efforts to make Mexico a priority, since he recognizes that illegal immigration will not cease until the standard of living in Mexico is raised.[46]

And if they—and we—do not succeed? Robert S. Leiken ominously predicts that "if emigration is deterred without development, what is migration today could be felony or rebellion tomorrow. Mexican development is in the United States' interest because stagnation will produce more crime, corruption, unemployment, migration, instability, and the temptation to blame the United States, and hence tension between the two countries."[47] In the meantime, there are many joint programs that continue to bring results, such as the Partnership for Prosperity, "launched in 2001 as a public-private alliance of Mexican and U.S. governmental and business leaders to promote economic development in Mexico, especially in areas with high migration rates,"[48] and the Overseas Private Investment Corporation (OPIC), which fosters American investments and the establishment of joint ventures.

CHAPTER 9

Other Countries

"Lisa Martinez" is one of many illegal immigrants who "reap few bene-fits," and who face "low wages, long hours, grueling conditions and paying kickbacks. ... It's not unusual, for instance, for factory workers to flip-flop weeks between night and day shifts, or for employers to require workers to put in unpaid overtime. ... Martinez has held 13 jobs in 11 years here, but never with health insurance. She pays her own medical expenses—even after she scalded her hand in a vat of broth at a soup plant and after stomach and back pain immobilized her at a tile-painting factory where workers wore no masks." She was also cheated of some $1,000 in withholding taxes.[1]

Sound familiar? Martinez, who comes from Peru, is not in the United States, however, but in Japan, which prides itself on its homogeneous character and doesn't welcome strangers. "*Wareware nihonjin . . .*" "We Japanese people," one hears often, as though they speak with one voice. It's a country that practices citizenship by *jus sanguinis*, by descent, not birth, even excluding native-born Koreans whose grandparents arrived many years ago. Up until 1993, foreign residents were required to be fingerprinted, including Koreans, although "an estimated 90 percent of this population was born in Japan and the majority are not fluent in Korean."[2]

Even homogeneous Japan, however, must face the realities of demographics. With a life expectancy of over eighty-one years and a birth rate of 1.4 children per woman, the Japanese face the same problems that confront many of the countries of the developed world. In 2003 the official estimate of the illegal population was 220,000 out of a population of almost 128,000,000, but there may be many more than that.[3]

Immigration is certainly not a new phenomenon. As long as there are haves and have-nots, some of the poor will seek a better life elsewhere. The projected increase in the population of Third World countries, added to the ease of transportation and a communication system that allows the poor to see how the richer half lives, will continue to push those with get-up-and-go, or those desperate enough, to get up and go.

Egypt, with a population of some 72 million, hosts between two and five million refugees from Sudan, while in the state of São Paulo in Brazil, "it is estimated that forty percent of the alien population is illegal." Immigrants to Brazil come especially from Bolivia, Paraguay, Peru, and Chile.[4]

Thousands fleeing African violence and poverty risk their lives in small boats to sail the five hundred miles from Mauritania, west of North Africa, to Spain's Canary Islands, or attempt the shorter but closely watched route between Morocco and Spain. Many drown in the process. Or they struggle to reach Melilla or Ceuta, Spanish enclaves in Morocco. The law states that from there they are to be sent to Spain to be interviewed. Once in Europe, it's an easy matter to slip away.

When would-be immigrants from Africa learned that workers were doubling the height of the razor-wire fence around Melilla, hundreds rushed to scale the barrier before the work was completed, 400 in one night. Five died in the attempt, and many were injured.[5] About 200 succeeded, as had 100 the night before.[6] In 2005, some 11,000 migrants had attempted to get over the fence.[7] Spain has added another 400 border guards to try to deter the flood of desperate Africans. Those who do make it to Spain have reached one of Europe's more tolerant countries, where "a succession of amnesties has given hundreds of thousands of immigrants at least a theoretical path to legal status."[8] It has also initiated a guest worker program with Senegal that offers passage and renewable one-year visas and job opportunities.[9]

Morocco, in the meantime, has found itself "caught between weak sub-Saharan countries that do nothing to stop the flow of migrants north and European countries angry that the flow reaches their southern shores"—and accused of violating the human rights of the travelers, even abandoning them in the desert.[10]

Italy, too, "has been inundated with illegal immigrants setting sail from North Africa," many of whom don't survive the crossing.[11] In 2004 a group of 100 left Libya for Sicily, but without enough food and water, more than a dozen had died by the time they were rescued nine days later. Italy's minister fears that now the migrants are heading for Lampedusa, another Italian island, where 9,500 migrants had landed in the first six months of 2006, while Greece's minister claims that 500 illegal migrants sail to his country every year.[12]

Once arrived in Europe, the newcomers find that affordable housing doesn't exist. In Italy, the *International Herald Tribune* reports, "faced with the impossibility of finding an apartment, some immigrants resort to living in makeshift camps in abandoned industrial areas or next to rail yards outside large cities, including Rome, Milan, and Turin," without plumbing, water, heat, or electricity.[13]

Government estimates indicate that there are some 200,000 to 400,000 illegal immigrants in France.[14] In 2005 a series of fires in Paris killed forty-eight West African immigrants, including children. Many of those living in the rundown buildings were there illegally, but even those in the country with permission had no place to go: "The plan to evacuate large numbers of squatters was dismissed by city officials as unrealistic given the dearth of housing."[15]

Even tiny landlocked Switzerland, with a population of 7.5 million, has its share of problems—90,000 foreigners are living there illegally. Switzerland, which (along with Japan) in a government study ranked among the top in limiting immigration, has introduced even stricter sanctions. "Japan and Switzerland are effective in enforcing immigration laws because illegal immigration is viewed as harmful," although in the Zurich region in 2005 only 5.5 percent of crimes reported were committed by illegal aliens.[16]

It was fear of immigration, especially from Eastern Europe, that led Austrian elections in 2006 to take a turn to the right. The governing People's Party lost ground to the Social Democrats, who "promised to crack down on crimes committed by foreigners," especially illegal immigrants.[17]

The recent extension of the European Union to Eastern European countries has made them, too, magnets for the poor of the world, including Africans, Middle Easterners, and gypsies. The Czech Republic alone may have 200,000 illegal immigrants. They, along with those who have entered legally, "take jobs Czechs do not want, like cleaning, construction and restaurant work." With a population that is aging even faster than America's, the whole question of immigration has given rise to "an active, if rancorous, debate about attracting immigrants." The country's top immigration official in the Ministry of Labor and Social Affairs, Michal Meduna, says, "We are quite serious about eliminating the negative impacts of demographic aging"; but the president, Vaclav Klaus, is more concerned about preserving national character.[18] Poland, which after a transition period will become the new border of Western Europe, at EU insistence is strengthening its border to keep out would-be immigrants from Ukraine.[19] In 2007 Poland began participating in the Schengen

Agreement, which allows free movement among the signatories. The agreement has been signed by all European Union states with the exception of Ireland and the United Kingdom, plus the non-EU members Iceland, Norway, and Switzerland. For this reason Poland's border becomes especially important.

Moving farther east, Russia has experienced "a wave of punitive measures against Georgian migrants and businesses." Under Putin's government the minority, who may number as many as a million, was blamed for organized crime, and many were deported. Critics call it "racism" and even "ethnic cleansing."[20] An anti-immigration group in Russia claims thousands of members who would rid the country of its many immigrants from the former Soviet Union, and even those from Chechnya and the Northern Caucasus, who are Russian citizens.[21]

Germany acknowledges that it needs immigration to offset the demographics of an aging population, but on its own terms: A new law will allow immigration for those who possess certain skills and establish services to promote assimilation. Germany has Europe's largest foreign population, some seven million, most of whom are Eastern Europeans of German heritage or guest workers. There are 300,000 first- and second- generation Muslims in Berlin alone, a legal but troublesome situation.

NOT ALL IMMIGRANT PROBLEMS DEAL WITH ILLEGALITY. THE REAL PROBLEM arises when the newcomers do not assimilate, as with the current large Muslim populations throughout Europe. In Germany the concept of the equality of the sexes has collided with the culture of a large Turkish minority that believes otherwise; numerous "honor killings" of daughters who won't submit to arranged marriages are the most shocking manifestation of this clash.

Hatun Surucu, a Turkish Kurd and one such victim, was born and raised in Berlin. When she had finished the eighth grade, her parents sent her off to Turkey for an arranged marriage. She eventually divorced her husband and returned to Berlin with her infant son, moved into a women's shelter, and continued her education, while she enjoyed the freedom of wearing makeup and jewelry, leaving her hair uncovered, and even going dancing. She was shot and killed by three of her brothers; "evidently," says the German writer Peter Schneider, "in the eyes of her brothers Hatun Surucu's capital crime was that, living in Germany, she had begun living like a German." A dangerous "parallel society" has arisen within the country, one that has little to do with the host culture, and even despises it.[22]

The tendency for young ethnic Turks to arrange for brides from the home country perpetuates the problem, and the new generation the unions produce will add to ethnic enclaves. In order to discourage such marriages, the German government has instituted immigration reforms that would raise the legal age of foreign-born spouses to eighteen.[23]

In Holland, 10 percent of the population are first-generation foreigners, from the Middle East and from throughout Africa and Asia. It is the Moroccans, though, that are "the most problematic minority." The offspring of Moroccan immigrants who came in the booming '80s and '90s on work visas were allowed to stay and enjoy extensive social benefits. And yet they see Holland's tolerance as decadence and find they can never be part of the country's affluence. Their resentment culminated in the murders of the filmmaker Theo Van Gogh and the politician Pim Fortuyn.[24] And the resentment is mutual. One reason the Dutch, as well as the French, rejected the EU Constitution was to show their frustration with the influx of immigrants. Fear of the admission of Turkey played a part among countries that already feel threatened by a large Muslim population in their midst.[25]

Of Europe's estimated 12 million Muslims, about half live in France.[26] Riots in France's suburban ghettos demonstrate the native-immigrant friction in that country. While first-generation arrivals from Muslim countries kept a low profile, fearing that if they were noticed they might be expelled, the third generation, born and raised in France and legal citizens, are angry. They know they can never fit into the rigid mold of Frenchness that society, and the government, demands. Unlike in America, where the national character is always evolving, France would like to hold onto its concept of what constitutes a Frenchman. Government policy of keeping no figures on race or ethnicity has backfired. A *New York Times* editorial sums up the problem:

> France clings to its cherished approach to immigration, which has been to declare that once in France, everyone is French and therefore equal, and that's that. The truth is that everyone is not French, nor equal, especially in an era of soaring immigration. The old approach gets in the way of real affirmative action or community outreach. Efforts at imposed integration, like the ban that keeps Muslim girls from wearing head scarves in state schools, have only antagonized immigrants.[27]

Although official policy would like to pretend that France is color-blind—there are no census figures on race, and job applications never include racial identity—French ambassador Jean-David Levitte admits that it's a lot easier to get a job if your name is Dupont than it is if you're called Mohammed.[28] French Muslims, like those in Germany, live in a parallel society, separate but not equal. The unemployment rate in France has been a high 10 percent, but for those in France's immigrant areas it has been a higher 21 percent,[29] and for Muslim youth the highest of all, close to 40 percent.[30] Even with generous social benefits, French immigrants, especially youth, feel alienated and disenfranchised, a discontent spawned by "poor, rundown living conditions, substandard education, massive unemployment, and social prejudice,"[31] and by the "deep-seated, searing, soul-destroying racism that the unemployed and profoundly alienated young of the ghettos face every day of their lives, both from the police and when trying to find a job."[32] It's not surprising that, according to one study, over half of the prison population in France is Muslim.[33]

Even though the economic picture has been much better in Britain, with its lower unemployment rate, the country has had its own problems with an underclass of Muslims who don't know to which culture they belong. American invasion of Iraq has exacerbated the identity crisis, united the discontented young Muslims of England's industrial cities, and sparked acts of terrorism, as many feel the West has turned against Islam itself. With 745,000 people of Pakistani origin living in Britain, many of whom feel closer to Pakistan than they do to their country of residence, the UK has become "a key location for international terrorist activity."[34] Bomb attacks in July 2005 on London's subway system were perpetrated by young men born and raised in England's industrial city of Leeds. They formed part of a larger group of Muslim youth "who turned their backs on what they came to see as a decadent, demoralized Western culture. Instead, the group embraced an Islam whose practice was often far more fundamentalist than their fathers', and always more political, focused passionately on Muslim suffering at Western hands."[35]

The terrorist attacks in London gave rise to much discussion over the immigrant situation in the United Kingdom, which had come to pride itself on its diversity. Because of the influx of immigrants, including some 230,000 from Eastern Europe since the EU's expansion, Britain's population has increased by 1.1 million in ten years; in London, one quarter of the population is foreign-born.[36] In addition to those arriving with permission, some 50,000 people attempting to enter illegally are detained each year.[37] Estimates of the number of illegals range from 250,000 up to 500,000 in a total population of about 60 million.[38] The problem of the UK's illegal minorities was brought to the forefront when thirty-two Chinese cockle pickers were drowned in a rising tide. One survivor described the deplorable conditions in which she lived in a small apartment in Liverpool, where she shared a mattress with five other people.

Rather than ignore its minorities, as France has done, Britain has embraced them, lauding the contributions of its immigrants. The think tank Civitas claims, however, that such a multicultural policy "is breeding racial hatred." In its report titled *The Poverty of Multiculturism*, Patrick West says:

> The fruits of 30 years of state-endorsed multiculturism have seen increased inter-racial tension and inter-racial sectarianism. . . . The fact that the London suicide bombers were born and bred in Britain, and encouraged by the state to be different, illustrate that hard multiculturism has the capacity to be not only divisive but decidedly lethal.[39]

The picture in Sweden is somewhat different, according to Peter Ericson of the Swedish Embassy. Because Sweden has signed the Schengen Agreement, border control is not exercised by the country, but rather by those states that form the boundary of the Schengen area. In the booming 1970s, Sweden attracted immigrants from Latin America and has also been accepting refugees for decades. In the 1980s came those fleeing the Iran-Iraq War, including many Kurds, and later those escaping the Balkan War. Many languished for years, unable to work while authorities determined their status. Today, as if to prove the adage "No good deed goes unpunished," large groups of immigrants remain unassimilated, blamed for an increased crime rate. Citizens of other countries make up 26 percent of Sweden's prison population, but about half of those sentenced for serious crimes are foreign-born.[40] As in other European countries, Sweden's foreign underclass lives on the fringes of the cities, where most of the residents are fellow foreigners and where unemployed young men are blamed for the surge in vandalism and petty crime. Alienated Muslim youth in particular are prey for radical groups that, according to the writer Kassem Hamadé, convey the message that "Sweden will never accept you."[41] As Christopher Caldwell says, "Sweden's immigrants are far from the poorest in Europe, but they are among the most excluded."[42] Peter Ericson of the Swedish embassy asks, "How do you integrate hundreds of thousands of relatively recent immigrants with cultural differences? It is very difficult, because we really don't know how to make a Swede out of somebody, because we are not really aware ourselves of what makes us Swedish. Can anybody become a Swede?" It's a question made more difficult by Swedish indifference to religion when faced with Muslim immigrants who care very much about their faith.

The problem of alienated minorities is endemic throughout Western Europe. "Europe is not a melting pot," says Thomas Friedman, "and has never adequately integrated its Muslim minorities, who, as The Financial Times put it, often find themselves 'cut off from their country, language and culture of origin without being assimilated into Europe, making them easy prey for peddlers of a new jihadist identity.'"[43] How is Europe confronting the many challenges presented by the situation?

Since the Revolution, France has depended upon its education system to unite the nation, making "peasants into Frenchmen."[44] In the late nineteenth century, as in the United States, it was in the schools that newcomers learned the language and culture of their country. Schools still loom as a prime influence for molding children into good European citizens, but today's schools in France's suburban ghettos are overcrowded, substandard, and "frequently staffed by weary, cynical, indifferent teachers." And yet there is hope that the schools will once again be a positive influence. Along with combating job discrimination, the government is working toward affirmative action programs, tripling the number of scholarships and boarding-school programs for students from troubled neighborhoods, and sponsoring mentorship and apprenticeship programs. The elite university Sciences Po is actively recruiting underprivileged students in "ZEPS—zones the government has designated as lacking educational and economic resources."[45] Nicolas Sarkozy, former interior minister and current president, is among those who have promoted the establishment of government-supported schools for the training of imams, who presumably would be more loyal to France than those who are imported from other countries today.

One surprising twist in education is that it may be the Muslim schools in Germany, Holland, Britain, Italy, and Spain that can offer part of the solution. "If the European educational system does not play a constructive role in the religious education of devout European Muslims, then where will that education come from, and how will it be shaped?" asks Jay Tolson. Abdullah Trevathan, head teacher in north London's Islamia Primary School, says Tolson, argues that schools such as his "can play a vital role in hammering out a new Muslim identity, one that combines being a good Muslim with being a good citizen in a pluralist society." Good Muslim schools might offer an antidote to the poisonous message of the extremists, because they would introduce children to the rich history of the religion that benefited from an openness to changing cultural conditions. Students would also gain more confidence in their own identity as Muslims, and as British citizens.[46]

It is education that Alison Kelly of the Irish Embassy credits with the *lack* of problems in her country, whose immigrants come from all over the world but who "mix quite well." Even in the face of an economic slowdown, Ireland continues to attract immigrants;[47] it makes *Foreign Policy*'s list of "The World's Best Places to Be an Immigrant," along with Spain, Canada, Israel, and New Zealand.[48]

In addition to pouring money into schools and social services—France has budgeted some $35 billion for housing and crime prevention, as well as education[49]—EU countries with immigration problems are individually and collectively working to strengthen their borders, increase security measures, and restrict immigration.

The British government is well aware that change is needed. In the wake of the terrorist attacks, British law will now allow suspects to be detained for up to twenty-eight days without charges, an act that the American government has considered emulating.[50] It will also attempt to check the flow of immigrants by restricting the numbers permitted from the former Eastern Bloc and by limiting benefits.[51]

The French, in a get-tough measure under then interior minister Sarkozy, have deported foreigners who advocate violence, and stepped up its program to expel illegal immigrants. Its goal for 2006: 25,000 out of the estimated 200,000 to 400,000.[52]

One thing that France is not advocating is amnesty for its many illegal aliens. It's a step that Spain took in 2005 and that Germany and Italy have been considering. The European Commission strongly opposes such a move, claiming that amnesty does not solve the underlying problems and merely serves to encourage others to enter illegally.[53]

THE EUROPEANS COULD TAKE A LESSON FROM THE UNITED STATES IN CONSIDering amnesty, in view of the results of the disastrous Immigration Reform and Control Act of 1986. On the other hand, perhaps we could learn from the European experience. Obviously, ignoring minorities to the point that there is no way to identify their problems by race or ethnicity does not work; Muslims and blacks in France feel they suffer from a not-so-benign neglect. "What the French government sees as a color-blind neutrality, many blacks see as an obstacle to their social progress," says John Tagliabue.[54] Nor does Britain's multiculturism serve to integrate all its citizens. Promoting a unifying language and culture is an essential role of education, a need that flies in the face of bilingual education.

We can continue to learn from one another as the Europeans wrestle with their own problems, many of which are similar to our own. At a conference on immigration in Morocco attended by representatives of fifty-eight European and African countries, they tackled the subjects of "border controls, workplace enforcement, economic development south of the border, questions of assimilation and national identity,"[55] a very familiar agenda for our own lawmakers.

WHILE EUROPE IS HAVING PROBLEMS INTEGRATING ITS NEWCOMERS, IN Canada, lauded by some as the country most welcoming to immigrants, a recent poll shows that 73 percent of Canadians think that immigrants exert a positive influence—and they have averaged 220,000 a year in recent years.[56] With an area of close to 4 million square miles and a population roughly one-tenth that of the United States, they have plenty of room for newcomers. Canada, Joseph H. Carens explains, "has special provisions for providing temporary visas for seasonal agricultural workers and for live-in caregivers. After two years, the latter (but not the former) are entitled to convert their status to that of a permanent resident without restrictions on work."[57]

In order to determine who may immigrate, Canada, as well as Australia and New Zealand, relies on a point system that takes into account education, occupation, language ability, age, and family connections. It's not without its problems, though. There's a backlog of more than 800,000 applicants, some of whom must wait four years or more for admittance. In addition, critics say the preference for the highly educated has led to a shortage of blue-collar workers, especially in the oil fields of western Canada.[58]

The economist George Borjas describes how New Zealand's policy works toward assimilation, providing financial incentives for learning the language. Families are required to post a bond, forfeiting portions of the bond progressively if family members do not pass an English test within stipulated periods.[59]

CHAPTER 10

The Good News

Compared to other countries, the United States, through luck or skill, has been able to embrace its immigrant population with relatively few problems. "In general, Europe, which has never developed an immigration culture, seems to have been less successful than the United States at integrating foreigners and giving them a stake in a new national identity," says Richard Bernstein. "At the same time, European immigrants seem to have been less eager than immigrants to the United States to take on a new identity, instead adhering to their traditional identities, languages and customs for generation after generation."[1]

Peter Ericson, who wonders what it takes to become a Swede, has observed that, unlike in his own country, "you move to the U.S., you say that you want to be an American and you embrace the basic values that anybody can do. That's about it. Then you are an American. Here in America there are all kinds of colors. Some of the people emigrated from Iran in the 1980s, some of them from Ireland in the 1700s, and everybody is American."

Stanley Crouch explains what assimilation means. In spite of all the talk of multiculturism, "assimilation is not, as advocates of separatism would teach us, a matter of domination and subordination, nor the conquest of one culture by another. On the contrary, it's about the great intermingling of cultural influences that comprises the American condition: the fresh ideas brought forward in our folklore, our entertainment, our humor, our athletic contests, our work places, even our celebrity trials and political scandals." He claims, in fact, "that American society is now so demonstrably open to variety, and so successful at gathering in those who would join it, that it is the international model of a free and progressively integrated nation."[2]

Chicago's Devon Avenue, the center of the Pakistani community in that city, may in some ways resemble similar neighborhoods in Britain, but residents spell out the difference. Nizam Arain, a native Chicagoan of Pakistani descent, says, "There is integration even when you have an enclave. . . . You don't have the same siege mentality."[3] Although the British may give lip service to the importance of their immigrants, the fact is that the chances for success are much greater in the United States. "Britain remains far more rigid," says the journalist Neil MacFarquhar. "In the United States, for example, Pakistani physicians are more likely to lead departments at hospitals or universities than they are in Britain," and "nationwide, Pakistanis appear to be prospering." Unlike the British, we are unburdened by a "collective history here of frustrated efforts to assimilate into a society where a shortened form of Pakistani is a stinging slur, and there are no centuries-old grievances nursed from British colonial rule over what became Pakistan."[4] Yet another "major difference between the United States and Britain, some say, is the United States' ideal of being a melting-pot meritocracy."[5]

As for France, according to Robert A. Levine of the RAND Corporation:

> The central difference—between the United States and France and between France's past and its future—lies in numbers. France absorbs individuals into its classic culture; until the current ingress of North African Muslims, it had not experienced mass immigration, and neither its beliefs nor its policies have adapted to the new wave. The United States has absorbed mass migrations over a several-generation period and has continually adapted its own culture and policies. The difference does not make either country morally or politically "better" or "worse" than the other, but American practice is likely to preserve its essential institutions; unless France changes direction, the difference may lead to dire consequences for that admirable nation.[6]

"'You can keep the flavor of your ethnicity, but you are expected to become an American,' said Omer Mozaffar, 34, a Pakistani-American raised here who is working toward a doctorate in Islamic studies at the University of Chicago."[7]

Ihsan Alkhatib, who is president of the American Arab Anti-Discrimination Committee, thinks we could teach Europe a thing or two. He compares the European experience of "residential segregation, low high-school graduation rates, and high un-employment rates" to the situation in the United States, "where Muslim-Americans are better off economically than many Americans. Western Europe," he says, "needs to learn from the U.S. how to accept and integrate its Muslim communities into the larger society politically, economically and socially."[8]

Assimilation may work for the relatively small numbers of Pakistanis and Muslims in our midst, but what about the millions of Hispanics? All the indicators of integration—language, intermarriage, and homeownership—point to their integration into American society as well. Consider the learning of English—and the forgetting of Spanish. Tamar Jacoby suggests that if we visit even the most isolated Latino enclave, the adults will be speaking Spanish, "but the children—even very young children, and even small siblings in families of Spanish-speaking adults—can often be heard speaking English among themselves. Even if they don't learn much at school, children pick up English from TV and other popular culture; their parents know it is the key to their futures."[9]

Although it is a loss for her country, Remedios Gómez-Arnau, Mexico's consul general in Atlanta, describes what happens. The first generation maintains strong ties with Mexico, but "if you're talking about the second or third, they tend to lose their ties. You see it right here. You see the labor force here, their parents aren't here, and you rarely go to the country where your parents live. Your relatives are here in the United States. You know that there is some kind of tie with Mexican culture, but that's it. A kid who is born here, attends school here, he speaks English. Many of them tend to lose Spanish. From the second generation they don't speak Spanish anymore; they only communicate in English. So the people who complain that Latinos don't integrate are just taking a very specific moment in time, and that's not the best way to look at any human phenomenon, social phenomenon. You need to look at the dynamic perspective. The second generation is born here and they attend school. Which language do they speak to them in school? English. And they sing the American anthem, and they are taught to pay respect to the American flag. People need to look at the second and third generation."[10]

According to figures from the Pew Hispanic Center, "most second-generation Latinos are either bilingual (47%) or English-dominant (46%). By the third generation eight in ten are English-dominant."[11] Churches in Chicago's large Hispanic community are well aware of these changes; they're adding English-language services "in an effort to meet the demands of second- and third-generation Hispanics," as well as appeal to non-Latinos. "As the children of immigrants grow up," says Eric Gorski, "it's either bolster Spanish with English or give up on the future."[12]

By every definition of assimilation, Hispanics become a part of the American culture at the same rate that immigrants always have. Take intermarriage, which

Nathan Glazer says "marks the highest degree of social acceptance."[13] Tamar Jacoby finds this "ultimate measure" in the United States today to be "nothing short of astounding. Among U.S.-born Asians and Hispanics," she says, "between a third and a half marry someone of a different ethnicity. By the third generation, according to some demographers, the rates reach over 50 percent for both groups."[14] Robert A. Levine asserts that "like the data on language, figures on intermarriage show steady acculturation," adding that "Hispanics seem to be headed in the same direction" as the Jews and Italians who came before them.[15] As for home ownership, another indication of integration into American life, "within 20 years," says Tamar Jacoby, "60% are homeowners."[16] Even though the immigrants who come to America generally suffer from a lower level of education than natives, which puts them at a disadvantage as wage earners, RAND Corporation economist James P. Smith claims that "2nd and 3rd-generation Hispanic men have made great strides in closing the economic gaps with native whites. The reason is simple—each successive generation has been able to close the schooling gap with native whites which then has been translated into generational progress in incomes."[17]

And they share the same dominant values as mainstream Americans. While still placing a higher level of importance on family than do non-Hispanic whites, Latinos lose the fatalistic attitude of their Spanish-only parents and embrace American optimism: "Nearly 60 percent of Spanish-speakers, for instance—compared to 15 percent of non-Hispanic whites—were so fundamentally fatalistic that they saw no point in planning for the future. But among second-generation and English-dominant Hispanics, 75 percent felt they were in charge of their lives. America had already changed them that much—they had assimilated that thoroughly."[18] From numerous polls, Amitai Etzioni concludes that "there is ample evidence that Americans of all racial and ethnic backgrounds hold their most important beliefs in common."[19] On everything from what they consider American characteristics ("hardworking and diligent," "ambitious") to concerns over children's excessive materialism, percentages of the responses of all groups surveyed were surprisingly close. And they all agree on the importance of spending money on education. In one poll of New York residents, more Hispanics (88 percent) than whites (70 percent) judged "teaching 'the common heritage and values that we share as Americans' to be 'very important.'"[20]

Hispanic newcomers soon come to enjoy the same pop culture, for better or worse, since, say researchers Matt S. Meier and Feliciano Ribera, "Mexican American children, regardless of the environment and language at home, are constantly exposed to American mass culture—national products and tastes, Anglo heroes and social values."[21] Victor Davis Hanson regrets the Mexicanization of his home state of California, but he takes hope from the lowbrow consumer culture in which we all partake:

At a time when illegal immigration is at an all-time high, and formal efforts at forging a common culture and encouraging assimilation are at an all-time low, the habits, tastes, appetites and expressions of everyday people have offered a rescue of sorts—perhaps deleterious to the long-term moral health of the United States, but in the short term about the only tool we possess to prevent racial separation and ethnic tribalism. Informality in dress, slang speech, movies, videos, television—all this makes assimilation easier, even at a time when professional racialists are calling for highbrow separatism.[22]

Once those here without documents obtain legal status, will this new population also become integrated into American society? Every indication is that it will, and at the same rate as previous immigrants. Huntington claims that the "educational achievements" of Mexican-American immigrants "continue to lag."[23] But it is only in education, says Michael Barone, that Hispanic immigrants are behind,[24] while other factors indicate that they are following the path of previous arrivals to America.

Robert Toonkel of U.S. English recalls how important the schools were for the acculturation process at the turn of the century. Not only the schools, but the whole community worked toward immigrants acquiring English fluency, because "you're not going to become a productive member of society if you can't speak English," he says, citing the many polls that indicate that between 80 and 85 percent of Americans support making English our official language. "English puts people on the path to citizenship and it puts people on the direction to where they could survive anywhere in this nation." Hispanics know this, too: according to a Pew Hispanic Center survey, by "a large majority" they believe "that immigrants have to speak English to be a part of American society and even more so that English should be taught to the children of immigrants."[25] Herman Badillo, a former congressman, self-styled ex-liberal, and erstwhile activist for bilingual education, has come to agree. "The only answer to Hispanic poverty and assimilation . . . is education"—in English, he says.[26]

Rather than look at those who have just stepped over the border, it might be more productive to look ahead at the children of the newcomers, many of whom are American citizens. The statistics show that our schools, especially in the South, are seeing a surge in school-age children, thanks to the increase in the Hispanic population.[27] From 1993 to 2003, our school-age population increased by 4.7 million, of which 64 percent were Hispanic.[28]

Just as those in Europe are discovering that education is the key to integrating their minority populations, we, too, have the opportunity, through education, to prepare our new Americans to be an integral part of our society.

As Americans, although they may still maintain their culture, in a few years they will acquire a unique identity that will set them apart from their roots, as other groups have done. On my first visit to England, I had hoped to sense some sort of atavistic genetic connection to my British forebears. I was surprised at how different we were. An African American friend told us that it was only when he went to Africa that he realized how American he was. In Japan I watched a group of tourists come down a garden path on Shikoku Island. Although their features were pure Japanese, their clothes, the way they walked, and the way they held themselves were pure American. Sure enough, when they came closer, one man called out informally, "Hey, where're you folks from? We're from L.A.!"

Through the presence of the immigrants, America will change, too, as it is already doing. "Acculturation has always been a two-way street in the United States," says Robert A. Levine.[29] In sports, in the music we listen to, and the food we eat, we can hardly ignore the Latino influence. Among other things, Hispanics are bringing new life to the troubled American Catholic church. According to Monsignor Jarlath Cunnane, "The renewal we've experienced has not just been in numbers but in terms of vibrancy of faith and in the sense of community."[30]

In his book *Who Are We?* Samuel Huntington infers that the massive influx of Spanish-speaking immigrants is eroding our Anglo-Protestant national identity. Levine's response would be: "Is America's Anglo-Protestant-African-Catholic-Indian-German-Irish-Jewish-Italian-Slavic-Asian society in danger of 'Hispanicization?' The obvious answer is 'no.'"[31]

It's apparent that Hispanics are assimilating in the same way that other immigrants have in the past, especially as they move out of the border states. But what's happening on the economic front in the meantime?

Apart from legal and ethical considerations, most economists agree that the newcomers affect the economy as a whole in a positive manner. Although George J. Borjas notes that competition from immigrant workers has a negative effect on what low-skilled native workers earn[32]—a report by the anti-immigration think tank Center for Immigration Studies puts it at 12 percent[33]— mainstream economists like Gianmarco I. P. Ottaviano and Giovanni Peri claim that "overall immigration generates a large positive effect on the *average* wages of U.S.-born workers" (italics added). They admit that, in the period from 1990 to 2000, "the inflow lowered the real wage of native workers without a high school degree by 1%," but, on the other hand, "it increased the real wage of native workers with at least a high-school degree as much as 3–4%."[34] Stephen Moore of the *Wall Street Journal* says that while "immigrants compete with American workers in some industries and in localized labor markets," and "often do displace American workers and push wages downward," that "on a macrolevel . . . there is no evidence of wage suppression by immigrants, because natives have generally migrated into other professions with higher wages."[35] John Tierney asks us to consider two options:

1. Restricting immigration to protect some of the lower-paid workers in America from a decline in wages that would be no more than 8 percent, if it occurred at all.
2. Expanding immigration to benefit most Americans while also giving some non-Americans living in dire poverty the chance to quadruple their income.[36]

It's obvious which choice he thinks we would make.

David Card, an economist at UC Berkeley, states that "data from the 2000 Census shows that relative wages of native dropouts are uncorrelated with the relative supply of less-educated workers, as they were in earlier years. At the aggregate level, the wage gap between dropouts and high school graduates has remained nearly constant since 1980, despite supply pressure from immigration and the rise of other education-related wage gaps. Overall, evidence that immigrants have harmed the opportunities of less educated natives is scant."[37] He finds that "there is a surprisingly weak relationship between immigration and less-skilled native wages."[38] What's more, like consul general Remedios Gómez-Arnau, he believes that you have to take a long view:

> Few of the 40 percent of immigrants who come to the U.S. without completed high school education will ever catch up with the average earnings of natives. Most of their U.S.-born children, however, will catch up with the children of natives. Evidence on the intergenerational progress of immigrants' children is now becoming available, and points to above-average levels of educational attainment, even for children whose fathers had much lower schooling than native-born fathers. The relatively strong educational progress of second generation immigrants, together with the limited evidence of adverse effects on less skilled natives, suggest that the new immigration may not be so bad after all.[39]

In a *New York Times* interview, Card conceded that "some might argue that a larger population raises housing prices and causes more pollution. . . . But there can be advantages to size, too. 'If you have population growth, you can finance intergenerational transfer systems' like Social Security and Medicare. . . . 'And lest we forget,' he said, 'Big countries have more power.'"[40] In the same article, William H. Frey of the Brookings Institution "agreed that waves of immigration could help to solidify a country's position in the world. In that respect, he said, 'Europe and Japan have a problem. They have a very aging society because they don't like immigrants. . . . They're going to end up on the back burner of the global economy.'"[41]

The editors of the *Wall Street Journal* also recognize the economic importance of immigrants, even those here without documentation:

In 2001, undocumented immigrants filled 1.4 million jobs in the wholesale and retail trades alone, according to the Pew Hispanic Center. More than one million worked in manufacturing, and another 1.2 million worked in agriculture. Without these immigrants, employers would be forced to raise wages to attract Americans, perhaps to levels above what productivity and competition allow. Certain jobs would simply not get done, as is now the case in Europe as companies automate or move more jobs overseas. Far from costing the United States jobs, immigrants today allow some industries to survive and expand.[42]

"Immigrants also contribute to the creation of new jobs by circulating their wages in the local economy and adding to the regional and federal tax base," says Jorge Ramos.[43] In addition to contributing to the local economy through paying sales taxes where they apply, immigrants often have taxes withheld from their payroll. Even if they are illegal, most do pay taxes, since employers must follow the book when it comes to payroll deductions, although the identification the employees present may be fake. Such deductions are bolstering our Social Security program: "Illegal immigration, Marcelo Suárez-Orozco, co-director of immigration studies at New York University, noted sardonically, could provide 'the fastest way to shore up the long-term finances of Social Security.'"[44]

The buying power of millions of Hispanic immigrants, both legal and illegal, has not gone unnoticed by the nation's businesses. Financial institutions, real estate agents, insurance companies, and those who create and sell consumer products such as Coca-Cola, Anheuser-Busch, Kellogg's, and Unilever, are among the companies looking for ways to appeal to the burgeoning market. Travel agencies and telecom companies have discovered that family-oriented Hispanics are especially good customers, with their need to keep in touch with other family members. The Hispanic media are thriving, and marketing companies like LaVerdad in Cincinnati and Vargas & Amigos in Atlanta are helping businesses reach Latinos. The Hispanic market has been estimated to reach $1 trillion in 2010, says the U.S. Bureau of Economic Analysis.[45] Not so, Daniel Vargas tells me. It was almost there long before that date.

Immigrants are revitalizing old industrial cities like Chicago and Boston, to the point that other cities, like Cleveland, are actively seeking to attract newcomers to bring new life to their urban areas.[46]

Contrary to conventional wisdom, "as immigration soars, crime falls," says Eyal Press. Criminal-justice professor Ramiro Martinez Jr. has examined homicide records in cities with high numbers of Mexican immigrants, such as San Diego and El Paso, and discovered that "almost without exception . . . the homicide rate for Hispanics was lower than for other groups, even though their poverty rate was very high, if not the *highest*, in those metropolitan areas." Criminologist Andrew Karmen discovered the same trend in New York City, where "he found that 'the disproportionately youthful, male and poor immigrants' who arrived during the 1980s and 1990s 'were surprisingly law-abiding' and that their settlement into once-decaying neighborhoods helped 'put a brake on spiraling crime rates.'" In Chicago, too, "the rate of violence among Mexican-Americans was significantly lower than among both non-Hispanic whites and blacks."[47] According to the *Economist*, poor immigrants, "as studies have repeatedly shown, are much better behaved than natives of similar means."[48] As David Brooks notes:

> The facts show that the recent rise in immigration hasn't been accompanied by social breakdown, but by social repair. As immigration has surged, violent crime has fallen by 57 percent. Teen pregnancies and abortion rates have declined by a third. Teenagers are having fewer sexual partners and losing their virginity later. Teen suicide rates have dropped. The divorce rate for young people is on the way down. . . . . The anti-immigration crowd says this country is under assault. But if that's true, we're under assault by people who love their children. . . . Immigrants work hard. They build community groups. They have traditional ideas about family structure, and they work heroically to make them a reality.[49]

Carlos Martinez believes that both sides benefit from immigration. Mexicans in America are learning that it is possible to have a voice in what happens to them; they return to Mexico with the attitude that they can change their government. They are learning from us—small things like agricultural improvements or major changes in attitudes toward authority. Dr. Sandra Nichols, a research analyst at California for Rural Studies, has investigated what she calls "transnational communities," focusing especially on relations between the Napa Valley and a town in Mexico. She notes that many immigrants maintain strong ties with their home community, which gains from American innovations like the "drip irrigation" method, which allows water to get directly to the roots of the plant. Transfer of knowledge is not limited to technology, she says. "A lot of anthropologists and people who work in the Mexican villages have noticed for a long time that people coming back bring back new styles, new ways of thinking, new kinds of behavior. Like women standing up for their rights a little more." And what do we gain from the exchange? Dr. Nichols recalls what happened when a sister-city relationship was established between Napa and Jerez in Mexico: "When we start to bridge the gap, I think we get what's missing in the Anglo Protestant culture, where we sometimes overlook that human warmth and connection, the passion, and all those qualities that the Northern Europeans seek when they go to Italy and the Mediterranean." And, as Sister Maria Stacy of

Dayton's Catholic Hispanic Ministry says, how can the influx of family-oriented, hard-working people be anything but a good influence on our society?

For those who are concerned about the huge influx from Mexico, there are some indications that fewer Mexicans will be heading north in the future. For one thing, Mexicans are having fewer children; the birth rate has dropped 30 percent in the last ten years.[50] In 2005 the birth rate hit an all-time low of 2.1 children per woman—in 1962 it was 7.3—which Mexican population expert Carlos Welti thinks is "due to the increasing education level of women and their participation in economic life."[51] Looking some twenty years into the future, the population is expected to stop growing, which will initiate "some dramatic changes," says the National Population Council: "This process of change will free up resources that were once dedicated to attending a continuously growing population of minors, . . . generating a virtuous cycle of more savings, investment and employment."[52]

We don't need to look that far ahead to see some indications for optimism. Foreign investors—both European and American—are investing in Mexican real estate, encouraged by the country's strong economic growth; gross domestic product was some 3.5 percent in 2005.[53] The *Wall Street Journal* editors note that Mexico has made progress in recent years on various fronts: with the privatization of thousands of government-owned businesses, the lowering of trade tariffs, the signing of the North American Free Trade Agreement, and the institution of free elections, which led to the unseating of the PRI (Institutional Revolutionary Party), which had held power for so long. Felipe Calderón, elected president in 2006, promised "to simplify the tax regime, allow private 'partnerships' for deep water oil exploration, and rid the country of monopoly privilege. He has also committed to preserving fiscal and monetary stability," all of which bode well for the future. What is more, "a stable peso has . . . led to low inflation, and interest rates have followed. In recent years markets for consumer credit and mortgages have developed. Retail competition has given Mexican consumers a taste of what is possible. . . . If Mexicans are able to build on the liberalizing trends of the past 20 years, their appetite for El Norte is bound, over time, to diminish."[54]

The *Economist* predicts that Mexico will remain "an attractive destination for foreign direct investment," especially in the long term, with predicted GDP growth figures of 3.9 percent for 2010; 3.6 percent for 2011; and 3.5 percent for 2012, after a short downturn in line with the American economy.[55] The publication gives Calderón good marks for his attempts at fiscal reform, although his authority is challenged by long-standing problems with drug-related crime.[56] There is room for hope here, too, with the promise of substantial U.S. cooperation to fight the problem.

Business Week is also optimistic about Mexico, which, in spite of its woes, "has quietly become more competitive" with China and India. Thanks to some "crucial factors" vis-à-vis its Asian competitors when it comes to "costs, logistics, skills, trade, and risk," "business is standing its ground," the publication explains.[57]

In the meantime, the new immigrants, like their predecessors, will continue to change—and to change America.

Conclusion

BEGINNING WITH THE FIRST STEP OF THE JOURNEY, THOSE WHO ENTER OUR country without the protection of the law are at risk, for first the travelers must face the dangers of the no-man's-land at the border. Once arrived at their destination, illegal immigrants are vulnerable to abuse at work or at home, afraid to report crimes because of the possibility of deportation. They must live a life in hiding, in constant fear of losing their homes and security.

When pro-immigration rallies throughout the country in the spring of 2006 brought rumors that the ICE would descend in force, many were led to hide behind closed doors, keeping their children home from school and not attending church. Although ICE officials denied that they would retaliate for the rallies, those on the side of the immigrants complained that people were worried. "You wonder if the immigration Gestapo are coming to get you," said the owner of a nursery, and a pastor lamented that such ugly rumors "intimidated people who are already afraid. They are living in the shadows of society, wondering who is going to knock on the door."[1]

Nina Bernstein writes that during federal crackdowns in rural western New York, "farm hands have simply disappeared by twos and threes, picked up on a Sunday as they went to church or to the laundry. Whole families have gone into hiding, like the couple who spent the night with their child in a plastic calf hutch." The spring raids caught dozens of workers "on their way to milk parlors, apple orchards and vineyards, and prompted more to flee, affecting hundreds of farms. Some longtime employees with American children were deported too quickly for goodbyes, or remain out of reach in the federal detention center in Batavia, N.Y., where immigrants are tracked by alien registration number, not by name."[2]

Hundreds fled the county when federal agents conducted a raid in little Still-more, Georgia, many heading for the woods, where they camped out for days. Residents worried that some were still hiding weeks later without enough food. At least one child, an American citizen toddler, was left behind with a babysitter when his father was deported and his weeping mother fled. After residents of his trailer park were taken away in handcuffs, David Robinson hung an American flag upside down in protest and said, "These people might not have American rights, but they've . . . sure got human rights. . . . There ain't no reason to treat them like animals."[3] Once arrested, immigrant families, including young children, "are being kept in jail-conditions" in some parts of the country, say immigrant rights' groups.[4]

In June 2007, it was reported that since 2004, sixty-two immigrants had died while being held in "a secret detention system."[5] Many of the deaths could have been prevented by prompt medical treatment, like that of Sandra M. Kenley, a Barbados native who didn't receive her high-blood-pressure medication, or Guinea-born Abdoulai Sall, who failed to get treatment for his serious kidney ailment.[6]

Even those who most avidly oppose illegal immigration must agree that this is not the way to handle the problem. The treatment of undocumented immigrants looms as a major human rights issue.

Workers who cross the border without documentation are not the only ones who suffer in an environment in which the law is not respected. As consul general Remedios Gómez-Arnau has pointed out, when we do not know who is crossing our border, we "get all kinds of people," including criminals. The U.S. Justice Department estimated that in 2003, roughly 270,000 illegal immigrants had served time in jail, while some estimates indicated that up to half of California's prison population are in the country illegally. Steven Camarota of the Center for Immigration Studies said in 2004 that "roughly 17 percent of the prison population at the federal level are illegal aliens," and California governor Pete Wilson thought the figure was even higher: "One in five in our prison population were illegal immigrants who had been convicted of a felony after entering the country illegally," he claimed.[7] More Justice Department figures show that "immigrants arrested for being in the United States illegally may have been charged up to six more times, for serious crimes, after they were released by local authorities. In a sample group of 100 examined, 73 immigrants were later arrested a collective 429 times."[8] Cox Newspapers reported in 2006 that thousands of high-risk criminals were being released rather than deported;[9] 20 percent of those illegal immigrants who had been incarcerated in Georgia were set free rather than deported as the law requires.[10] And those criminals are not just preying on their fellow immigrants.

Many of the increasing number of identity thefts can be blamed on illegal immigrants using stolen ID in order to obtain jobs. Audra Schmierer of California discovered that her social security number had been used by at least 81 people in seventeen states, most of whom were probably unauthorized immigrants looking for work.[11] In December 2006, 1,282 immigrants who were arrested at meatpacking plants in six states were suspected of this offense.[12] In a 2007 raid of a Smithfield Foods plant in North Carolina, 25 of the 29 illegal immigrants were charged with stealing the identities of American citizens.[13] Eagle County, Colorado, is just one of the many areas where such crimes are a common occurrence. Says Avon police detective Paul Arnold, "I'd say probably three-quarters of the illegals I've dealt with here get false documents. . . . With the number of illegals here in the valley, I'd say there are thousands of them."[14]

In the face of the chaos that illegal immigration presents, not all the outrage that farmers have expressed has been on behalf of the immigrants. At harvest time in 2006 they were furious at the U.S. Congress, by whom they felt betrayed, blaming its members for losses like that of $10 million for California's pear growers alone. Like Sheriff Richard Jones, they complain that all they get from Congress is "lip service," rather than action on a guest worker program. The current program, which grants a limited number of visas for seasonal workers, does not fulfill farmers' needs, especially since employers cannot apply until 120 days before they are needed.[15] In spite of their illegal status, those who come across the border to work in our farms and businesses are very necessary to keep America running, say their employers. When workers failed to show up at harvest time, deterred by stricter border controls, farmers growing sweet potatoes and onions in Georgia, oranges in Florida, vegetables in California, and apples in Washington all suffered.[16] In California, Nick Ivicevich's joy at his beautiful, record-breaking pear crop turned to heartbreak when no one was there to harvest them. In the future, "unless those workers somehow get across that border," the farmers agree, "agriculture here once again will be hard hit, if not crippled."[17] In Colorado, where tougher restrictions on immigration caused immigrant workers to flee, farmers turned to prison labor.[18]

Other businesses, too, clamor for a guest worker program that would legalize employees and help them face a shortage of labor that will only become worse as baby boomers retire. Shawn McBurney of the American Hotel and Lodging Association says that resorts and hotels can't find enough American employees to fill the cleaning, cooking, food-serving, and landscaping jobs they offer.[19] The U.S.

Chamber of Commerce supports a legalization plan, estimating that by 2010, "the United States will have 168 million jobs and only 158 million Americans to fill them."[20] Eliseo Medina of the Service Employees International Union is vocal in his support of a plan for temporary workers.

Labor unions, too, support immigration reform. While the AFL-CIO and its rival the Change to Win Federation oppose an expanded guest worker program, they have agreed to work together to support the legalization of undocumented immigrants already here. They call for a program to control through a national commission the number of future immigrants, both permanent and temporary, based upon the need for labor.[21]

Economists continue to argue over whether immigration, even illegal, is a financial plus or minus. A Heritage Foundation report says that each immigrant household receives $3 for every dollar it pays,[22] while the President's Council of Economic Advisers states that immigrants contribute some $30 billion a year to the economy.[23] But it's not just a question of economics. Do we really want the creation of an underclass, outside the law, that is often mistreated, underpaid, ill-housed, and placed at risk, afraid to complain for fear of deportation?

Americans are united by two things: the rule of law and the English language. It's important that these pillars of our unity not be eroded. It is the question of legality that is the most troubling feature of a problem affecting health providers, law enforcement, education, social services, and employment, as well as the immigrants themselves. Controversial sheriff Richard K. Jones has been criticized for overstepping the bounds in his get-tough approach to illegal immigrants, but he makes a valid point when he says that when we ignore the justice system under which we operate, "the basic rule of law breaks down."

Americans are well aware of the dangers to this basic tenet of our "unifying core." Although there has been no national referendum like that which Jim Wolfe of the forum in Jackson, Wyoming, envisions, there have been plenty of polls to let us know what Americans think. In a survey of public-opinion polls in 2006, the Pew Hispanic Center reported that "a significant majority of Americans see illegal immigration as a very serious problem and most others see it at least as a serious problem."[24] At the same time, according to a 2007 *U.S.A. Today*/Gallup poll, most Americans—78 percent—are willing to allow illegal immigrants a chance to remain here legally if certain provisions are made.[25] A *New York Times/CBS News* poll gave similar results. Many of those provisions that Americans favor—tighter security at the border, guest worker programs, and earned citizenship among them—are compatible with the very measures that reformers in Congress are seeking.

It is in our favor that along with respect for the rule of law, Americans also value compromise. As Congress begins to address illegal immigration, there will be many issues that warrant such give-and-take.

General amnesty is not the answer, as we saw in 1986. It only encouraged others to come in the hope that they, too, might be rewarded some day with residency. Nor is it practical to consider mass deportation, even if it would be possible to round up all of the undocumented. Rajeev Goyle and David A. Jaeger of the Center for American Progress estimate that such a move would cost from at least $206 billion to perhaps more than $230 billion over a five-year period. The low figure of $41 billion a year would still be more than Homeland Security's 2006 budget, twice the amount spent on border and transportation security annually, half the annual cost of the Iraq War, and "more than double the annual cost of military operations in Afghanistan."[26] As it is, in 2004 the federal government had a backlog of some 460,000 fugitive "absconders" who had been ordered deported, 80,000 of whom had criminal records. The estimated cost of apprehending and deporting fugitives in 2005: almost $67 million.[27]

Stricter enforcement of immigration laws, as in the recent crackdown on employers, however, must be matched with a way to help those who most depend on such labor. (It's estimated that at least 70 percent of those working on farms are here illegally.[28])

Guest worker programs that would contain safeguards lacking in earlier *bracero* programs and provide health-care insurance, among other things, would help those who want to be on the right side of the law, employee and employer alike, as would plans for earned legalization.

As for the second unifying force, learning English must be a top priority if the newcomers are to be welcomed into our society and not become part of a separate, permanent underclass. Robert Toonkel of U.S. English notes that "the language thing is so strong. If you go into a football stadium and you look around, you could say if we were in any other country on this earth, we'd probably be warring with the people sitting next to us, because they look different or they have a different background. Here in the United States we can stand together side by side and have a conversation over anything because we can speak that one language."

The importance of education—in English—is a recurring theme throughout the book. Education today is as important as it was for the "huddled masses" of the Great Wave who assimilated and produced today's citizens. It was education that lifted José from his Ecuadorean peasant background to life as a productive middle-class American. Recognizing its importance, the Mexican government offers education, including English lessons, at its consulates, while in Europe, too, leaders are looking to education to redress the problems of disadvantaged immigrant youth.

The great numbers of immigrant children, many of them American citizens, who are entering our schools offer the same chances for us. It's an opportunity we must not pass up. If ever we needed a clinching argument for the importance of investing in education, this is it.

The immigration problem will not go away overnight, and its resolution will not be cheap. For example, although preliminary figures indicated that federal spending for the failed Comprehensive Immigration Reform Act of 2007—up to $38 billion over the 2008–2017 period—could have been offset by increases in federal revenue, additional expenses were anticipated for such things as law enforcement grants and verification of employment eligibility, amounting to an estimated $40 billion for 2008–2017.[29]

Nor will any arrangement be perfect. There will undoubtedly be unexpected consequences, as in the case of some Medicare patients who lacked treatment because of crackdowns on abuses by illegal immigrants. Some—like the Southern Poverty Law Center—will argue that guest worker programs exploit immigrants, placing them in near-slavery conditions.[30] Others will argue that an "earned legalization" program will reward those who break the law and be tantamount to amnesty, encouraging even more to cross the border—while others fear that few immigrants will take the chance on returning home to apply for legal admittance, should that be required. Employers complain of a government-imposed point system that won't help them find the kinds of employees they need. [31] Others claim that valuing skills over family ties would break up families, and many immigrants complain that the plan would be too costly. There may be a grain of truth in all of the objections, but the alternative of doing nothing is far worse.

Immigration reform will mean some of us will have to sacrifice personal gain for the good of all—everyone from Republicans, who, it is said, support businesses in their attempts to lower costs, and Democrats, who are accused of seeking more Hispanic voters, to those of us who will have to pay more for the services we've grown accustomed to.

It will be a small price to pay, however, to reject a devil's bargain and restore the rule of law that unites us—and be on the side of the angels again.

NOTES

PREFACE

1. Jeffrey S. Passel, "Size and Characteristics of the Unauthorized Migrant Population in the U.S.," Pew Hispanic Center Report, 7 March 2006, http://pewhispanic.org/reports/report.php?Report ID=61.

2. Julia Preston, "A Slippery Place in the U.S. Work Force," *New York Times*, 22 March 2009, 1.

CHAPTER 1. GETTING HERE

1. Some names and details have been changed to protect privacy.

2. Quoted in "Outside Reading," *Arizona Water Resource* (May-June 2001): 1–2, http://ag.Arizona.edu/AZWATER/awr/mayjune/01.

3. Randal C. Archibold, "Risky Measures by Smugglers Increase Toll on Immigrants," *New York Times*, 9 August 2006, A12.

4. Mark Randall, "People Stacked like 'Cord Wood' in Fatal Vehicle; 9 Die in Rollover," *Yuma Sun*, 7 August 2006, http://sun.yumasun.com/cgi-bink/artman/exec/view.cgi/17125844.

5. Luis Alberto Urrea, *The Devil's Highway* (New York: Little, Brown and Company, 2004), 19.

6. "Arizona MinuteMan Project to Patrol Border," 26 January 2005, http://www.securityarms.com/cgi-local.

7. Marc Cooper, "High Noon on the Border," *The Nation*, 6 June 2005, 21.

8. Quoted in John Annerino, *Dead in Their Tracks: Crossing America's Desert Borderlands* (New York: Four Walls, Eight Windows, 1999), 114.

9. Urrea, *Devil's Highway*, 19.

10. Bob Keefe, "High-tech Eyes along Border Give Blurred View," (Cox News Service) *Dayton Daily News*, 17 May 2006, A15.

11. Leo R. Chavez, *Shadowed Lives: Undocumented Immigrants in American Society* (Fort Worth, TX: Harcourt Brace College Publishers, 1991), 42.

12. Urrea, *Devil's Highway*, 20.

13. "Border Patrol Agents Deliver New Citizen in Back of Truck," (AP) *Dayton Daily News*, 4 March 2005, A3.

14. Ralph Blumenthal, "Trial Starts in Nation's Deadliest Human Smuggling Case," *New York Times*, 9 March 2005, A13.

15. Tom Buechele, "Missing the Welcome Mat: New Border Rules Stifle U.S. Boast As 'Mother of Exiles,'" *Episcopal Life*, December 2004, 22.

16. Brenda Zurita, "Christians Shine the Light on Sex Trafficking," *Family Voice* (July-August 2005).

17. "Sex Slavery: The Growing Trade," *CNN.com/World*, 8 March 2001, http://archives.cnn.com/2001/WORLD/Europe/03/08/women.trafficking/.

18. Susan Carroll, Republic Nogales Bureau, "Migrant Death Toll Sets Grim Record," 5 September 2003, 1, http://www.azcentral.com/specials/specia103/articles/0905recorddeaths.05.htm.

19. Richard Alba and Victor Nee, *Remaking the American Mainstream: Assimilation and Contemporary Immigration* (Cambridge, MA: Harvard University Press, 2003), 40.

20. Gerald F. Kicanas, "Never Again! (Illegal immigrants in the U.S. face conditions similar to those in concentration camps)," *America Magazine*, 3 November 2003, 7.

21. Arthur H. Rotstein, "U.S. Wildlife Refuges Face Threats from People, Development," (AP) *Dayton Daily News*, 10 October 2004, A7.

22. Leo W. Banks, "Minutemen Are People, Too," *Wall Street Journal*, 19 May 2005, A15.

23. Ibid.

24. "The Minuteman Project—MMP—A Citizens' Neighborhood along Our Border," http//minutemanproject.com, 30 April 2005, 1.

25. Dennis Durband, "Minuteman and Congressional Candidate Gilchrist Aims to Re-Ignite Reagan Republicanism," *The Arizona Conservative*, 19 September 2005, http://www.azconservative.org/NFRA_Gilchirst/htm.

26. "Border Breaches Worry Rice," *Dayton Daily News*, 11 March 2005, A6.

27. Kathleen Parker, "Hillary Waffles While Security Suffers," (*Orlando Sentinel*), *Buffalo News*, 7 August 2005, H1.

28. Dennis Wagner, "Mexicans Go to Ariz. for Medical Help," *USA Today*, 18 May 2005, 3A.

CHAPTER 2. WORKING HERE

1. Clarence Page, "Low-Income Workers Hurt by Illegal Immigrants," *Dayton Daily News*, 30 March 2006, A21.

2. Steven Greenhouse, "Among Janitors, Labor Violations Go with the Job," *New York Times*, 13 July 2005.

3. Quoted in Anna Gorman, "Survey Reveals Widespread Abuse of Day Laborers," *Los Angeles Times*, 23 January 2006, B3.

4. Justin Pritchard, "Mexicans' Deaths on Job an Epidemic," *Atlanta Journal-Constitution*, 14 March 2004.

5. Quoted in ibid.

6. David K. Shipler, *The Working Poor: Invisible in America* (New York: Alfred K. Knopf, 2004), 114.

7. Quoted in Kim Lewicky, "Invisible in Plain Sight," *Highlands (NC) Newspaper*, 18 March 2005.

8. "Cosecha de Dolor, " *Sin Fronteras*, 11 June 2005.

9. "Migrants to Stay While Birth Defects Investigated," (AP) *St. Petersburg Times*, 27 March 2005, http://www.sptimes.com/2005/03/27news_pf/States/Migrants_to_stay_whil.shtml.

10. Ken Silverstein, "FoodSpeak," 2–3, http://www.cspinet.org/foodspeak.

11. Laura Bischoff, "Buckeye Egg Ordered to Shut Down," *Dayton Daily News*, 9 July 2003.

12. Ibid.

13. Ann V. Millard and Jorge Chapa, *Apple Pie and Enchiladas: Latino Newcomers in the Rural Midwest* (Austin: University of Texas Press, 2004), 17.

14. Kelly Lecker, "Ohio Fresh Eggs Facing $212,000 Fine," *Columbus Dispatch*, 16 June 2005, C11.

15. Ben Sutherly, "Egg Farm's Permits Revoked When State Finds Falsified Applications," *Dayton Daily News*, 1 December 2006, A4.

16. Quoted in Dan Herbeck, "Contractor Gets 46 Months in Prison for 'Despicable' Abuse of Farm Labor," *Buffalo News*, 27 May 2005, D1.

17. Ibid., D2.

18. "What Meat Means," *New York Times*, 6 February 2005.

19. Bob Herbert, "Where the Hogs Come First," *New York Times*, 15 June 2006, A23.

20. Eric Schlosser, *Fast Food Nation: The Dark Side of the All-American Meal* (New York: Perennial/HarperCollins, 2002), 172.

21. Ibid., 203.

22. "Kosher Meat Plant Leaders Face 9,000 Labor Charges," *Dayton Daily News*, 10 September 2008, A13; Julia Preston, "Former Manager of Kosher Slaughterhouse in Iowa is Acquitted of Labor Charges," *New York Times*, 8 June 2010, A13.

23. Nathan Thornburgh, "Inside the Life of the Migrants Next Door," *Time*, 6 February 2006, 34–45.

24. Kim Cobb, "For Migrants, Jobs Come with a Price," *Houston Chronicle*, 7 June 2003, http://are.Berkeley.edu/APMP/pubs/agworkvisa/jobsprice060703.html.

25. Richard Alba and Victor Nee, *Remaking the American Mainstream: Assimilation and Contemporary Immigration* (Cambridge, MA: Harvard University Press, 2003), 46.

26. Quoted in "Hamilton Contractors Praise Illegal Immigrants Bust," *Dayton Daily News*, 26 May 2006, A11.

27. Victor Davis Hanson, *Mexifornia: A State of Becoming* (San Francisco: Encounter Books, 2003), 35–36.

28. Quoted in Elliott Minor, "Trouble down on the Farm," (AP) *Dayton Daily News*, 15 March 2006, D1.

29. George J. Borjas, *Heaven's Door* (Princeton, NJ: Princeton University Press, 1999), 19.

30. Matthew Philpott, letter to the editor, *New York Times*, 8 August 2005, A18.

31. Bruce Wilcox, letter to the editor, *USA Today*, 10 May 2006, 11A.

32. Ginger Thompson, "Mexico: Meeting Set on Fox's Comment," *New York Times*, 18 May 2005, A11.

33. Bob Herbert, "Who's Getting the New Jobs," *New York Times*, 23 July 2004, A23.

34. David C. Holzman, letter to the editor, *New York Times*, 21 July 2004, A22.

35. Stephen Moore, "More Immigrants, More Jobs," *Wall Street Journal*, 11 July 2005, A13.

36. Quoted in "Why Are Latinos Leading Blacks in the Job Market?" *Business Week*, 15 March 2004, 70.

37. Quoted in Peter Applebome, "Seeking Pride in a Day's Work," *New York Times*, 31 July 2005, 20.

38. Evan Pérez and Corey Dade, "An Immigration Raid Aids Blacks—For a Time," *Wall Street Journal*, 17 January 2007, 1.

CHAPTER 3. STRANGERS IN A STRANGE LAND

1. Jeffrey S. Passel, *Estimates of the Size and Characteristics of the Undocumented Population*, Pew Hispanic Center Report, 7 March 2006, http://pewhispanic.org/reports/reportphp?ReprtID=61.

2. Nina Bernstein, "Tax Returns Rise for Immigrants in U.S. Illegally," *New York Times*, 16 April 2007, A1.

3. Randy Capps, The Urban Institute, and Michael Fix, Migration Policy Institute, "Undocumented Immigrants: Myth and Reality," 25 October 2005, http://www.urban.org/uploadedPDF/900898_undocumented_immigrants.pdf-9k.

4. Kris Axtman, "IRS Seminars, IDS Help Illegal Immigrants Pay US Taxes," *Christian Science Monitor*, 21 March 2002, http://www.csmonitor.com/2002/0321/p02s01-ussc.html.

5. David Luhnow and John Lyons, "In Latin America, Rich-Poor Chasm Stifles Growth," *Wall Street Journal*, 18 July 2005, A1.

6. Richard Alba and Victor Nee, *Remaking the American Mainstream: Assimilation and Contemporary Immigration* (Cambridge, MA: Harvard University Press, 2003), 188.

7. Roger Waldinger, "The 21st Century: An Entirely New Story," in *Reinventing the Melting Pot*, ed. Tamar Jacoby (New York: Penguin/Basic Books, 2004), 215.

8. Lionel Sosa, *The Americano Dream: How Latinos Can Achieve Success in Business and in Life* (New York: Dutton/Penguin, 1998), 7.

9. Ibid., 8.

10. Michael Barone, *The New Americans: How the Melting Pot Can Work Again* (Washington, DC: Regnery Publishing, 2001), 168.

11. Ken R. Crane and Ann V. Millard, "To Be With My People," in *Apple Pie and Enchiladas*, ed. Ann V. Millard and Jorge Chapas (Austin, TX: University of Texas Press, 2004), 179.

12. Cameron Stracher, "Much Depends on Dinner," *Wall Street Journal*, 29 July 2005, W13.

13. Quoted in Elisabeth Malkin, "Study Challenges Assumptions about Money Being Remitted to Mexico," *New York Times*, 7 July 2005, C4.

14. Leo R. Chavez, *Shadowed Lives: Undocumented Immigrants in American Society* (Fort Worth, TX: Harcourt Brace College Publishers, 1991), 151.

15. Thomas Black, "Mexico Remittances to Surge 20%, Central Bank Says," *Agonist News*, http://agonist.org/20060810/mexico_remittances_to_surge_20_central_bank_says, 10 August 2006.

16. Zoran Stanisljevic, "Microcapital Story: Microfinance Continues to Play a Key Role in Developing Economies as Remittances to Latin America and the Caribbean Decline in 2009," 23 March 2009, http://www.microcapital.org/microcapital-story-microfinance-continues-to-play-a-key-role.

17. Nina Bernstein, "Diversity and Unity on Display at Immigration Rally in New York," *New York Times*, 11 April 2006, C12.

18. Quoted in Wayne Tompkins, "Hispanics Changing Area Profile," *Courier-Journal News*, 2 March 2003, 7, http://www.courier-journal.com/localnews/2003/03/02/ke0302035374642.htm.

19. "Hispanic Health Woes Detailed," (AP) *Dayton Daily News*, 2 March 2006, A11.

20. Quoted in Tompkins, "Hispanics Changing Area Profile," 6.

21. "Latinos in North Carolina," *Children's Services Practice Notes*, June 2002, 6, http://ssw.unc.edu/fcrp/Cspn/vo17_n3/cspn_v7n3.pdf.

22. Anita Wadhwani, "Negativism about Hispanics Rising, Poll Says," *Tennessean.com.*, 14 November 2002, 2, http://www.tennessean.com/local/archives/02/11/25263988.

23. Kevin Johnson, "Center Ties Hate Crimes to Border Debate," *USA Today*, 17 May 2006, 3A.

24. Adam Nossiter, "Day Laborers Are Easy Prey in New Orleans," *New York Times*, 16 February 2009, 1.

25. Jennifer Levitz, "Scams Use Leased Radio Time to Target Immigrant Listeners," *Wall Street Journal*, 31 October 2006, 1.

26. Gary Rivlin, "Dollars and Dreams: Immigrants as Prey," *New York Times*, 11 June 2006, 3:1.

27. Victor Davis Hanson, *Mexifornia* (San Francisco: Encounter Books, 2003), 63.

CHAPTER 4. LIVING HERE

1. David K. Shipler, *The Working Poor: Invisible in America* (New York: Knopf, 2004), 97–99.

2. Paul Cuadros, "Hispanic Poultry Workers Live in New Southern Slums," *APF Reporter*, http://www.aliciapatterson.org/APF2001/Cuadros/Cuadros.html.

3. Bruce Lambert, "Mexican Official Says a Long Island Community Should Relocate Evicted Workers," *New York Times*, 9 July 2005, A13.

4. Marilyn Rosenblum, letter to the editor, *New York Times*, 30 March 2006, A26.

5. "Immigrant Working Families Nearly 70 Percent More Likely Than Their Native-Born Counterparts to Spend over Half Their Income on Housing," National Housing Conference, 30 July 2003, http://www.nhc.org/index/ImmigrantsStudy-pr-073003, 1.

6. Jeffrey S. Passel, "Estimates of the Size and Characteristics of the Undocumented Population," Pew Hispanic Center report, 7 March 2006, 3, http://pewhispaniccenter.org/reports/reportphp?ReportID=61.

7. Rakesh Kochar, Roberto Suro, and Sonya Tafoya, "The New Latino South: The Context and Consequences of Rapid Population Growth," Pew Hispanic Center, 26 July 2005, 18, http://pewhispanic.org/reports/report.php?ReportID=50.

8. Passel, "Estimates of the Size and Characteristics of the Undocumented Population," 3.

9. Nicolas C. Vaca, *The Presumed Alliance* (New York: HarperCollins, 2004), 23–24.

10. Kochar, Suro, and Tafoya, "The New Latino South."

11. "Illegals on the Rise in Southeast," (AP) *Dayton Daily News*, 24 February 2010, A14.

12. Ann V. Millard and Jorge Chapa, *Apple Pie and Enchiladas: Latino Newcomers in the Rural Midwest* (Austin: Texas University Press, 2004), 35.

13. Millard and Chapa, *Apple Pie and Enchiladas*, 35.

14. Eric Schlosser, *Fast Food Nation* (New York: Perennial/HarperCollins, 2002), 162.

15. Gregory Rodriguez, "Mexican-Americans and the Mestizo Melting Pot," in *Reinventing the Melting Pot*, ed. Tamar Jacoby (New York: Penguin/Basic Books, 2004), 136.

16. Roberto Suro, *Strangers Among Us* (New York: Vintage/Random House, 1998), 279–80.

17. Marc Cooper, "Border Justice," *The Nation*, 2 February 2005, 22.

18. Roberto Suro, "Attitudes toward Immigrants and Immigration Policy: Surveys among US Latinos and in Mexico," Pew Hispanic Center report, 2005, http://pewhispanic.org/reports/report.php?ReportID=52.

19. Rosendo Majano, "Survey: Latinos Have Sharp Internal Differences over Immigration," *HispanicBusiness.com*, 8 January 2006, http://www.hispanicbusiness.com/news/newsbyid.asp?id=27453&cat=headlines&more=/n.

20. "Migration between Mexico and the United States/Estudio Binacional Mexico-Estados Unidos sobre Migración," a Binational Study, 1997, 43, http://utexas.edu/lbj/uscir/binational.html.

21. Douglas S. Massey, "International Migration in a Globalizing Economy," *Great Decisions 2007* (Hanover, NH: Foreign Policy Association, 2007), 47.

22. Hector Tobar, *Translation Nation* (New York: Riverhead/Penguin, 2005), 153.

23. Vicki Smith, "Big-City Latin American Gang Creeps into West Virginia Town," (AP) *Dayton Daily News*, 14 August 2005, A3.

24. Schlosser, *Fast Food Nation*, 162.

25. Matthew Brzezinski, "Hillbangers: Hispanic Gangs Are Going Rural, Following the Flow of Immigrant Labor—and the Profits in Heartland Street Drugs—to the American Countryside," *New York Times Magazine*, 15 August 2004, 41.

26. Leo R. Chavez, *Shadowed Lives* (Fort Worth, TX: Harcourt Brace College Publishers, 1991), 148.

27. Hector Tobar, *Translation Nation*, 110–11.

28. Ibid., 105–6.

29. Ibid., 109.

30. Ibid., 111–12.

31. Chavez, *Shadowed Lives*, 151.

32. Millard and Chapa, *Apple Pie and Enchiladas*, 106.

33. Pam Belluck, "Town Uses Trespass Law to Fight Illegal Immigrants," *New York Times*, 13 July 2005, A14.

34. Abby Goodnough, "A Florida Mayor Turns to an Immigration Curb to Fix a Fading City," *New York Times*, 10 July 2006, A12.

35. Lawrence Downes, "Day Laborers, Silent and Despised, Find Their Voice," *New York Times*, 10 July 2006, A20.

36. Bruce Lambert, "Mexican Official Says a Long Island Community Should Relocate Evicted Workers," *New York Times*, 9 July 2005, A13.

37. Duncan Mansfield, "More Striving to Curb Illegal Immigration: Minutemen-Type Activism Spreading throughout U.S.," (AP) *Columbus Dispatch*, 18 July 2005, A5.

38. Anita Madhwani, "Negativism about Hispanics Rising, Poll Says," *Tennessean*, 14 November 2002.

39. Suro, *Strangers Among Us*, 47.

40. "Tenn. Driving Papers a Hot Item Nationally," *Washington Post*, 30 January 2006, A8.

41. Quoted in Steve Striffler, "Underground in a Chicken Factory," *Utne Reader* (January-February 2004), 74.

42. Ibid., 72.

43. Kochar, Suro, and Tafoya, "The New Latino South," 38.

CHAPTER 5. COMMUNITY REACTION

1. "Latinos in North Carolina," *Children's Services Practice Notes* 7, no. 3, Jordan Institute for Families, June 2002.

2. Sandra Noble Canon, Marta Miranda, and David R. Rich, "Let's Move Forward, Not Sideways, for Latino Community Incorporation into Lexington," National Conference for Community and Justice, undated.

3. Spring Miller, "Latino Immigrants in Tennessee: A Survey of Demographic and Social Science Research," University of Tennessee College of Law, June 2004, 3.

4. Hector Tobar, *Translation Nation* (New York: Riverhead/Penguin, 2005), 106.

5. Quoted in ibid., 107.

6. Quoted in ibid., 108.

7. Eunice Moscoso, "Hispanic Kids Bolster Boom at U.S. Schools," *Atlanta Journal-Constitution*, 6 October 2006, A6.

8. "English-Only Immersion Debated for Schools," *Arizona Republic*, 28 February 2006.

9. Karina Bland, "State Struggles to Help English-Learners Achieve," *Arizona Republic*, 26 February 2006.

10. "Bilingual Education," Ohio ESL, Ohio University, 18 October 2002, http://cscwww.cats.ohiou.edu/esl/project/bilingual.

11. John M. Broder, "Immigration Issue Plays Out in Arizona Education Fight," *New York Times*, 3 February 2006, A12.

12. Quoted in Samuel G. Freedman, "On Education: Latino Parents Decry Bilingual Programs," *New York Times*, 14 July 2004, A21.

13. Joseph Berger, "For Hispanic Parents, Lessons on Helping with the Homework," *New York Times*, 1 November 2006, A23.

14. Matt S. Meier and Feliciano Ribera, *Mexican Americans/American Mexicans* (New York: Hill and Wang, 1993), 233, 226.

15. "Immigration: Catholic Campaign for Immigration Reform 2005," *Houston Catholic Worker* 25, no. 5 (July-August 2005).

16. Hernan Rozemberg, "Catholic Bishops: Halt Raids," (*San Antonio Express-News*) *Dayton Daily News*, 12 September 2008, A10.

17. Wayne Thompkins, "Hispanics Changing Area Profile," *Louisville Courier-Journal*, 2 March 2003, http://www.courier-journal.com;localnews/2003/03/03.

18. United Conference of Catholic Bishops, Inc. and Conferencia del Episcopado Mexicano, "A Pastoral Letter Concerning Migration from the Catholic Bishops of Mexico and the United States," 22 January 2003.

19. Gerald F. Kicanas, "Never Again! (Illegal immigrants in the U.S. face conditions similar to those in concentration camps)," *America Magazine*, 3 November 2003, 7, http://www.americamagazine.org/gettext.cfm?articleType ID=3252&issueID=458.

20. Maggie Burnett, "A Perilous Crossing: Arizona Episcopalians Visit Mexico to Understand Migrants' Plight," *Episcopal Life* (June 2004): 9.

21. Paula Voell, "Effort Shows Humanity Knows No Borders," *Buffalo News*, 2 July 2005, C1.

22. Andrea Tunarosa, "Houses of Worship: Spreading the Word—Fast," *Wall Street Journal*, 28 July 2006, W11.

23. Wayne Tompkins, "Hispanics Changing Area Profile," *Courier-Journal News*, 2 March 2003, 7, http://www.courier-journal.com;pca;mews2003/03/02/keo32o3s374642.htm.

24. Michael Arnold Glueck and Robert J. Cihak, "High Cost of Medical Care for Illegal Immigrants," *New York Times*, 27 December 2005, http://www.newsmax.com/archives/articles/2005/12/26/170334.shtml.

25. Ibid., 2; Dennis Wagner, "Mexicans Go to Ariz. for Medical Help," *USA Today*, 18 May 2005, 3A.

26. Kim Cobb, "For Migrants, Jobs Come with a Price," *Houston Chronicle*, 7 June 2003.

27. Julia Preston, "Texas Hospitals' Separate Paths Reflect the Debate on Immigration," *New York Times*, 18 July 2006, A1.

28. Ibid.

29. Robert Pear, "U.S. Is Linking Status of Aliens to Hospital Aid," *New York Times*, 10 August 2004, A1.

30. "FDA OKs Test to Get Chagas Disease out of Blood Supply," (AP) *Dayton Daily News*, 14 December 2006, A21.

31. Robert Pear, "Lacking Papers, Citizens Are Cut from Medicaid," *New York Times*, 12 March 2007, A1.

32. Russ Oates, "Tennessee Officers Get Intense Training in Spanish Language, Culture," *Hispanicvista*, 28 May 2003, 1, http://www.hispanicvista.com/htm13/060203he.htm.

33. Ibid., 1–3.

CHAPTER 6. LAW AND DISORDER

1. Gary Althen, *American Ways*, 2nd ed. (Yarmouth, ME: Intercultural Press, 2003), 80.

2. In at least one case, however, it has led to family estrangement: Steven M. Lonegan, as mayor of Bogota, New Jersey, has promoted anti-immigration measures, while his brother Bryan is a well-known immigration-rights activist. See Nina Bernstein, "Immigration Debate Pits Brother against Brother," *New York Times*, 4 September 2007, A19.

3. "'Solve It' or 'Complain about It,'" *USA Today*, 30 May 2007, 13A.

4. Julia Preston, "Immigration Is at Center of New Laws around U.S.," *New York Times*, 6 August 2007, A12.

5. Katie Kelley, "A Deal in Colorado on Benefits for Illegal Immigrants," *New York Times*, 12 July 2006, A16.

6. Rick Lyman, "As Congress Dithers, Georgia Tackles Immigration," *New York Times*, 12 May 2006, A17.

7. William Hershey, "House Leaders Plan Measure to Crack Down on Illegal Immigration," *Dayton Daily News*, 3 August 2006.

8. James H. Walsh, "Sanctuary Cities, States: Undermining the American Republic," *The Social Contract* (Spring 2005): 196, www.thesocialcontract.com/pdf/fifteen-three/xv-3-192.pdf.

9. Kelley, "A Deal in Colorado on Benefits for Illegal Immigrants," A16.

10. Anabelle Garay, "Dallas Suburb Trying to Be 1st in Texas with a Law Barring Illegal Immigrants," (AP) *Dayton Daily News*, 13 November 2006, A18.

11. "Judge: Immigrants Not Trespassing," *North County (California) Times*, 13 August 2005, A20.

12. Michael Kiefer, "Maricopa Court Upholds Migrant Smuggling Laws," *Arizona Republic*, 10 June 2006, http://www.azcentral.com/arizonarepublic/local/articles/0610.html.

13. Miriam Jordan, "New Backlash: In Immigrant Fight, Grassroots Groups Boost Their Clout," *Wall Street Journal*, 28 September 2006, Al.

14. Quoted in Bruce Lambert, "Two Leaders, in Agreement on Immigration," *New York Times*, 17 August 2006, A22.

15. Quoted in "Hamilton Contractors Praise Illegal Immigrants Bust," *Dayton Daily News*, 26 May 2006, A11.

16. Mary Lolli, "Butler County Mounts Drive to Oust Illegal Immigrants," *Dayton Daily News*, 22 October 2005, B4.

17. "Utah Senate Approves Immigrant Driver's Card," *New York Times*, 20 February 2005, N25.

18. "The Move toward a National ID," *Parade*, 24 February 2008, 14.

19. Mary Lolli, "Butler Gets Feds' OK to Bust Illegals in County," *Dayton Daily News*, 14 December 2006, A4.

20. Tom Tancredo, "Two Views: Should 'Sanctuary Cities' Have Federal Funds Cut?" *Dayton Daily News*, 10 April 2006, A13.

21. Hector Becerra, "Welcome to Maywood, Where Roads Open Up for Immigrants," *Los Angeles Times*, 21 March 2006.

22. Walsh, "Sanctuary Cities, States," 192, 196.

23. Edward J. Erler, "Sanctuary Cities: A New Civil War," The Claremont Institute, 7 September 2005, 2–3, http://www.eco.freedom.org/articles/erler-706.shtml.

24. Huyen Pham, "The Inherent Flaws in the Inherent Authority Position: Why Inviting Local

Enforcement of Immigration Laws Violates the Constitution," *Florida State University Law Review* 31 (2004): 987, 965, http://www.law.txwes.edu/pham.

25. Huyen Pham, "Sovereignty and Immigration Power," *University of Cincinnati Law Review* 74 (2006): 1379, http://www.law.txwes.edu/pham.

26. Ibid., 1375.

27. Ibid., 983.

28. Richard Winton and Daniel Yi, "Police Split on Plan for Migrant Checks," *Los Angeles Times*, 23 January 2006, B1.

29. Quoted in Dennis Sadowski, "Bishops Concerned about Proposed Immigration Bill," *Catholic Universe Bulletin*, http://www.ohiocathconf.org/I/IM/ubstoryimm.pdf.

30. Rosalba Piña, "Los inmigrantes indocumentados también tienen derechos legales," *(Chicago) Nuevo Siglo*, 5 December 2003, http://www.nuevosiglonews.com/moxie/columnas/2+5/336. shtml. (My translation.)

31. Edward Sifuentes, "Mexico Urges Illegal Immigrants to Sue," *North County (California) Times*, 16 March, 2004.

32. "Rancher Who Detained Immigrants On Trial," *Arizona Republic*, 13 November 2006.

33. Quoted in Tom Baxter and Jim Galloway, "GOP to Use Immigration As Battle Cry," *Atlanta Journal-Constitution*, 16 October 2006, B4.

34. Immigrant Voting Project, http://www.immigrantvoting.org/.

35. Dudley L. Poston, Jr., Steven A. Camarota, and Amanda K. Baumle, "Remaking the Political Landscape," Center for Immigration Studies, October 2003, http://www.cis.org/articles/2003/ back1404.html.

36. Quoted in Steven Greenhouse, "Immigration Sting Puts 2 U.S. Agencies at Odds," *New York Times*, 16 July 2005, A1.

37. Quoted in ibid.

38. Stephen Ohlemacher, "Bureau Wants No Immigration Raids during 2010 Census Count," (AP) *Dayton Daily News*, 17 August 2007, A14.

39. Kris Axtman, "IRS Seminars, IDS Help Illegal Immigrants Pay US Taxes," *Christian Science Monitor*, 21 March 2002, http://www.csmonitor.com/2002/0321/p02s01-ussc.html.

40. Laura Green, "Church Sees Clear 'Moral' Choice in Immigration Debate," *International Herald Tribune*, 30 April 2006.

CHAPTER 7. LOOKING BACK

1. Jared Diamond, *Guns, Germs, and Steel* (New York: Norton, 1997), 16.

2. "Immigration Statistics—USA Census numbers," http://www.allcountries.org/uscensus/5_ immigration.html.

3. Evangeline Lindsley and Nancy Diggs, *My Century: An Outspoken Memoir* (Dayton, OH: Landfall Press, 1997), 108.

4. Thomas Sowell, *Ethnic America: A History* (New York: Basic Books, 1981), 22.

5. Quoted in Herbert Asbury, *The Gangs of New York* (New York: Knopf, 1927), 10–11.

6. Richard Alba and Victor Nee, *Remaking the American Mainstream: Assimilation and Contemporary Immigration* (Cambridge, MA: Harvard University Press, 2003), 156.

7. Thomas Sowell, *Ethnic America*.

8. Ibid., 81.

9. Thomas Sowell, *Black Rednecks and White Liberals* (San Francisco: Encounter Books, 2005), 90.

10. Sowell, *Ethnic America*, 277.

11. "Knownothingism," *Catholic Encyclopedia*, http://www.newadvent.org/cathen/086776a.htm.

12. John E. Kleber, "Aug. 6, 1855: Bloody Monday," *Louisville Courier-Journal*, 31 July 2005, H1.

13. Sowell, *Ethnic America*, 79.

14. Tamar Jacoby, "What It Means to Be American in the 21st Century," in *Reinventing the Melting Pot*, ed. Tamar Jacoby (New York: Basic Books, 2003), 296.

15. Alba and Nee, *Remaking the American Mainstream*, 69.

16. William Wei, "The Chinese-American Experience: An Introduction," http://www.immigrants. harpweek.com/ChineseAmericans/1Introduction/BillWeiIntro.htm. Nor were Europeans ever forced to enter what my Nisei friend calls "concentration camps," when legal Japanese residents, including many American-born citizens, were interned during World War II.

17. Michael Powell, "U.S. Immigration Debate Is a Road Well Traveled," *Washington Post*, 8 May 2005, A4.

18. Alba and Nee, *Remaking the American Mainstream*, 172.

19. George J. Borjas, *Heaven's Door* (Princeton, NJ: Princeton University Press, 1999), 9.

20. Nicolas C. Vaca, *The Presumed Alliance* (New York: HarperCollins, 2004), 30.

21. Victor Davis Hanson, *Mexifornia* (San Francisco: Encounter Books, 2003), 32.

22. Matt S. Meier and Feliciano Ribera, *Mexican Americans/American Mexicans* (New York: Hill and Wang, 1972, 1993), 87.

23. Vaca, *Presumed Alliance*, 31.

24. Ibid., 35.

25. Meier and Ribera, *Mexican Americans/American Mexicans*, 264.

26. Sowell, *Ethnic America*, 249.

27. Meier and Ribera, *Mexican Americans/American Mexicans*, 105.

28. Nina Bernstein, "100 Years in the Back Door, Out the Front," *New York Times*, 21 May 2006, 4.

29. Quoted in Wendy Koch, "U.S. Urged to Apologize for 1930s Deportations," *USA Today*, 5 April 2006, 1.

30. Ibid., 2A.

31. Quoted in Bernstein, "100 Years in the Back Door, Out the Front," 4.

32. Vaca, *Presumed Alliance*, 43–44.

33. Meier and Ribera, *Mexican Americans/American Mexicans*, 186.

34. Alba and Nee, *Remaking the American Mainstream*, 6.

35. Hanson, *Mexifornia*, 122, 117, 121.

36. Sowell, *Ethnic America*, 256.

37. Alba and Nee, *Remaking the American Mainstream*, 128.

38. Vaca, *Presumed Alliance*, 4.

CHAPTER 8. MEXICO

1. Phil Bryant, "The Impact of Illegal Immigration on Mississippi: Costs and Population Trends," Office of the State Auditor, Mississippi, 21 February, 2006, http://www.osa.state.ms.us/documents/performance/illegal-immigration.pdf.

2. *México y la Protección de sus Nacionales en Estados Unidos* (Mexico City: CISAN/UNAM, 1991).

3. "El nuevo Muro de Berlín," editorial, *(Atlanta, GA) Mundo Hispánico*, 5–11 October 2006, A48. (My translation.)

4. "México rechaza muro fronterizo," *Telemundo47.com*, 26 October 2006, http://www.azcentral.com/lavoz/Spanish/latin-america/articles/latin-america_177429.html.

5. Embassy of Mexico, "Border Fences Are No Solution for Immigration Nor Will They Increase Border Security," 26 October 2006, http:///www.embassyofmexico.org/eng/index.php?option=com_content&task=view&id=21.

6. Sergio Sarmiento, "Migración illegal: El muro y los políticos," *Cato Institute*, 23 May 2006, http://elcato.org/node/1572.

7. Quoted in "Urgen a crear una estrategia contra la 'fuga de cerebros," *El Universal.com*, 30 May 2006, http://www.eluniversal.com.mx/nacion/vi_138891.html. (My translation.)

8. Government of Mexico, "Mexico frente al Fenómeno Migratorio," 16 February 2006, http://www.sre.gob.mx/eventos/fenomenomigratorio/doics/mexicofrentealfenommigr.pdf.

9. Demetrios G. Papademetriou, "The Mexico Factor in US Immigration Reform," *Migration Information Source*, 1 March 2004, http://www.migrationinformation.org.Feature/display.cfm?ID=210.

10. Francesc Relea, "Mexico exige una 'solución integral' al problema migratorio," *El Pais Internacional*, 30 March 2006, http://www.elpais.es/articulo/elpporint/20060330elpepiin t_14Tes/internacional/Mexico/e.

11. Federico Novelo Uradanivía, "Situación actual y perspectivas de la migración México-Estados Unidos," *Observatorio de la Economía Latinoamericana*, no. 28 (July 2004), http://www.eumed.net/cursecon/ecolat/mx/2004/fn-migra.htm.

12. "Migration between Mexico and the United States/Estudio Binacional Mexico-Estados Unidos sobre Migración," a report of the Binational Study on Migration, 1997, 40, http://www.utexas.edu/lbj/uscir/binational.html.

13. Quoted in "Urgen a crear una estrategia contra la 'fuga de cerebros," *El Universal*, 30 May 2006, http://www.eluniversal.com.mx/nacion/vi_138891.html.

14. Government of Mexico, "La emigración hacia Estado Unidos," http://www.conapo.gob. .mx/prensa/carpetas/carpeta2002_15.htm. (My translation.) See also "Registra el 96% de municipios del país algún tipo de migración," *El Siglo de Torreón*, Durango, Mexico, 27 March 2003.

15. Nathan Thornburgh, "Inside the Life of the Migrants Next Door," *Time*, 6 February 2006, 42.

16. Kelly Lecker, "Turning Dollars to Pesos: Mexican Workers in Columbus Create Lifeline for Hometown," *Columbus Dispatch*, 28 March 2005, 4.

17. Marc Lacey, "Mexican Migrants Carry H.I.V. Home to Unready Rural Areas," *New York Times*, 17 July 2007, A1.

18. Chris Kraul, "Youth Suicides Soar in Wake of Ecuador's Exodus," *Los Angeles Times*, 28 January 2007, http:www.latimes.com/news/nationworld/world/la-fg=suicides 28jan28,-,3590996.story?c.

19. "Migration between Mexico and the United States," 18.

20. Government of Mexico, "Mexico's Public Policies to Foster Circular Migration," http://www.embassyofMexico.org/. 2006. See also Government of Mexico, "A Message from Mexico About Migration, www.SanDiego.edu/peacestudies/documents/tbi/Mexico_about_migration.pdf.

21. Jorge Castañeda, "America's Misguided Immigration Debate," *Project Syndicate*, 2006, http://www.project-syndicate.org/commentary/castaneda8/English.

22. Jorge Castañeda, "The 2004 John L. Manion Lecture: North America in the 21st Century," 2004, http://www.asu.edu/clas/nacys/bna/archive/Castaned.NA31stCen,2004.pdf.

23. Victor Davis Hanson, *Mexifornia* (San Francisco: Encounter Books, 2003), 27.

24. David Fitzgerald, "State Responses to Labor Emigration: A View from Arandas, Jalisco, Mexico," 5–6, presented at the Institute for Labor and Employment Graduate Student Conference, 20–21 February 2004, Pt. Reyes, CA, http://www.iir.ucla.edu/research/grad_conf/2004/Fitzgerald.pdf.

25. "Mexico Wants Whole Immigration Enchilada," *WorldNetDaily*, 4 July 2001, http://www.wnd.com/news/article.aso?ARTICLE_ID=23499.

26. Samuel P. Huntington, *Who Are We?* (New York: Simon & Schuster, 2004), 279.

27. Fitzgerald, "State Responses to Labor Emigration," 7.

28. Ibid., 9.

29. Ibid., 11.

30. Ibid., 13–28.

31. Hanson, *Mexifornia*, 29.

32. Jon E. Dougherty, *Illegals* (Nashville, TN: WND Books, 2004), 37.

33. "A Guide for the Illegal Migrant," *New York Times*, 9 January 2005, 5.

34. Federico Novelo Uradanivía, "Situación actual y perspectivas de la migración México-Estados Unidos" (my translation), July 2004.

35. Robert Leiken, "A Change in Course? Mexican Foreign Policy after Castañeda," *In the National Interest*, 15 January 2003.

36. "Migration between Mexico and the United States," 57, 59.

37. Robert Leiken, "Enchilada Lite: A Post-9/11 Mexican Migration Agreement," Center for Immigration Studies, http://www.cis.org/articles/2002/leiken.html.

38. Jose Carreno, "From High Hopes to Disenchantment," *Foreign Service Journal*, March 2003, 19.

39. Leiken, "A Change in Course?" 1.

40. Leiken, "Enchilada Lite," 6.

41. Ibid., 21.

42. Luis Ernesto Derbez, "Mexico and the Free Trade Area of the Americas," *Economic Perspectives, Electronic Journal of the U.S. Department of State*, October 2002, http://usinfo.state.gov/journals/ites/1002/ijee/ijee1002.pdf.

43. K. Larry Storrs, "Mexico-United States Dialogue on Migration and Border Issues, 2001–2005," *CRS Report for Congress*, updated 2 June 2005, CRS-6, http://www.fas.org/sgp/crs/row/RL327.35.pdf.

44. Castañeda, "The 2004 John L. Manion Lecture," 21.

45. "Calderón: Inmigración no es todo," *TelemundoLA.com*, 9 November 2006, http://www.telemundola.com/inmigracion/10284182/detail.html.

46. James C. McKinley, Jr., "From Mexico Also, the Message to Bush Is Immigration," *New York Times*, 14 March 2007, A11.

47. Leiken, "Enchilada Lite," 19.

48. Storrs, "Mexico-United States Dialogue on Migration and Border Issues, 2001–2005," unnumbered page.

CHAPTER 9. OTHER COUNTRIES

1. Sharon Noguchi, "Hard Work, Furtive Living: Illegal Immigrants in Japan," *YaleGlobal*, 2 March 2006, 4, http:/www.yaleglobal.yale.edu/display.article?id=7067.

2. Erin Aeran Chung, "Korean Voluntary Associations in Japanese Civil Society," Japan Policy Research Institute, JPRI Working Paper No. 69: July 2000, 1, http://ww.jpri.org/publications/workingpapers/wp69.html.

3. "Immigration Law Sanctions and Enforcement in Selected Foreign Countries," Report for Congress, Law Library of Congress, April 2006, 1, http://judiciary.house.gov/media/pdfs/lawlibrimmreport5506.pdf.

4. Ibid., 1.

5. Renwick McLean, "5 African Migrants Killed and Scores Hurt at Spanish Enclave Fence," *International Herald Tribune*, 30 September 2005, 3.

6. "Madrid: 400 More Africans Try to Scramble to Asylum," (Reuters) *International Herald Tribune*, 29 September 2005, 8.

7. "Madrid: Spanish Police Thwart Migrants from Africa," (Reuters) *International Herald Tribune*, 28 September 2005, 7.

8. Lawrence Downes, "As an Immigration Tide Swells, Europe Treads Water," *New York Times*, 1 August 2006, A18.

9. Burnett, Victoria, "To Curb Illegal Migration, Spain Offers a Legal Route," *New York Times*, 11 August 2007, A3.

10. Craig S. Smith, "Morocco Again Expels Africans Trying Risky Path to Europe," *New York Times*, 17 October 2005, A8.

11. Jason Horowitz, "Survivors Rescued on Boat Smuggling Africans to Italy," *New York Times*, 9 August 2004, A8.

12. "Bloc at Odds on Illegal Sea Migration," *New York Times*, 25 July 2006, A6.

13. Katrin Bennhold, "In Egalitarian Europe, a Not-So-Hidden World of Squalor," *International Herald Tribune*, 17 October 2005, http://www.iht.com/bin/print_ipub.php?file=/articles/2005/10/17/news/housing.php.

14. Katrin Bennhold, "Expulsion of Illegals Stepped Up by France," *International Herald Tribune*, 2–3 September 2006, 3.

15. Katrin Bennhold, "Unsafe Paris Buildings Targeted," *International Herald Tribune*, 1 September 2005, 3.

16. "Immigration Law Sanctions," 2–3.

17. Mark Landler, "Social Democrats Defeat Governing Party in Austria," *New York Times*,

2 October 2006, http://www.nytimes.com/2006/10/02/world/Europe/01austriak.html?_
r=1&oref=slogin.

18. Ian Fisher, "Czech Republic Faces Debate on Immigration," *New York Times*, 25 April 2004, 4.

19. Richard Bernstein, "Poland Worries about Creating a New Divide," *New York Times*, 25 April 2004, 4.

20. Steven Lee Myers, "Russia Deports Georgians and Increases Pressures on Businesses and Students," *New York Times*, 7 October 2006, A6.

21. Steven Lee Myers, "In Anti-Immigrant Mood, Russia Heeds Gadfly's Cry," *New York Times*, 22 October 2006, 4.

22. Peter Schneider, "The New Berlin Wall," translated by Philip Boehm, *New York Times Magazine*, 4 December 2005, 69.

23. Christopher Caldwell, "Where Every Generation Is First-Generation," *New York Times Magazine*, 27 May 2007, 49.

24. Ian Buruma, "Letter from Amsterdam: Final Cut," *New Yorker*, 3 January 2005, 27.

25. Leon de Winter, "Tolerating a Time Bomb," *New York Times*, 16 July 2005, A27.

26. "France's Shattered Image," *USA Today*, 6 November 2005.

27. "In Paris, Tough Talk Isn't Enough," *New York Times*, 4 November 2005, A24.

28. Alan B. Nichols, "Civil Unrest in France Triggers Massive Reform," *Washington Diplomat*, February 2006, 10.

29. "France's Shattered Image."

30. "An Underclass Rebellion," *Economist*, 12 November 2005, 24.

31. Nichols, "Civil Unrest in France," 10.

32. Doug Ireland, "Why Is France Burning?" *The Nation*, 28 November 2005.

33. "An Underclass Rebellion," 25.

34. Michael Elliott, "Such Lovely Lads," *Time*, 21 August 2006, 28.

35. Amy Waldman, "British Bombers' Rage Formed in a Caldron of Discontent," *New York Times*, 31 July 2005, 1.

36. James Slack and Matthew Hickley, "One in Every 13 Is Now a Migrant," *(London) Daily Mail*, 8 September 2005, 8.

37. Ibid.

38. Alan Cowell, "Britain Joins Others in Europe in Limiting Immigrant Workers," *New York Times*, 24 February 2004, A5.

39. Quoted in "Multicultural Policy 'Is Breeding Racial Hatred,'" *London Times*, 30 September 2005, 31.

40. Christopher Caldwell, "Islam on the Outskirts of the Welfare State," *New York Times Magazine*, 5 February 2006, 56.

41. Quoted in Caldwell, "Islam on the Outskirts," 58.

42. Ibid.

43. Thomas Friedman, "A Poverty of Dignity and a Wealth of Rage," *New York Times*, 15 July 2005, A21.

44. David A. Bell, "The Shorn Identity," *The New Republic*, 28 November and 5 December 2005, 28.

45. Tami Abdollah, "French Test Affirmative Action," *Wall Street Journal*, 27 July 2005, A11.

46. Jay Tolson, "An Education in Muslim Integration," *U.S. News & World Report*, 21 November 2005, 37–38.

47. "Migration News," http://www.migration.ucdavis.edu/mn/comments.php[?id=3490_0_4_0.

48. "The List: The World's Best Places to Be an Immigrant," *Foreign Policy*, February 2008, http://www.foreignpolicy.com?story/cms.php?story_id=4185.

49. Anna Mulrine, "After the Flames," *U.S. News & World Report*, 21 November 2005, 37.

50. Eric Lichtblau, "In Wake of Plot, Justice Dept. Will Study Britain's Terror Laws," *New York Times*, 15 August 2006, A15.

51. Cowell, "Britain Joins Others," A5.

52. Katrin Bennhold, "Expulsion of Illegals Stepped Up by France," *International Herald Tribune*, 2–3 September 2006, 3.

53. "EU Parliament Speaks against Mass Regularization of Illegal Immigrants," (AP) *International Herald Tribune*, 28 September 26, http://www.iht.com/bin/print.ipub.php?file=/articles/apk/2006k09/28/euope/EU_GEN_E.

54. John Tagliabue, "Blacks in France Fight Equality Bind," *International Herald Tribune*, 21 September 2005, 3.

55. Downes, "Immigration Tide Swells," A18.

56. "Immigrant Friendly Canada," *International Herald Tribune*, 29 September 2005, 6.

57. Joseph H. Carens, "Crossing the Border: Belonging," *Boston Review* (Summer 2005): 19.

58. Christopher Mason and Julia Preston, "Canada's Policy on Immigrants Brings Backlog," *New York Times*, 27 June 2007, A1.

59. George J. Borjas, "Economic Assimilation: Trouble Ahead," in *Reinventing the Melting Pot*, ed. Tamar Jacoby (New York: Penguin/Basic Books, 2004), 209.

CHAPTER 10. THE GOOD NEWS

1. Richard Bernstein, "Despite Minor Incidents, Chances of Large-Scale Riots Elsewhere in Europe Is Seen as Small," *New York Times*, 8 November 2005, A15.

2. Stanley Crouch, "Goose-Loose Blues for the Melting Pot," in *Reinventing the Melting Pot*, ed. Tamar Jacoby (New York: Penguin/Basic Books, 2004), 271–72.

3. Quoted in Neil MacFarquhar, "Pakistanis Find U.S. an Easier Fit Than Britain," *New York Times*, 21 August 2006, A1.

4. MacFarquhar, "Pakistanis Find U.S. an Easier Fit," A15.

5. MacFarquhar, A1.

6. Robert A. Levine, "Assimilating Immigrants: Why America Can and France Cannot," RAND Corporation, July 2004, 1–2, http://www.rand.org/pubs/authors/1/levine_robert_a.html.

7. MacFarquhar, "Pakistanis Find U.S. an Easier Fit," A15.

8. Ihsan Alkhatib, letter to the editor, *Wall Street Journal*, 25 July 2005, A15.

9. Tamar Jacoby, "The New Immigrants: A Progress Report," in *Reinventing the Melting Pot*, ed. Tamar Jacoby, 24.

10. Interview of 17 October 2006.

11. Quoted in Tamar Jacoby, "Defining Assimilation for the 21st Century," in *Reinventing the Melting Pot*, ed. Tamar Jacoby, 4.

12. Eric Gorski, "Hispanic Churches Adding English," *Lexington Herald-Leader*, 1 September 2007, E4.

13. Nathan Glazer, *We Are All Multiculturists Now* (Cambridge, MA: Harvard University Press, 1997), 128.

14. Tamar Jacoby, "The New Immigrants," 25.

15. Robert A. Levine, "Assimilation, Past and Present," *Public Interest* (Spring 2005), http://findarticles.com/p/articles/mi_m0377/is_159/ai_n13779494/.

16. Jacoby, "The New Immigrants: A Progress Report," 24.

17. Quoted in Levine, "Assimilation, Past and Present."

18. Jacoby, "The New Immigrants," 28.

19. Amitai Etzioni, "Assimilation to the American Creed," in *Reinventing the Melting Pot*, ed. Tamar Jacoby, 213.

20. Ibid., 213–15.

21. Matt S. Meier and Feliciano Ribera, *Mexican Americans/American Mexicans* (New York: Hill and Wang, 1993), 247.

22. Victor Davis Hanson, *Mexifornia* (San Francisco: Encounter Books, 2003), 133.

23. Samuel P. Huntington, *Who Are We?* (New York: Simon & Schuster, 2004), 233.

24. Michael Barone, *The New Americans: How the Melting Pot Can Work Again* (Washington, DC: Regnery Press, 2001), 169.

25. "Hispanic Attitudes toward Learning English," Pew Hispanic Center Factsheet, 7 June 2006, http:www.pewhispanic.org/files/factsheets/20pdf.

26. Herman Badillo, *One Nation, One Standard* (New York: Sentinel, 2006), 195.

27. Eunice Moscoso, "Hispanic Kids Bolster Boom at U.S. Schools," *Atlanta Journal-Constitution*, 6 October 2006, A6.

28. Rick Fry, "The Changing Landscape of American Public Education: New Students, New Schools," Pew Hispanic Center, 5 October 2006, http://pewhispanic.org/reports/report.php?ReportID=72.

29. Robert A. Levine, "Assimilation, Past and Present," *Public Interest* (Spring 2005).

30. Quoted in David Rieff, "Nuevo Catholics," *New York Times Magazine*, 24 December 2006, 43.

31. Levine, "Assimilation, Past and Present."

32. George J. Borjas, *Heaven's Door* (Princeton, NJ: Princeton University Press, 1999), 86.

33. Michelle Mittelstadt, "Immigrant Competition Reduces Wages," (AP) Center for Immigration Studies, 21 January 1998, http://www.cis./org/articles/1998/wagestudy/wage_coverage.html.

34. Gianmarco I. P. Ottaviano and Giovanni Peri, "Rethinking the Gains from Immigration: Theory and Evidence from the U.S.," *Social Science Research Network*, NBER Working Paper No. W11672, 3 October 2005, 1, 4, http://papers.ssrn.com/so13/papers.cfm?abstract_id=819833.

35. Stephen Moore, "More Immigrants, More Jobs," *Wall Street Journal*, 11 July 2005, A13.

36. John Tierney, "Sense and Sandwiches," *New York Times*, 2 May 2006, A27.

37. David Card, "Is the New Immigration Really So Bad?" January 2005, unnumbered page, http://www.phil.frb.org/econ/conf/immigration/card.pdf.

38. Ibid., 11.

39. Ibid., 25–26.

40. Quoted in David Altman, "Immigration Math: It's a Long Story," *New York Times*, 18 June 2006, 4.

41. Altman, "Immigration Math," 4.

42. "Our Border Brigades," *Wall Street Journal*, 27 January 2004, A14.

43. Jorge Ramos, *The Other Face of America* (New York: Rayo/HarperCollins, 2002), 180.

44. Eduardo Porter, "Workers Illegally in U.S. Bolster Social Security," *Times Digest*, 5 April 2005, 5.

45. "U.S. Hispanic Purchasing Power: 1978–2010," Research and Markets, http://www.research-andmarkets.com/reports75036/75036.htm, 1 August 2003.

46. Joe Frolik, "City's Appeal to Immigrants Has Declined," *Cleveland Plain Dealer*, 23 June 2005, B9.

47. Eyal Press, "Do Immigrants Make Us Safer?" *New York Times Magazine*, 3 December 2006, 20.

48. "New Model Police," *Economist*, 9 June 2007, 30.

49. David Brooks, "Immigrants to Be Proud Of," *New York Times*, 30 March 2006, A27.

50. Mireya Navarro, "For Younger Latinos, a Shift to Smaller Families," *New York Times*, 5 December 2004.

51. Chris Hawley, "Smaller Families Evidence of Cultural Shift in Mexico," *Arizona Republic*, 4 April 2006, 1, http://www.azcentral.com/arizonarepublic/news/articles/0404nobabies.html.

52. Quoted in Hawley, "Smaller Families," 3.

53. Sara Seddon Kilbinger, "Foreign Investors Look to Mexico, Lured by Growth," *Wall Street Journal*, 31 May 2006, B3.

54. "Mexican Watershed," editorial, *Wall Street Journal*, 29 June 2006, A14.

55. See also the "2009 Mexico Consensus Economic Forecast," issued by Arizona State University's W.P. Carey School of Business.

56. "Country Profile," Country Briefings: Mexico, *Economist.com*, 16 June 2008, http://www.economist.com/countries/Mexico/PrinterFriendly.cfm?Story_ID=111522926.

57. Pete Engardio and Geri Smith, "Business Is Standing Its Ground," *Business Week*, 20 April 2009, 34–37.

CONCLUSION

1. Raid Rumors Scare Some Illegals," (AP) *Dayton Daily News*, 29 April 2006, A11.

2. Nina Bernstein, "A Climate of Fear as Immigration Agents Raid New York Farms," *New York Times*, 24 December 2006, 20.

3. Russ Bynum, "Immigration Raid Outrages Small Georgia Town," (AP) *Louisville Courier-Journal*, 16 September 2006.

4. "Call to Shut Migrant 'Jail,'" *New Zealand Herald*, 23 February 2007, B2.

5. "Gitmos across America," *New York Times*, 27 June 2007, A22.

6. Nina Bernstein, "New Scrutiny As Immigrants Die in Custody," *New York Times*, 26 June 2007, A19.

7. "Justice Dept. Figures on Incarcerated Illegals," *NewsMax.com*, http://www.newsmax.com/archives/ic/2006/3/27/114208.shtml.

8. Lara Jakes Jordan, "Study: Some Immigrants Re-Arrested 6 Times on Average," (AP) *North County (California) Times*, 8 January 2007, http://www.nctimes.com/articles/2007/01/09/nes/nation/13_34_791_8_-8.txt.

9. Julia Malone, "Many Illegal Immigrants Are Going Free Instead of Going Back Home," (Cox News Service) *Dayton Daily News*, 23 May 2006, A10.

10. Rebecca Carr, "Immigration Convict Data Sought," *Atlanta Journal-Constitution*, 15 October 2006, A7.

11. "California Woman's Identity Stolen by Dozens," (AP) *Dayton Daily News*, 17 June 2006, A1.

12. Jennifer Talhem, "Feds Arrest 1,282 in Raids; Evidence Shows ID Theft Used as a Tool to Get Work," (AP) *Dayton Daily News*, 14 December 2006, A17.

13. "Illegal Immigrants Accused of ID Theft," *Dayton Daily News*, 29 August 2007, A16.

14. J. K. Perry, "Workers Buy Edwards Man's Identity," *Vail Daily*, 7 December 2006, A3.

15. John Seewer, "Foreign Worker Shortage Threatens Seasonal Companies," (AP) *Dayton Daily News*, 4 April 2005, D2.

16. Elliott Minor, "Trouble down on the Farm," (AP) *Dayton Daily News*, 15 March 2006, D1.

17. John Quinones, *ABC News*, 24 November 2006, http://www.abcnews.go.com/WNT/US/story?id=2677661&page=1.

18. Frosch, Dan, "Inmates Will Replace Wary Migrants in Colorado Fields," *New York Times*, 4 March 2007, 20.

19. Eunice Moscoso, "Businesses Making a Push to Legalize Guest Workers," *Dayton Daily News*, 10 April 2005, A10.

20. Ibid.

21. Julia Preston and Steven Greenhouse, "Immigration Accord by Labor Boosts Obama Effort," *New York Times*, 13 April 2009.

22. Cal Thomas, "Politicians Refuse to Tell Truth about Immigration," *Dayton Daily News*, 6 June 2007, A15.

23. "Immigration Heritage," editorial, *Wall Street Journal*, 8 June 2007, A16.

24. "The State of American Public Opinion on Immigration in Spring 2006: A Review of Major Surveys," Pew Hispanic Center Factsheet, 17 May 2006, 1, http://www.pewhispanic.org/factsheets/factsheet.php?FactsheetID=18-.

25. Kathy Kiely, "Public Favors Giving Illegal Immigrants a Break," *USA Today*, 19 April 2007, 7A.

26. "Deporting the Undocumented: A Cost Assessment," Center for American Progress, July 2005, http://www.americanprogress.org/issues/2005/07/b913099.html.

27. Laura Wides, "Task of Deporting Illegal Immigrants Too Big," (AP) *Dayton Daily News*, 19 September 2004.

28. Julia Preston, "Farmers Call Crackdown on Illegal Workers Unfair," *New York Times*, 11 August 2007, A9.

29. Peter R. Orszag, Congressional Budget Office, letter to the Honorable Kent Conrad, 23 May 2007.

30. Matthew Bigg, "U.S. 'Guest' Worker Program Exploitative: Report," (Reuters) 12 March 2007, http://www.reuters.com/articlePrint?articleId=USN1237714820070312.

31. Robert Pear, "After Aiding Bill on Immigration, Employers Balk," *New York Times*, 21 May 2007, A1.

REFERENCES

Abdollah, Tami. "French Test Affirmative Action." *Wall Street Journal*, 27 July 2005, A11.

Ajami, Fouad. Letter to the editor. *Foreign Policy* (May/June 2004): 7–8.

Alba, Richard, and Victor Nee. *Remaking the American Mainstream: Assimilation and Contemporary Immigration.* Cambridge, MA: Harvard University Press, 2003.

Alkhatib, Ihsan. Letter to the editor. *Wall Street Journal*, 25 July 2005, A15.

Altman, David. "Immigration Math: It's a Long Story." *New York Times*, 18 June 2006, 4.

Alonso-Zaldivar, Ricardo. "Immigrants' Cut of New Jobs Is Bad for Bush." (*Los Angeles Times*) *Atlanta Journal-Constitution*, 17 June 2004, C2.

Alltucker, Ken. "Numbers Reveal Flow of Hispanics into Area." *Cincinnati Enquirer*, 17 March 2001. http://www.enquirer.com/editions/2001/03/17/loc_numbers_refeal_flow.html.

Althen, Gary. *American Ways: A Guide for Foreigners in the United States.* 2nd edition. Yarmouth, ME: Intercultural Press, 2003.

Andes, Jodi, and Kevin Mayhood. "911 Call: 'We can't get out.'" *Columbus Dispatch*, 14 September 2004, A1.

Annerino, John. *Dead in Their Tracks: Crossing America's Desert Borderlands.* New York: Four Walls, Eight Windows, 1999.

Ante, Spencer E. "Keeping Out the Wrong People." *Business Week*, 4 October 2004, 90–94.

Applebome, Peter. "Seeking Pride in a Day's Work, amid the Jeers." *New York Times*, 31 July 2005, 20.

Archibold, Randal C. "Risky Measures by Smugglers Increase Toll on Immigrants." *New York Times*, 9 August 2006, A12.

"Arizona Governor Vetoes Measures on Immigration." *New York Times*, 22 May 2005.

"Arizona MinuteMan Project to Patrol Border." 26 January 2005. http/www.securityarms.com.

Armas, Genaro C. "Hispanics, Asians Fuel Population Explosion." (AP) *Dayton Daily News*, 15 June 2004.

———. "Immigrant Wave Still Floods U.S." (AP) *Dayton Daily News*, 22 March 2005, A5.

Asbury, Herbert. *The Gangs of New York*. New York: Knopf, 1927.

"Authorities Try to ID Driver in Deadly Wreck." (AP) *Dayton Daily News*, 18 October 2004, A3.

Axtman, Kris. "IRS Seminars, IDS Help Illegal Immigrants Pay US Taxes." *Christian Science Monitor*, 21 March 2002. http://www.csmonitor.com/2002/0321/p02s01-ussc.html.

Bacon, David. "Which Side Are You On?" 25 January 2006. http://www,truthout.org/.

Badillo, Herman. *One Nation, One Standard*. New York: Sentinel, 2006.

Balive, Marcelo. "Integración de las Americas." *El Tecolote*, 11 September 2003. http://news.eltecolote.org/news/view.

Banks, Leo W. "Minutemen Are People, Too." *Wall Street Journal*, 19 May 2005, A15.

Barnes, Steve. "Texas: Guilty Plea in Border Case." *New York Times*, 28 September 2004, A21.

Barone, Michael. "New Americans after September 11." In *Reinventing the Melting Pot*, ed. Tamar Jacoby. New York: Penguin/Basic Books, 2004.

———. *The New Americans: How the Melting Pot Can Work Again*. Washington, DC: Regnery Publishing, 2001.

Barringer, Felicity. "Bitter Division for Sierra Club on Immigration." *New York Times*, 16 March 2004, A2.

Bartels, Chuck. "Wal-Mart Pays $11M, Settles: Ends Federal Inquiry into Use of Illegal Immigrants to Clean Its Stores." (AP) *Dayton Daily News*, 19 March 2005, D1.

Bartlett, Donald L., and James B. Steele. "Who Left the Door Open?" *Time*, 20 September 2004, 51–66.

Baxter, Tom, and Jim Galloway. "GOP to Use Immigration As Battle Cry." *Atlanta Journal-Constitution*, 16 October 2006, B4.

Bebbington, Jim. "Dayton to Accept Foreign ID Cards." *Dayton Daily News*, 14 April 2005.

Becerra, Hector. "Welcome to Maywood, Where Doors Open Up for Immigrants." *Los Angeles Times*, 23 January 2006, B1.

Becker, Elizabeth. "Immigrant Workers Send Billions Home." (New York Times News Service) *Lexington (KY) Herald-Leader*, 19 May 2004, C1.

Bedard, Paul. "Washington Whispers: More Spanish for the Speaker." *U.S. News & World Report*, 20 June 2005, 4.

Bell, David A. "The Shorn Identity." *The New Republic*, 28 November and 5 December 2005, 28.

Belluck, Pam. "Town Uses Trespass Law to Fight Illegal Immigrants." *New York Times*, 13 July 2005, A14.

Bennhold, Katrin. "Expulsion of Illegals Stepped Up by France. *International Herald Tribune*, 2–3 September 2006, 3.

———. "In Egalitarian Europe, A Not-So-Hidden World of Squalor." *International Herald Tribune*, 17 October 2005. http://www.iht.com/bin/print_ipub.php?file=/articles/2005/10/17/news/housing.php.

————. "Unsafe Paris Buildings Targeted." *International Herald Tribune*, 1 September 2005, 3.

Berger, Joseph. "For Hispanic Parents, Lessons on Helping with the Homework." *New York Times*, 1 November 2006, A23.

Bernstein, Nina. "A Climate of Fear as Immigration Agents Raid New York Farms." *New York Times*, 24 December 2006, 20.

————. "Immigration Debate Pits Brother against Brother." *New York Times*, 4 September 2007, A19.

————. "New Scrutiny As Immigrants Die in Custody." *New York Times*, 26 June 2007, A1.

————. "New Study Paints Clearer Picture of Mexicans in New York City." *New York Times*, 3 March 2005, A23.

————. "100 Years in the Back Door, Out the Front." *New York Times*, 21 May 2006, 4.

————. "Tax Returns Rise for Immigrants in U.S. Illegally." *New York Times*, 16 April 2007, A1.

Bernstein, Richard. "Despite Minor Incidents, Chance of Large-Scale Riots Elsewhere in Europe Is Seen As Small." *New York Times*, 8 November 2005, A15.

————. "Poland Worries about Creating a New Divide." *New York Times*, 25 April 2004, 4.

Berry, Amelia. "Trouble in a New Land: Violencia Doméstica." *Midwest Latina*, 23 September 2005.

Betancourt, Antonio. "Mexico: Federal Forces Sent to Border City." *New York Times*, 14 June 2005, A7.

Beteta, Ignacio. "Cinco razones para el optimismo: Mejoran las perspectivas." (Economía) (augurando la economía; Mexico). *Siempre!* 9 May 2002.

Bigg, Matthew. "U.S. 'Guest' Worker Exploitative: Report." Reuters, 12 March 2007. http://www.reuters.com/articlePrint?articleId=USN12377148200770312.

"Bilingual Education." Ohio ESL, Ohio University, 18 October 2002. http://cscwww.cats.ohiou.edu/esl/project/bilingual.

Bischoff, Laura. "Buckeye Egg Ordered to Shut Down." *Dayton Daily News*, 9 July 2003.

Black, Thomas. "Mexico Remittances to Surge 20%, Central Bank Says." *The Agonist News*. http://agonist.org/20060810mexico_remittances_to_surge_20_central_bank_says, 10 August 2006.

Bland, Karina. "State Struggles to Help English-Learners Achieve." *Arizona Republic*, 26 February 2006.

Bleier, Ronald. Letter to the editor. *New York Times*, 26 July 2004, A18.

"Bloc At Odds on Illegal Sea Migration." *New York Times*, 25 July 2006, A6.

Blumenthal, Ralph. "New Strains and New Rules for Agents along Mexican Border." *New York Times*, 12 August 2004, A13.

————. "Trial Starts in Nation's Deadliest Human Smuggling Case." *New York Times*, 9 March 2005, A13.

Borden, Teresa. "Applications for Temporary Visas Near Cap." *Atlanta Journal-Constitution*, 8 September 2004, F3.

"Border Patrol Agents Deliver New Citizen in Back of Truck." (AP) *Dayton Daily News*, 4 March 2005, A3.

"Border Patrol Begins Using Unpiloted Aircraft for Surveillance." *New York Times*, 27 June 2004, 15.

"Border Patrol Considering Use of Volunteers, Official Says." *New York Times*, 21 July 2005, A12.

Borjas, George J. "Economic Assimilation: Trouble Ahead." In *Reinventing the Melting Pot*, ed. Tamar Jacoby. New York: Penguin/Basic Books, 2004.

————. *Heaven's Door: Immigration Policy and the American Economy*. Princeton, NJ: Princeton University Press, 1999.

Boshnakova, Tina. "Border Patrol: Friend or Foe?" *Avance* (January-February 2005): 11–22.

Broder, John M. "Immigration Issue Plays Out in Arizona Education Fight." *New York Times*, 3 February 2006, A16.

———. With Congress's Blessing, a Border Fence May Finally Push through to the Sea." *New York Times*, 4 July 2005, A8.

Brooks, David. "The Americano Dream." *New York Times*, 24 February 2004, A27.

———. "Immigrants to Be Proud Of." *New York Times*, 30 March 2006, A27.

Bryant, Phil. "The Impact of Illegal Immigration on Mississippi: Costs and Population Trends." Office of the State Auditor, Mississippi, 21 February 2006. http://www.osa.state.ms.us/documents/performance/illegal-immigration.pdf.

Brzezinski, Matthew. "Hillbangers: Hispanic gangs are going rural, following the flow of immigrant labor—and the profits in heartland street drugs—to the American countryside." *New York Times Magazine*, 15 August 2004, 38–43.

Buchanan, Patrick. Letter to the editor. *Foreign Policy* (May/June 2004): 12–13.

"Buckeye Egg Workers to Be Deported: Raid by Federal Agents Uncovers 36 Illegal Aliens." (AP) *Cincinnati Enquirer*, 8 November 2000.

Buechele, Tom. "Missing the Welcome Mat: New Border Rules Stifle U.S. Boast As 'Mother of Exiles.'" *Episcopal Life* (December 2004): 22.

Burnett, Maggie. "A Perilous Crossing: Arizona Episcopalians Visit Mexico to Understand Migrants' Plight." *Episcopal Life* (June 2004): 1.

Burnett, Victoria. "To Curb Illegal Migration, Spain Offers a Legal Route." *New York Times*, 11 August 2007, A3.

Burnham, Philip. "Interview with Tohono O'odham Nation's Vivian Juan-Saunders." *Indian Country Today*, 6 November 2004.

Buruma, Ian. "Letter from Amsterdam: Final Cut." *New Yorker*, 3 January 2005, 27.

Bush, George W. "State of the Union Address." 21 January 2004, Washington, DC.

Bynum, Russ. "Immigration Raid Outrages Small Georgia Town." (AP) *Louisville Courier-Journal*, 16 September 2006.

"Calderón: Inmigración no es todo." *TelemundoLA.com*, 9 November 2006. http://www.telemundola.com/inmigracion/10284182/detail.html.

Caldwell, Christopher. "Islam on the Outskirts of the Welfare State." *New York Times Magazine*, 5 February 2006, 56.

———. "Where Every Generation Is First-Generation." *New York Times Magazine*, 27 May 2007, 44–49.

"California Here We Come: Immigrants Make It into the Middle Class." *Wall Street Journal*, 23 February 2004, A16.

"California: Illegal Immigrants Down Helicopter." *New York Times*, 26 August 2005, A14.

"California Woman's Identity Stolen by Dozens." (AP) *Dayton Daily News*, 17 June 2006, A1.

"Call to Shut Migrant 'Jail.'" (AP) *New Zealand Herald*, 23 February 2007, B2.

Canon, Sandra Noble, Marta Miranda, and David L. Rich. "Let's Move Forward, Not Sideways, for Latino Community Incorporation into Lexington." The National Conference for Community and Justice. Undated.

Capps, Randy (The Urban Institute), and Michael Fix (Migration Policy Institute). "Undocumented

Immigrants: Myth and Reality." 25 October 2005. http://www.urban.org/Uploaded-PDF/900898_undocumented_immigrants.pdf-9k.

Card, David. "Is the New Immigration Really So Bad?" January 2005. http://www.phil.frb.org/econ/conf/immigration/card.pdf.

Carens, Joseph H. "Crossing the Border: On Belonging." *Boston Review* (Summer 2005): 16–19.

Carr, Rebecca. "Immigration Convict Data Sought." *Atlanta Journal-Constitution*, 15 October 2007, A7.

Carroll, Susan. "Migrant Death Toll Sets a Grim Record." Republic Nogales Bureau. 5 September 2003. htpp://www.azcentral.com/specials/specia103/articles/0905recorddeaths.05.htm.

Castañeda, Jorge. "The 2004 John L. Manikon Lecture: North America in the 21st Century." 2004. http://www.asu.edu/clas/nacys/bna/archive/Castaned.NA21stCen, 2004.pdf.

———. "America's Misguided Immigration Debate." *Project Syndicate.* 2006. http://www.project-syndicate.org/commentary/castañeda8.

Cevallos, Diego. "Mexico: Crece cerco en torno de emigración a Estados Unidos." *Inter Press Service News Agency*, 11 August 2004. http://www.ipsespanol.net/ataque/1809_5.shtml.

Chang, Anita. "Fire Victims Strived to 'Be with Friends and Family.'" (AP) *Dayton Daily News*, 13 September 2004, A1.

———. "Suspicious Fire Kills 10 Near Columbus: Victims All Mexican Immigrants." (AP) *Dayton Daily News*, 13 September 2004, A5.

Chavez, Leo R. *Shadowed Lives: Undocumented Immigrants in American Society/Case Studies in Anthropology.* Edited by George and Louise Spindler. Fort Worth, TX: Harcourt Brace College Publishers, 1991.

"Child Labor in the US: An Overview of Federal Child Labor Laws." *Child Labor Coalition*, 16 June 2005. http://www.stopchildlabor.org/Uschildlabor/fact1.htm.

"Children Are Left Behind after Immigration Raid in Arkansas." *New York Times*, 31 July 2005, 13.

Cho, David. "Some Laborers Arrested in Virginia Face Deportation: Frightening of Immigrant Community Decried." *Washington Post*, 27 October 2004, A1.

Chung, Erin Aeran. "Korean Voluntary Associations in Japanese Civil Society." Japan Policy Research Institute, JPRI Working Paper No. 69: July 2009. http://www.jpri.org/publications/workingpapers/wp69.html.

Cobb, Kim. "For Migrants, Jobs Come with a Price." *Houston Chronicle*, 7 June 2003.

Cohn, D'Vera. "Area Immigration Booming: Census Finds Steady Flow Despite Economy, 9/11." *Washington Post*, 23 November 23, 2004, A1.

Cooper, Marc. "Border Justice." *The Nation*, 2 February 2005, 22.

———. "High Noon on the Border." *The Nation*, 6 June 2005, 20–24.

Cornelius, Wayne. Letter to the editor. *Foreign Policy* (May/June 2004): 86–87.

"Cosecha de Dolor." *Sin Fronteras* (Mexican television program). 4 June 2005.

"Cost of Illegal Immigrants Growing." *Dayton Daily News*, 26 August 2004, A3.

Cowell, Alan. "Britain Joins Others in Europe in Limiting Immigrant Workers." *New York Times*, 24 February 2004, A5.

Crane, Ken R., and Ann V. Millard. "'To Be with My People': Latino Churches in the Rural Midwest." In *Apple Pie and Enchiladas: Latino Newcomers in the Rural Midwest*, ed. Ann V. Millard and Jorge Chapa, 172–96.

Crockett, Roger O. "Why Are Latinos Leading Blacks in the Job Market?" *Business Week*, 15 March 2004, 70.

Crouch, Stanley. "Goose-Loose Blues for the Melting Pot." In *Reinventing the Melting Pot*, ed. Tamar Jacoby, 271–83. New York: Penguin/Basic Books, 2004.

CNN Headline News, 29 March 2004.

Crary, David. "Kids of Illegal Immigrants at Center of Policy Struggle." (AP) *Dayton Daily News*, 5 June 2005, A18.

Crawford, Byron. "American Dream Is a Working Reality." *Louisville Courier-Journal*, 28 January 2004, B1.

Cuadros, Paul. "Hispanic Poultry Workers Live in New Southern Slums." *APF Reporter*. http://www. aliciapatterson.org/APF2001/Cuadros/Cuadros.html.

Cummings, James. "More Agencies Willing to Talk the Talk." *Dayton Daily News*, 26 October 2005, B1.

Curiel, Carolyn. "In Los Angeles, the Inevitable Is Reflected in a New Hispanic Mayor." *New York Times*, 28 May 2005, A22.

Custred, Glynn. "Where Are My Juice and Crackers? Citizens along America's Southwestern Border Have Organized A Neighborhood Watch." *American Spectator* (July/August 2005): 21–25.

Daniels, Roger. Letter to the editor. *Foreign Policy* (May/June 2004): 8–10.

"Deadly Incompatibility." *Washington Post*, 9 March 2004.

"Deporting the Undocumented: A Cost Assessment." Center for American Progress. July 2005. http://www.americanprogress.org/issues/2005/07/b913099.html.

Derbez, Luis Ernesto. "Mexico and the Free Trade Area of the Americas." *Economic Perspectives, Electronic Journal of the U.S. Department of State*, October 2002. http://usinfo.state.gov/ journals/ites/1002/ijee/ijee1002.pdf.

DeStigter, Todd. *Reflections of a Citizen Teacher: Literacy, Democracy, and the Forgotten Students of Addison High*. Urbana, IL: National Council of Teachers of English, 2001.

DeWinter, Leon. "Tolerating a Time Bomb." *New York Times*, 16 July 2005, A27.

Diamond, Jared. *Guns, Germs, and Steel*. New York: Norton, 1997.

Dorazio, David. Letter to the editor. *Newsweek*, 27 June 2005, 20.

Dougherty, Geoff. "'Taperos' Break Down Union Walls: More Mexicans Enter Chicago Trades." *Chicago Tribune*, 26 September 2004, 1.

Dougherty, Jon E. *Illegals*. Nashville, TN: WND Books, 2004.

Dowd, Matthew. "The Mexican Evolution." *New York Times*, 1 August 2005, A17.

Downes, Lawrence. "As an Immigration Tide Swells, Europe Treads Water." *New York Times*, 1 August 2006, A18.

———. "Day Laborers, Silent and Despised, Find Their Voice." *New York Times*, 10 July 2006, A20.

Doyle, Rodger. "Coming to America: Immigration Today Rivals the Influx of a Century Ago." *Scientific American*, August 2005, 25.

Durband, Dennis. "Minuteman and Congressional Candidate Gilchrist Aims to Re-Ignite Reagan Republicanism." *The Arizona Conservative*, 19 September 2005. http://www.azconservative. org/NFRA_Gilchrist.htm.

Ehrenreich, Barbara. *Nickel and Dimed: On (Not) Getting By in America*. New York: Henry Holt, 2001.

El Nasser, Haya. "Mexicans Feel Strong Pull to USA: Poll Finds Desire to Immigrate in 'Whole Breadth' of Society." *USA Today*, 17 August 2005, 1A.

"El nuevo Muro de Berlin." Editorial. *(Atlanta, GA) Mundo Hispánico*, 5–11 October 2006, A48.

Elliott, Michael. "Such Lovely Lads." *Time*, 21 August 2006, 28.

"Emergency Order Forces Megafarm to Control Flies, Repair Water Leaks." *Dayton Daily News*, 11 August 2005, B3.

"Empleados fuera de la ley: Indocumentados, motor laboral de EU." *Vanguardia*, 7 January 2004.

Erler, Edward J. "Sanctuary Cities: A New Civil War." The Claremont Institute. 7 September 2005, 3. http://www.eco.freedom.org/articles/erler-706.shtml.

Estrada, Richard. "Whom Do Hispanic Leaders Speak For?" *Boston Globe*, 24 July 1996, 11.

Etzioni, Amitai. "Assimilation to the American Creed." In *Reinventing the Melting Pot*, ed. Tamar Jacoby, 211–20. New York: Penguin/Basic Books, 2004.

"EU Parliament Speaks against Mass Regularization of Illegal Immigrants." (AP) *International Herald Tribune*, 28 September 2006. http://www.iht.com/bin/print.ipub.php?file=/articles/apk/2006k09/28/Europe/EU_GEN_E.

"FDA OKs Test to Get Chagas Disease out of Blood Supply." (AP) *Dayton Daily News*, 14 December 2006, A21.

Federation for American Immigration Reform. "Immigration Issue Centers: Illegal Immigration." 3 June 2005. http://www.fairus.org/immigrationIssueCenters/ImmigrationIssueCentersList.cfm?c=13.

Figueredo, D. H. *The Complete Idiot's Guide to Latino History and Culture.* Indianapolis: Alpha, 2000.

"First, They Took On Taco Bell, Now, the Fast-Food World." *New York Times*, 22 May 2005, 21.

Fisher, Ian. "Czech Republic Faces Debate on Immigration." *New York Times*, 25 April 2004, 4.

Fitzgerald, David. "State Responses to Labor Emigration: A View from Arandas, Jalisco, Mexico." Presented at the Institute for Labor and Employment Graduate Student Conference, 20–21 February 2004, Pt. Reyes, CA. http://www.iir.ucla.edu/research/grad_conf/2004/fitzgerald.pdf.

Flowers, Christine. Letter to the editor. *New York Times*, 8 August 2005, A18.

Flynn, Stephen E. "Rethinking the Role of the U.S. Mexican Border in the Post-9/11 World." *Council on Foreign Relations*. 24 March 2004. http://www.cfr.org/pub6906.

"Foreign-Born Population of the USA." *USA Today*, 22 February 2005, 8A.

Foster, David, and Farrell Kramer. "America's Secret Child Labor Force." *AP Child Labor Series*. 14 December 1997. http://www.ufw.org/ap1214.htm.

"France's Shattered Image." *USA Today*, 6 November 2005.

Freedman, Samuel G. "On Education: Latino Parents Decry Bilingual Programs." *New York Times*, 14 July 2004, A21.

Friedman, Thomas. "Innovation Gives America Its Edge: People in Other Countries Not Used to Independent Thinking." *Dayton Daily News*, 9 March 2004, A6.

———. "A Poverty of Dignity and a Wealth of Rage." *New York Times*, 15 July 2005, A21.

———. *The World Is Flat*. New York: Farrar, Straus and Giroux, 2005.

Frolik, Joe. "City's Appeal to Immigrants Has Declined." *Cleveland Plain Dealer*, 23 June 2005, B9.

Frosch, Dan. "Inmates Will Replace Wary Migrants in Colorado Fields." *New York Times*, 4 March 2007, 20.

Fry, Rick. "The Changing Landscape of American Public Education: New Students, New Schools." Pew Hispanic Center. 5 October 2006. http://pewhispanic.org/reports/report.php?ReportID=72.

Fuentes, Annette. "Comprende doctor?" *USA Today*, 21 February 2006, 19A.

Garay, Annabelle. "Dallas Suburb Trying to Be 1st in Texas with a Law Barring Illegal Immigrants." (AP) *Dayton Daily News*, 13 November 2006, A18.

Garcia, Anita, and Cynthia Morgan, "A 50 State Survey of Requirements for the Education of Language Minority Children." The Read Institute. November 1997.

"Gitmos across America." Editorial. *New York Times*, 27 June 2007, A22.

Glazer, Nathan. "Assimilation Today: Is One Identity Enough?" In *Reinventing the Melting Pot*, ed. Tamar Jacoby, 61–73. New York: Penguin/Basic Books, 2004.

———. *We Are All Multiculturalists Now*. 1997; Cambridge, MA: Harvard University Press, 2003.

Glueck, Michael Arnold, and Robert J. Cihak. "High Cost of Medical Care for Illegal Immigrants." *New York Times*, 27 December 2005. http://www.newsmax.com/archives/articles/2005/12/26/170334.shtml.

Goldfarb, Zachary A. "Increasing Share of U.S. Uninsured Are Immigrants." *Wall Street Journal*, 14 June 2005, D6.

Goodnough, Abby. "A Florida Mayor Turns to an Immigration Curb to Fix a Fading City." *New York Times*, 10 July 2006, A12.

Goodstein, Laurie. "Catholic Groups to Work Together for Immigrants." *New York Times*, 10 May 2005, A13.

Gordon, Jennifer. "American Sweatshops." *Boston Review*, 13 June 2005, 11–15.

Gorman, Anna. "Survey Reveals Widespread Abuse of Day Laborers." *Los Angeles Times*, 23 January 2006, B3.

Gorski, Eric. "Hispanic Churches Adding English." (AP) *Lexington Herald-Leader*, 1 September 2007, E1.

"The Gospel vs. H.R. 4437." *New York Times*, 3 March 2006, A22.

"Gov. Champ of Immigrants, Minuteman Supporter." (AP) 30 April 2005. http://www.dailybulletin.com.

Green, Laura. "Church Sees Clear 'Moral' Choice in Immigration Debate." *International Herald Tribune*, 30 April 2006.

Greenhouse, Steven. "Among Janitors, Labor Violations Go with the Job." *New York Times*, 13 July 2005, A1.

———. "Broad Survey of Day Laborers Finds High Level of Injuries and Pay Violations." *New York Times*, 22 January 2006, 17.

———. "Crossing the Border into the Middle Class." *New York Times*, 3 June 2004, A22.

———. "Immigration Sting Puts 2 U.S. Agencies at Odds." *New York Times*, 16 July 2005, A1.

———. "Local 226, 'The Culinary,' Makes Las Vegas the Land of the Living Wage." *New York Times*, 3 June 2004, A22.

———. "Wal-Mart Is Said to Be in Talks to Settle Illegal-Immigrant Case." *New York Times*, 5 August 2004, C4.

Griswold, Daniel T. Letter to the editor. *Foreign Policy* (May/June 2004): 84–86.

"Group: Crackdown on Illegal Immigrants Misguided." *The (Ohio) Western Star*, 16 February 2006. http://www.western-star.com/police/content/new/police/stories/2006/02/16/ws0216butleri.

Grow, Brian. "Hispanic Nation." *Business Week*, 15 March 2004, 58–70.

"A Guide for the Illegal Migrant." *New York Times*, 9 January 2005, 5.

Hagenbuch, Stephen. "Presbyterian Leader Attacks Immigration Policy." *Buffalo News*, 6 July 2005, B2.

Hakim, Peter. "U.S.–Latin American Relations Post-9/11." *Great Decisions*. New York: Foreign Policy Association, 2004.

Hall, Mimi. "Feds Plan to Act on Border Problems: Chertoff: Illegal Immigration Gangs on List." *USA Today*, 24 August 2005, 3A.

Halloran, Liz. "Under the Sun: A New Wave of Immigrants Is Transforming Communities Nowhere Near the Border." *U.S. News & World Report*, 20 June 2005, 20–25.

"Hamilton Contractors Praise Illegal Immigrants Bust." *Dayton Daily News*, 26 May 2006, A11.

Hanson, Victor Davis. *Mexifornia*. San Francisco: Encounter Books, 2003.

Hawley, Chris. "Smaller Families Evidence of Cultural Shift in Mexico." *Arizona Republic*, 4 April 2006. http://www.azcentral.com/arizonarepublic/news/articles/0404nobabies.html.

Healy, Patrick. "Illegals Move In, and Long Island Grows Restive." *New York Times*, 29 November 2004, A1.

————. "In the Land of Four Wheels, Immigrants Walk in Peril." *New York Times*, 29 February 2004, 25.

"Heat Kills 12 Illegal Immigrants." *Dayton Daily News*, 24 May 2005, A3.

Herbeck, Dan. "Contractor Gets 46 Months in Prison for 'Despicable' Abuse of Farm Labor." *Buffalo News*, 27 May 2005, D1.

Herbert, Bob. "Where the Hogs Come First." *New York Times*, 15 June 2006, A23.

————. "Who's Getting the New Jobs." *New York Times*, 23 July 2004, A23.

Hershey, William. "House Leaders Plan Measure to Crack Down on Illegal Immigration." *Dayton Daily News*, 3 August 2006.

"Hidden Talent: Immigrants' Professional Skills Could Benefit All Central Ohioans." *Columbus Dispatch*, 14 September 2004, A10.

"Hispanic Attitudes toward Learning English." Pew Hispanic Center Factsheet. 7 June 2006. http://www.pewhispanic.org/files/factsheets/20.pdf.

"Hispanic Health Woes Detailed." (AP) *Dayton Daily News*, 2 March 2006, A11.

"Hispanic Heritage Month 2001 Events." Wright State University Asian/Hispanic/Native American Center. http://www.wright.edu/admin/ahna/archive/hhm2001.html.

Holzman, David C. Letter to the editor. *New York Times*, 21 July 2004, A22.

Horowitz, Jason. "Survivors Rescued on Boat Smuggling Africans to Italy." *New York Times*, 9 August 2004, A8.

"How Donated Cars Wind Up Helping Mexican Smugglers." *Wall Street Journal*, 4 October 2004, A1.

Howington, Patrick. "Spanish Media Blossom: Al Día in America Joins Other Publications to Serve Growing Louisville Population." *Louisville Courier-Journal*, 19 August 2004, D1.

Hughes, Clyde. "Latinos in Ohio: An Introduction: Latino Population Soars along with Opportunities." *Toledo Blade*, 15 October 2000.

Huntington, Samuel P. "The Hispanic Challenge." *Foreign Policy* (March/April 2004).

————. "Samuel P. Huntington Replies." *Foreign Policy* (May/June 2004): 90–91.

————. *Who Are We? The Challenges to America's National Identity*. New York: Simon and Schuster, 2004.

"Illegal Immigrants Accused of ID Theft." *Dayton Daily News*, 29 August 2007, A16.

"Illegals on the Rise in Southeast." (AP) *Dayton Daily News*, 24 February 2010.

"Immigrant Friendly Canada." *International Herald Tribune*, 29 September 2005, 6.

Immigrant Voting Project. http://www.immigrantvoting.org.

"Immigrant Workers Stay On Strike at Dairy Farm near Marshallville. *Dayton Daily News,* 9 November 2004, B3.

"Immigrant Working Families Nearly 70 Percent More Likely Than Their Native-Born Counterparts to Spend over Half Their Income on Housing." National Housing Conference, 30 July 2003. http://www.nhc.org, 1.

"Immigration: Catholic Campaign for Immigration Reform 2005." *Houston Catholic Worker* 25, no. 5 (July-August 2005).

"Immigration Heritage." Editorial. *Wall Street Journal,* 8 June 2007, A16.

"Immigration: Hoping for Amnesty." *Hispanic,* April 2004, 12.

"Immigration Law Sanctions and Enforcement in Selected Foreign Countries." Report for Congress. Law Library of Congress. April 2006. http://judiciary.house.gov/media/pdfs/lawlibrimmreport5506.pdf.

"In Paris, Tough Talk Isn't Enough." *New York Times,* 4 November 2005, A24.

Intermountain History Group, "La Guerra Mexico-EU y los pueblos del año 2000: Los datos de la política actual: Los inmigrantes 'indocumentados.'" http://www.sonic.net/~buscador/migraspa.htm.

"In Turner, Maine, Mexican Immigrants Dominate the Work Force at the Decoster Egg Farm." *Australia Visa.* Rural Laws: January, 1998—Number 8. http://www.migrationint.com.au/ruralnews/Belfast/jan_1998-08rmn.asp.

Iowa State University. "Extension Programming Efforts with Spanish Speaking Populations in Ohio." 11 September 2004. http://www.ncrcrd.iastate.edu/spanishconf/inventory/ohio.html.

Ireland, Doug. "Why Is France Burning?" *The Nation,* 28 November 2005.

Jackson, Gerard. "U.S. Immigration: *The Wall Street Journal* Gets It Wrong—Again." *BrookesNews. Com,* 25 July 2005, 1.

Jacoby, Tamar. "Defining Assimilation for the 21st Century." In *Reinventing the Melting Pot,* ed. Tamar Jacoby. New York: Penguin/Basic Books, 2004.

———. Letter to the editor." *Foreign Policy* (May/June 2004): 10—12.

———. "The New Immigrants: A Progress Report." In *Reinventing the Melting Pot,* ed. Tamar Jacoby. New York: Penguin/Basic Books, 2004.

———. "What It Means to Be American in the 21st Century." In *Reinventing the Melting Pot,* ed. Tamar Jacoby. New York: Penguin/Basic Books, 2004.

Jacoby, Tamar, ed. *Reinventing the Melting Pot: The New Immigrants and What It Means to Be American.* New York: Penguin/Basic Books, 2004.

Jelinek, Pauline. "Hispanics Make Up Half of U.S. Growth: Birth Rate Higher Than Other Groups in Country." (AP) *Dayton Daily News,* 9 June 2005, A5.

John, Butch. "Hispanics, Asians Flowing In." *Louisville Courier-Journal,* 6 September 2000. http://www.courier-journal.com/local news/2000/0009/06/000906cens.html.

Jordan, Lara Jakes. "Study: Some Immigrants Re-Arrested 6 Times on Average." (AP) *North County (California) Times,* 8 January 2007. http://www.nctimes.com/articles/2007/01/09/news/nation/13_34_791_8_07.txt.

Jordan, Miriam. "Immigrant Workers Are Curbside Attraction for Activists." *Wall Street Journal,* 18 July 2005, B1.

———. "Latinos Take the Lead in Job Gains." *Wall Street Journal,* 23 February 2004, A2.

———. "New Backlash: In Immigrant Fight, Grassroots Groups Boost Their Clout." *Wall Street Journal*, 28 September 2006, A1.

———. "The Sweat of Their Brows: Federal Plan Finances Homes of Low-Income Families Who Build Their Own Dwellings." *Wall Street Journal*, 10 August 2005, B1.

———. "Welcome Mat: Banks Open Doors to New Customers: Illegal Immigrants." *Wall Street Journal*, 8 July 2005, A1.

"Judge: Immigrants Not Trespassing." *North County (California) Times*, 13 August 2005, A20.

"Jury Acquits Tyson Foods in Immigrant Conspiracy Case." *CNN.com/LawCenter*, 26 March 2003. http://www.cnn.com/2003/LAW/03/26/tysons.food.ap/index.html.

"Justice Dept. Figures on Incarcerated Illegals." *NewsMax.com*. http://www.newsmax.com/archives/ic/2006/3/27/114208.shtml.

Kandell, Jonathan. "Cross Purposes: Mexican Immigrants Are Defying Expectations in This Country—and Changing the Landscape Back Home." *Smithsonian*, June 2005, 90–97.

Keefe, Bob. "High-Tech Eyes along Border Give Blurred View." (Cox News Service) *Dayton Daily News*, 17 May 2006, A15.

Kelley, Katie. "A Deal in Colorado on Benefits for Illegal Immigrants." *New York Times*, 12 July 2006, A16.

Kicanas, Gerald F. "Never Again! (Illegal immigrants in the U.S. face conditions similar to those in concentration camps)." *America Magazine*, 3 November 2003, 7. http://americamagazine.org/gettext.cfm?articleTypeID=458.

Kiefer, Michael. "Maricopa Court Upholds Migrant Smuggling Laws." *Arizona Republic*, 10 June 2006. http://www.azcentral.com/arizonarepublic/local/articles/0610.html.

Kiely, Kathy. "Public Favors Giving Illegal Immigrants in USA a Break." *USA Today*, 19 April 2007, 7A.

Kilbinger, Sara Seddon. "Foreign Investors Look to Mexico, Lured by Growth." *Wall Street Journal*, 31 May 2006, B3.

Kissell, Margo Rutledge. "Grandfather Taught Benefits of Hard Work." *Dayton Daily News*, 14 October 2004, E1.

———. "Health Center Sees Big Increase in Hispanic Patients." *Dayton Daily News*, 14 October 2004, E4.

———. "Hispanic Festival Is Just the Beginning of the Festivities." *Dayton Daily News*, 14 October 2004, E4.

———. "Language Made Man Feel Isolated." *Dayton Daily News*, 14 October 2004, E1.

———. "Restaurateur on a Mission to Share Culture." *Dayton Daily News*, 14 October 2004, E.

———. "Sinclair Graduate Encourages Education for Other Immigrants." *Dayton Daily News*, 14 October 2004, E4.

Kleber, John. E. "Aug. 6, 1855: Bloody Monday." *Louisville Courier-Journal*, 31 July 2005, H1.

"Knownothingism." *Catholic Encyclopedia*. http://www.newadvent.orgcathen086776a.htm.

Koch, Wendy. "U.S. Urged to Apologize for 1930s Deportations." *USA Today*, 5 April 2006, 1A.

Kochar, Rakesh, Roberto Suro, and Sonya Tafoya. "The New Latino South: The Context and Consequences of Rapid Population Growth." Pew Hispanic Center. 26 July 2005.

Kotlowitz, Alex. "Our Town." *New York Times Magazine*, 5 August 2007, 30.

Kramer, Farrell. "AP Finds Thousands of Child Laborers." *AP—Child Labor Series*, 14 December 1997. http://www.Ufw.org/ap1214.htm (16 June 2005).

Kraul, Chris. "Youth Suicides Soar in Wake of Ecuador's Exodus." *Los Angeles Times*, 28 January 2007. http://www.latimes.com/news/nationworld/world/la-fg-suicides28jan28,0,3590996.story?c.

"La emigración hacia Estados Unidos." http://www.conapo.gob.mx/prensa/carpetas/carpeta2002_15.htm.

"*La Vida* at Harvard." *Harvard Magazine*, July-August 2004, 62.

Lacey, Marc. "Mexican Migrants Carry H.I.V. Home to Unready Rural Areas." *New York Times*, 17 July 2007, A1.

Lambert, Bruce. "Mexican Official Says a Long Island Community Should Relocate Evicted Workers." *New York Times*, 9 July 2005, A13.

———. "Two Leaders, in Agreement on Immigration." *New York Times*, 17 August 2006, A22.

Landler, Mark. "Social Democrats Defeat Governing Party in Austria." *New York Times*, 2 October 2006. http://www.nytimes.com/2006/10/02/world/Europe/01austriak.html?_r=1&oref=slogin.

Lane, Mary Beth, and Kevin Mayhood. "Apartment Fire Kills 10." *Columbus Dispatch*, 13 September 2004, A1.

"Language Barriers." *Azcentral.com*. http://www.azcentral.com/specials/specia124/2006.

Lantigua, John. "Suburbanites, Day Laborers at Odds in Jupiter." *PalmBeachPost.Com*, 16 February 2004.

"Latinos in North Carolina." *Children's Services Practice Notes* 7, no. 3 (June 2002). Jordan Institute for Families. http://www.practicenotes.org/v017_no3/Latinos%20in%20NC.htm.

League of Women Voters Forum: "Immigration Myths vs. Reality." 17 November 2004, Dayton, Ohio.

Lecker, Kelly. "Crossing Cultural Borders: Mexican Traditions Survive with American Seasoning." *Columbus Dispatch*, 29 March 2005, A1.

———. "Life in the Shadows: Immigrants Long for Mexico As They Thrive in Columbus." *Columbus Dispatch*, 27 March 2005, A1.

———. "Ohio Fresh Eggs Facing $212,000 Fine." *Columbus Dispatch*, 16 June 2005, C11.

———. "Turning Dollars to Pesos: Mexican Workers in Columbus Create Lifeline for Hometown." *Columbus Dispatch*, 28 March 2005, A1.

LeDuff, Charlie. "Mexicans Who Came North Struggle As Jobs Head South." *New York Times*, 13 October 2004, A1.

———. "100 Members of Immigrant Gang Are Held." *New York Times*, 15 March 2005, A19.

Leiken, Robert S. "A Change in Course? Mexican Foreign Policy after Castañeda." *In the National Interest*, 15 January 2003. http://www.nationalinterest.org/article/a-change-in-course-mexican-foreign-policy-after-castañeda-2224.

———. "Enchilada Lite: A Post-9/11 Mexican Migration Agreement." Center for Immigration Studies. http://www.cis.org/articles/2002/leiken.html.

Levine, Robert A. "Assimilating Immigrants: Why America Can and France Cannot." Rand Corporation. July 2004. http://www.rand.org/pubs/authors/1/Levine_Robert_a.html.

———. "Assimilation Past and Present." *The Public Interest* (Spring 2005): 93–108. http://www.highbeam.com/doc/1G1-132292404.html.

Levitz, Jennifer. "Scams Use Leased Radio Time to Target Immigrant Listeners." *Wall Street Journal*, 31 October 2006, 1.

Lewicky, Kim. "Invisible in Plain Sight." *The (North Carolina) Highlands Newspaper*, 18 March 2005, 10.

Lichtbau, Eric. "In Wake of Plot, Justice Dept. Will Study Britain's Terror Laws." *New York Times,* 15 August 2006, A15.

———. "U.S. Takes Steps to Tighten Mexican Border." *New York Times,* 16 March 2004, A16.

Lindsley, Evangeline, and Nancy Diggs. *My Century: An Outspoken Memoir.* Dayton, OH: Landfall Press, 1997.

Lolli, Mary. "Butler County Mounts Drive to Oust Illegal Immigrants." (Cox News) *Dayton Daily News,* 22 October 2005.

———. "Butler Gets Feds' OK to Oust Illegal Immigrants." *Dayton Daily News,* 14 December 2006, A4.

Lopez, Edward, Jr. Letter to the editor. *Foreign Policy* (May/June 2004): 87–88.

"Lowest Wages Earned by Mexican Immigrants." *Diario de Juarez,* 4 February 2004. http://www.nmsu.edu/~frontera/old_1996/ju196/sumry/5.html.

Lozano, Juan A. "Smuggled Survivor Describes His Agony: Immigrants Were Trapped in Sweltering Tractor-Trailer." (AP) *Dayton Daily News,* 11 March 2005, A12.

Luhnow, David, and John Lyons. "In Latin America, Rich-Poor Chasm Stifles Growth." *Wall Street Journal,* 18 July 2005, A1.

Lyman, Rick. "As Congress Dithers, Georgia Tackles Immigration." *New York Times,* 12 May 2006, A17.

MacFarquhar, Neil. "Pakistanis Find U.S. an Easier Fit Than Britain." *New York Times,* 21 August 2006, A1.

Madhwani, Anita. "Negativism about Hispanics Rising, Poll Says." *Tennessean,* 14 November 2002. http://ww.tennessean.com/local/archives/02/11/25263988.shtml?Element_ID=25263988.

"Madrid: 400 More Africans Try to Scramble to Asylum." (Reuters) *International Herald Tribune,* 29 September 2005, 8.

"Madrid: Spanish Police Thwart Migrants from Africa." (Reuters) *International Herald Tribune,* 28 September 2005, 7.

Majano, Rosendo. "Survey: Latinos Have Sharp Internal Differences over Immigration." *Hispanic-Business.com,* January 2006. http://www.hispanicbusiness.com/news/newsbyid.asp?id+274 53&catk=headlines&more=/n.

Malkin, Elisabeth. "Study Challenges Assumptions about Money Being Remitted to Mexico." *New York Times,* 7 July 2005, C4.

Malone, Julia. "Many Illegal Immigrants Are Going Free Instead of Going Back Home." (Cox News Service) *Dayton Daily News,* 23 May 2006, A10.

Mansfield, Duncan. "More Striving to Curb Illegal Immigration: Minutemen-Type Activism Spreading throughout U.S." (AP) *Columbus Dispatch,* 18 July 2005, A5.

Marizco, Michael. "Experts Examine Immigration Proposal." *Arizona Daily Star,* 15 February 2004. http://www.dailystar.com.

Marosi, Richard. "Tons of Marijuana Found in Huge Tunnel." (LA Times/Washington Post Service) *Oregonian,* 27 January 2006, A12.

Mason, Christopher, and Julia Preston. "Canada's Policy on Immigrants Brings Backlog." *New York Times,* 27 June 2007, A1.

Massey, Douglas A. "The American Side of the Bargain." In *Reinventing the Melting Pot,* ed. Tamar Jacoby, 111–21. New York: Basic Books, 2004.

———. "An Exercise in Self-Deception: Mexican Immigration." *Newsweek International,* 29 January 2004, 41.

————. "International Migration in a Globalizing Economy." *Great Decisions 2007*, 41–51. Hanover, NH: Foreign Policy Association, 2007.

Mayhood, Kevin, and Sherri Williams. "Some Say Immigrants Should Learn English." *Columbus Dispatch*, 16 September 2004, A2.

Mcallister, Kristin. "Warren Deputies May Get Spanish Lessons." *Dayton Daily News*, 10 March 2004, B1.

McGee, M. J. "Desert Thirst As Disease." In "Outside Reading," *Arizona Water Resource* (May-June 2001): 1–2. http://ag.Arizona.edu/AZWATER/awr/mayjune/01.

McKinley, James C., Jr. "From Mexico Also, the Message to Bush Is Immigration." *New York Times*, 14 March 2007, A11.

————. "Leftist Outsider's Campaign Surges in Mexico." *New York Times*, 19 March 2006, 12.

————. "Mexico: Tighter Security Vowed along Border." *New York Times*, 3 August 2005, A8.

McLean, Renwick. "5 African Migrants Killed and Scores Hurt at Spanish Enclave Fence." *International Herald Tribune*, 30 September 2005, 3.

————. "Spain Scrambles to Cope with Tide of African Migrants." *New York Times*, 19 March 2006, 3.

Meier, Matt S., and Feliciano Ribera. *Mexican Americans/American Mexicans: From Conquistadors to Chicanos*. New York: Hill and Wang, 1993.

"Mexican Immigrants Found in Trailer." *Dayton Daily News*, 16 October 2004, A6.

"Mexican Watershed." Editorial. *Wall Street Journal*, 29 June 2006, A14.

"Mexico Announces Steps to Combat Red Tape." *Wall Street Journal*, 3 August 2005, A9.

Mexico, Government of. "Border Fences Are No Solution for Immigration Nor Will They Increase Border Security." 26 October 2006. http://www.embassyofmexico.org/eng/.

————. "México frente al Fenómeno Migratorio." 16 February 2006. http://sre.gob.mx/eventos/fenomenomigratorio/doics/mexicofrentealfenommigr.pdf.

————. "Mexico's Public Policies to Foster Circular Migration." http://www.embassyofMexico.org/images/pdfs/Circular%20Migration%2002%2003%202006.pdf.

"México rechaza muro fronterizo." *Telemundo47.com*, 26 October 2006. http://www.azcentral.com/lavoz/Spanish/latin-america/articles/latin-america_177429.html.

"Mexico Wants Whole Immigration Enchilada." *WorldNetDaily*, 4 July 2001. http://www.wnd.com/news/article.aso?ARTICLE_ID=23499.

"Migración." Undated. http://cuentame.inegi.gob.mex/poblacion/migracion.asp.

"Migración Internacional Boletín No. 2: Migración indocumentada a los Estados Unidos: Devoluciones realizadas por la Patrulla Fronteriza." *Consejo Nacional de Población*. http://www.conapo.gob.mx/. 12 September 2004.

"Migrants to Stay While Birth Defects Investigated." (AP) *St. Petersburg Times*, 27 March 2005. http://www.sptimes.com/2005/03/27news_pf/State/Migrants_to_stay-whil.schtml.

"Migration between Mexico and the United States/*Estudio Binacional Mexico-Estados Unidos sobre Migración*." A Report of the Binational Study on Migration, 1997. http://www.utexas.edu/lbj/uscir/binational.html.

Millard, Ann V., and Jorge Chapa. *Apple Pie and Enchiladas: Latino Newcomers in the Rural Midwest*. Austin: University of Texas Press, 2004.

Miller, Spring. "Latino Immigrants in Tennessee: A Survey of Demographic and Social Science Research." University of Tennessee College of Law. June 2004.

Millman, Joel. "Now, Complaints of Brand-Name 'Piracy' Go Both Ways." *Wall Street Journal*, 11 July 1005, B1.

Minor, Elliott. "Trouble down on the Farm." (AP) *Dayton Daily News*, 15 March 2006, D3.

The Minuteman Project. "MMP: A Citizens' Neighborhood Watch along Our Border." April 2005. http://minutemanproject.com/.

Mittelstadt, Michelle. "Immigrant Competition Reduces Wages." (AP) *Center for Immigration Studies*, 21 January 1988. http://www.cis.org/articles/1998/wagestudy/wage_coverage.html.

Moore, Stephen. "More Immigrants, More Jobs." *Wall Street Journal*, 11 July 2005, A13.

Moscoso, Eunice. "Businesses Making a Push to Legalize Guest Workers: Critics Dispute Idea That No Americans Could Fill the Jobs." *Dayton Daily News*, 10 April 2005, A10.

———. "Hispanic Kids Bolster Boom at U.S. Schools." *Atlanta Journal-Constitution*, 6 October 2006, A6.

Moss, Khalid. "Faith of Their Padres: Spanish Masses Draw Crowds at Holy Trinity." *Dayton Daily News*, 20 November 2004, E3.

Mulrine, Anna. "After the Flames." *U.S. News & World Report*, 21 November 2005, 37.

"Multicultural Policy 'Is Breeding Racial Hatred.'" *London Times*, 30 September 2005, 31.

Murphy, Dean E. "Imagining Life without Illegal Immigrants." *New York Times*, 11 January 2005, section 4, p. 1.

Myers, Steven Lee. "In Anti-Immigrant Mood, Russia Heeds Gadfly's Cry." *New York Times*, 22 October 2006, 4.

———. "Russia Deports Georgians and Increases Pressures on Businesses and Students." *New York Times*, 7 October 2006, A6.

Navarette, Ruben, Jr. "A 'Real American' on Border Control." *San Diego Union-Tribune*, 25 January 2006, B7.

Navarro, Mireya. "For Younger Latinos, a Shift to Smaller Families." *New York Times*, 5 December 2004, A1.

Nee, Victor, and Richard Alba. "Toward a New Definition." In *Reinventing the Melting Pot*, ed. Tamar Jacoby, 87–95. New York: Penguin/Basic Books, 2004.

Negative Population Growth. "Americans Talk about Illegal Immigration." March 2003. http://www.npg.org/immpoll.html.

"New Model Police." *The Economist*, 9 June 2007, 29–30.

"N.H. Won't Appeal Immigrant Ruling." *USA Today*, 24 August 2005, 3A.

Nichols, Alan B. "Civil Unrest in France Triggers Massive Reform." *The Washington Diplomat*, February 2006, 10.

Noel, Pamela. "Philadelphia Seeks Out Hispanic Visitors." *New York Times*, 29 May 2005, 5–2.

Noguchi, Sharon. "Hard Work, Furtive Living: Illegal Immigrants in Japan." *YaleGlobal*, 2 March 2006. http://www.yaleglobal.yale.edudisplay.artricle?id=7067.

Nossiter, Adam. "Day Laborers Are Easy Prey in New Orleans." *New York Times*, 16 February 2009, A1.

Novelo Uradanivía, Federico. "Situación actual y perspectivas de la migración México–Estados Unidos." *Observatorio de la Economía Latinoamericana* 28 (July 2004). http://www.eumed.net/cursecon/ecolat/mx/2004/fn-migra.htm.

Oates, Russ. "Tennessee Officers Get Intense Training in Spanish Language, Culture. *Hispanicvista*, 28 May 2003. http://www.hispanicvista.com/htm13/060203he.htm.

"Ohio Commission on Hispanic/Latino Affairs: Mission." 16 September 2004. http://www.ochla. ohio.gov/ochla/mission.htm.

Ohlemacher, Stephen. "Bureau Wants No Immigration Raids during 2010 Census Count." (AP) *Dayton Daily News*, 17 August 2007, A14.

Orszag, Peter R. Letter to Kent Conrad. Congressional Budget Office, U.S. Congress, Washington, DC, 23 May 2007.

Ottaviano, Gianmarco I. P., and Giovanni Peri. "Rethinking the Gains from Immigration: Theory and Evidence from the U.S." *Social Science Research Network.* NBER Working Paper No. W11672, 3 October 2005. http://papers.ssrn.com/so13/papers/cfm?abstract_id=819833.

"Our Border Brigades." *Wall Street Journal*, 27 January 2004, A14.

Page, Clarence. "Cooperation vs. Conflict: Blacks, Latinos Can Build Alliances on Common Ground." *Dayton Daily News*, 10 February 2004, A7.

———. "Immigration's Not-So-Hidden Costs: Low-Wage Workers Who Already Are Here Feel the Squeeze." *Dayton Daily News*, 17 May 2005, A6.

———. "Low-Income Workers Hurt by Illegal Immigrants." *Dayton Daily News*, 30 March 2006, A21.

Papademetriou, Demetrios G. "The Mexican Factor in Immigration Reform." *Migration Information Source*, 1 March 2004. http://www.migrationinformation.org.feature/display.cfm?Id=210.

Parker, Kathleen. "Hillary Waffles While Security Suffers." *Buffalo News*, 7 August 2005, H1.

Pascual, Aixa. "Risking It All for Work: They Come Illegally, Live in Uncertainty, Even Face Violence." *Atlanta Journal-Constitution*, 18 April 2004.

Passel, Jeffrey S. *Estimates of the Size and Characteristics of the Undocumented Population.* Washington, DC: Pew Hispanic Center Report, 7 March 2006. http://pewhispanic.org/reports/reportphp?Report ID=61.

———. "U.S. Immigration and Immigrants: Myth and Reality." Lecture, Chautauqua Institution. 25 July 2007.

Pear, Robert. "Payments to Help Hospitals Care for Illegal Immigrants." *New York Times*, 10 May 2005, A12.

———. "U.S. Is Linking Status of Aliens to Hospital Aid." *New York Times*, 10 August 2004, A1.

Perez, Evan. "Battered by Charley, Migrant Workers Fear Seeking Aid." *Wall Street Journal*, 18 August 2004, B1.

Perez, Evan, and Corey Dade. "An Immigration Raid Aids Blacks—For a Time." *Wall Street Journal*, 17 June 2007, 1.

Perry, J. K. "Workers Buy Edwards Man's Identity." *Vail Daily*, 7 December 2006, A3.

Pham, Huyen. "The Inherent Flaws in the Inherent Authority Position: Why Inviting Local Enforcement of Immigration Laws Violates the Constitution." *Florida State University Law Review* 31 (Summer 2004). http://www.law.txwes.edu/pham.

———. "Sovereignty and Immigration Power." *University of Cincinnati Law Review* 31 (2006). http://www.law.txwes.edu/pham.

Philpott, Matthew. Letter to the editor. *New York Times*, 8 August 2005, A18.

"Photographer Recounts Crossing U.S. Border with Mexican Illegal Immigrants." *National Geographic Adventure Magazine*, 23 January 2003. http://news.nationalgeographic.com/news/2003/01.

Piña, Rosalba. "Los inmigrantes indocumentados tambien tienen derechos legales." *(Chicago) Nuevo Siglo*, 5 December 2003. http://www.nuevosiglonews.com/moxie/colunmas/2_5/336.html.

PollingReport.com. "Race and Ethnicity." 30 November 2004. http://www.pollingreport.com/race. htm.

Poovey, Bill. "Tyson Accused of Smuggling Illegal Workers." (AP) *Law.Com*, 7 February 2003.

Porter, Eduardo. "In U.S. Groves, Cheap Labor Means Machines." *New York Times*, 22 March 2004, A1.

——. "Workers Illegally in U.S. Bolster Social Security." *(New York) Times Digest*, 5 April 2005, 5.

Porter, Eduardo, and Elisabeth Malkin. "Mexicans at Home Abroad: Will Millions Retire Here or Go South of Border?" *New York Times*, 4 August 2005, C1.

Poston, Dudley L., Jr., Steven A. Camarota, and Amanda K. Maumle. "Remaking the Political Landscape: The Impact of Illegal and Legal Immigration on Congressional Apportionment." Center for Immigration Studies. October 2003. http://www.cis.org/articles/2003/back1403ttp://www.cis.org/articles/2003/backcoverage.html.

Prengaman, Peter. "Businesses File Lawsuits on Hiring Illegal Immigrants." (AP) *Dayton Daily News*, 23 August 2006, A11.

——. "Catholics Work for Reform on Illegals." *Dayton Daily News*, 4 March 2006, A2.

Press, Eyal. "Do Immigrants Make Us Safer?" *New York Times Magazine*, 3 December 2006, 20.

Preston, Julia. "Farmers Call Crackdown on Illegal Workers Unfair." *New York Times*, 11 August 2007, A9.

——. "Former Manager of Kosher Slaughterhouse in Iowa is Acquitted of Labor Charges." *New York Times*, 8 June 2010, A13.

——. "Immigration Is at Center of New Laws around U.S." *New York Times*, 6 August 2007, A12.

——. "A Slippery Place in the U.S. Work Force. *New York Times*, 22 March 2009, A1.

——. "Texas Hospitals' Separate Paths Reflect the Debate on Immigration." *New York Times*, 18 July 2006, A1.

Preston, Julia, and Steven Greenhouse. "Immigration Accord by Labor Boosts Obama Effort." *New York Times*, 13 April 2009, A1.

Pritchard, Justin. "Dying for Work: Fatalities on Rise among Mexicans." (AP) *Dayton Daily News*, 14 March 2004, D1.

——. "Mexicans' Deaths on Job an Epidemic." (AP) *Atlanta Journal-Constitution*, 14 March 2004.

Quinones, John. ABC News, 24 November 2006. http://www.abcnews.go.com/WNT/US/story?id=2677661&page=1.

Radloff, Juliana. "Los Inmigrantes Mexicanos." April 2001. http://www.warren-wilson/edu~spanish/JulianaRadlof.html.

"Raid Rumors Scare Some Illegals." (AP) *Dayton Daily News*, 29 April 2006, A11.

Ramos, Jorge. *The Latino Wave: How Hispanics Will Elect the Next American President*. Translated by Ezra E. Fitz. New York: HarperCollins, 2004.

——. *The Other Face of America: Chronicles of the Immigrants Shaping Our Future*. Translated by Patricia A. Duncan. New York: HarperCollins, 2002.

"Rancher Who Detained Immigrants On Trial." http://www.azdauktsyb.articles.2006/11/14k/news/2006/1114_local_news_4.prt.

Randall, Mark. "People Stacked Like 'Cord Wood' in Fatal Vehicle; 9 Die in Rollover." *Yuma Sun*, 7 August 2006. http://sun.yumasun.com/cgi-bin/artrman/exec/view.cgi/17125844.

"Registra el 96% de municipios del país algún tipo de migración: CNP." *El Siglo Torreón*, 27 March 2003.

Reiter, Julie. Presentation at "An Immigration Forum: Dayton and Its Recent Immigrants." Dayton, Ohio, 17 May 2005.

Relea, Francesc. "México exige una 'solución integral' al problema migratorio." *El País.Internacional*, 30 March 2006. http://www.elpais.com/internacional/.

Rengifo, Patricia. "Farmers Unsure about Guest Worker Plan." *Coshocton Tribune*, 26 January 2004.

Rieff, David. "Nuevo Catholics." *New York Times Magazine*, 24 December 2006.

Riley, Michael. "Lawyers Use Anti-Mafia Law to Go After Wal-Mart. *Atlanta Journal-Constitution*, 7 September 2004, E5.

Rivlin, Gary. "Dollars and Dreams: Immigrants As Prey." *New York Times*, 11 June 2006, A3.

Rizzo, Holly Ocasio. "Under Attack: Bilingual Education Faces Uphill Fight." http//www.hispanic-magazine.com/2000/sep/Features/index2.html.

Rodriguez, Gregory. "Mexican-Americans and the Mestizo Melting Pot." In *Reinventing the Melting Pot*, ed. Tamar Jacoby, 125–38. New York: Penguin/Basic Books, 2004.

Rodriguez, Olga. "Criminals, Fear Rule Mexican Town: More Than 60 Killed since January in City near Laredo, Texas." (AP) *Dayton Daily News*, 11 June 2005, A5.

———. "Juarez Drug Gang Forms Alliances." (AP) *Dayton Daily News*, 13 February 2005, A12.

Rodriguez, Richard. "Border Line: The High Cost of Becoming a Gringo." *Sonoma County Independent*, 8 October 1998.

Rohe, John F. Letter to the editor. *Newsweek*, 27 June 2005, 20.

Rosenblum, Marilyn. Letter to the editor. *New York Times*, 30 March 2005, A26.

Rotstein, Arthur H. "Overnight Border Watch Starts Out Rather Uneventful: Minuteman Project Using Civilian Volunteers." (AP) *Dayton Daily News*, 10 April 2005, A7.

———. "U.S. Wildlife Refuges Face Threats from People, Development." (AP) *Dayton Daily News*, 10 October 2004, A7.

Ruiz, Juan Diez-Canedo. *La migración indocumentada de México a los Estados Unidos: Un nuevo enfoque*. Mexico City: Fondo de Cultura Económica, 1984.

Sadowski, Dennis. "Bishops Concerned about Proposed Immigration Bill." *Catholic Universe Bulletin*. http://www.ohiocathconf.org/I/IM/ubstoryimm.pdf.

Salamon, Julie. "Celebrating Mexican Life in New York." *New York Times*, 8 December 2004, B1.

Salgado, Gaspar Rivera. "Naa-Shioca Dav'I (Los que andan por tierras lejanas)." *Revista Ojarasca*. Undated. http://www.fiob/org/estudiosoaxacalifornia/ojarasca.htm.

Salins, Peter D. "The Assimilation Contract: Endangered but Still Holding." In *Reinventing the Melting Pot*, ed. Tamar Jacoby, 99–109. New York: Penguin/Basic Books, 2004.

Sarmiento, Sergio. "Migración illegal: El muro y los politicos." Cato Institute. http://www.elcato.org/node/1572.

Schiffrin, Anya. "Pay Now, Pay Later." *Mother Jones* (May/June 2005): 18–20.

Schlosser, Eric. *Fast Food Nation: The Dark Side of the All-American Meal*. New York: Perennial/HarperCollins, 2002.

Schneider, Peter. "The New Berlin Wall." Translated by Philip Boehm. *New York Times Magazine*, 4 December 2005, 69.

Schwartz, Jeremy. "Border Breaches Worry Rice: Fears Terror Group May Enter U.S. from Canada, Mexico." *Dayton Daily News*, 11 March 2005, A6.

Seewer, John. "Foreign Worker Shortage Threatens Seasonal Companies." (AP) *Dayton Daily News*, 4 April 2005, D2.

"Severe Birth Defects in the Migrant Farm Worker Population Have Ag-Mart Concerned." *News Target*, 2 April 2005. http://www.newstarget.com/006309.html.

"Sex Slavery: The Growing Trade." *CNN.Com/World*, 8 March 2001. http://archives.cnn.com/2001/WORLD/Europe/03/08/women.trafficking/.

Shawgo, Ron. "Indiana Sees Sharp Surge in Hispanics." *Fort Wayne Journal-Gazette*, 18 September 2003. http://www.fortwayne.com/mid/fortwayne/news/local/6801590.htm.

"Sheriff Wants to Arrest Illegals." *Dayton Daily News*, 3 March 2006, B2.

Shipler, David K. *The Working Poor: Invisible in America*. New York: Knopf, 2004.

Shteyngart, Gary. "The New Two-Way Street." In *Reinventing the Melting Pot*, ed. Tamar Jacoby, 285–92. New York: Penguin/Basic Books, 2004.

Sifuentes, Edward. "Mexico Urges Illegal Immigrants to Sue." *North County (California) Times*, 16 March 2004.

Silverstein, Ken. "Veggie Libel, Wilted Press." *The Nation*, 20 April 1998, 23.

Skerry, Peter. "'This Was Our Riot, Too': The Political Assimilation of Today's Immigrants." In *Reinventing the Melting Pot*, ed. Tamar Jacoby, 221–32. New York: Penguin/Basic Books, 2004.

Slack, James, and Matthew Hickley. "One in Every 13 Is Now a Migrant." *(London) Daily Mail*, 8 September 2005, 8.

Small, Dennis. "A Fifth of All Mexicans Are Now Economic Refugees in the U.S." *Executive Intelligence Review*, 10 September 2004.

Smith, Craig S. "Morocco Again Expels Africans Trying Risky Path to Europe." *New York Times*, 17 October 2005, A8.

Smith, Vicki. "Big-City Latin American Gang Creeps into West Virginia Town." (AP) *Dayton Daily News*, 14 August 2005, A3.

Sosa, Lionel. *The Americano Dream*. New York: Penguin, 1998.

Sowell, Thomas. *Black Rednecks and White Liberals*. San Francisco: Encounter Books, 2005.

———. *Ethnic America: A History*. New York: Basic Books, 1981.

Srivastava, Mehul. "Riverside Police May Meet with Hispanics." *Dayton Daily News*, 8 October 2004, B1.

Stanisljevic, Zoran. "Microcapital Story: Microfinance Continues to Play a Key Role in Developing Economies as Remittances to Latin America and the Caribbean Decline in 2009." 23 March 2009. http://www.microcapital.org/microcapital-story-microfinance-continues-to-play-a-key role.

"State Agency Proposes $212,000 Fine against Ohio Fresh Eggs." *Dayton Daily News*, 16 June 2005, D3.

"The State of American Public Opinion on Immigration in Spring 2006: A Review of Major Surveys." Pew Hispanic Center Factsheet. 17 May 2006. http://pewhispanic.org/factsheets/factsheet.php?Factsheet+D+18—.

"Statement by Ambassador E. Michael Southwick on the Report of the Special Rapporteur for the Human Rights of Migrant Workers on her Mission to the Border between Mexico and the United States." *Commission on Human Rights*, 10 April 2003. http://www.humanrights-usa.net/statements /0410Migrants.htm.

Stevens, Dana. "Film Review: Pilgrimage across the Border That Tempts but Dodges Fate." *New York Times*, 18 May 2005, B4.

Stewart, Nikita. "Jobs Lure Laborers to Site Despite Arrests." *Washington Post*, 27 November 2004, B3.

Storrs, K. Larry. "Mexico-United States Dialogue on Migration and Border Issues, 2001–2005."

CRS Report for Congress. Updated 2 June 2005. CRS-6. http://www.fas.org/sgp/crs/row/ RL327.35pdf.

Stracher, Cameron. "Much Depends on Dinner." *Wall Street Journal,* 29 July 2005, W13.

Striffler, Steve. "Underground in a Chicken Factory." *Utne Reader* (January-February 2004): 68–74.

"Study of Immigrants Notes Rising Obesity." *Washington Post,* 15 December 2004, A18.

"Study: Wealth Gap Widens for Minorities." (AP) *Dayton Daily News,* 18 October 2004, A2.

Steinberg, Stephen. "The Melting Pot and the Color Line." In *Reinventing the Melting Pot,* ed. Tamar Jacoby, 235–47. New York: Penguin/Basic Books, 2004.

Stephens, Caleb. "Hispanic Population Increases." *Dayton Business Journal,* 18 August 2002. http:// www.bizjournals.com/Dayton/stories/2002/08/19story3.html.

Suarez-Orozco, Marcelo, and Gary Orfield. Letter to the editor. *Foreign Policy* (May/June 2004): 88–89.

Sullivan, Kevin. "Border Agent a Hero, Then a Victim." (*Washington Post*) *Boston Sunday Globe,* 8 February 2004, A26.

Suro, Roberto. "Attitudes toward Immigrants and Immigration Policy: Surveys among US Latinos and in Mexico." Pew Hispanic Center Report. 2005.

———. Letter to the editor. *Foreign Policy* (May/June 2004): 5–6.

———. *Strangers Among Us: Latino Lives in a Changing America.* New York: Vintage/Random House, 1998. Afterword, 1999.

Sutherly, Ben. "Egg Farm's Permits Revoked When State Finds Falsified Applications." *Dayton Daily News,* 1 December 2006, A4.

Swarns, Rachel L. "Rift on Immigration Widens for Conservatives and Cardinals." *New York Times,* 19 March 2006, 4.

———. "Union Leader Backs Bush on Guest Worker Plan." *New York Times,* 24 February 2006, A14.

Svrivastava, Mehul. "Hispanic Surveillance Cost Riverside $2,000: Police Watched Soccer Games at Shellabarger Park." *Dayton Daily News,* 19 August 2004, A1.

———. "Riverside Police May Meet with Hispanics." *Dayton Daily News,* 8 October 2004, B1.

"Table Q: Estimates of the Unauthorized Resident Population in the Top 10 Countries of Origin and States of Residence: January 1990 and 2000." *2002 Yearbook of Immigration Statistics* (2003). http://www.uscis.gov.

Tagliabue, John. "Blacks in France Fight Equality Bind." *International Herald Tribune,* 21 September 2005, 3.

Takaki, Ronald. *A Different Mirror.* Boston: Little, Brown and Co., 1993.

Talhem, Jennifer. "Feds Arrest 1,282 in Raids; Evidence Shows ID Theft Used as a Tool to Get Work." (AP) *Dayton Daily News,* 14 December 2006, A17.

Tancredo, Tom. "Two Views: Should 'Sanctuary Cities' Have Federal Funds Cut?" *Dayton Daily News,* 10 April 2006, A13.

Tanner, Robert. "Immigration Concerns Governors." (AP) *Dayton Daily News,* 27 February 2006, A5.

Tedford, Michelle. "About the Series." *Dayton Daily News,* 29 July 2002, C1.

———. "Communicating Needs: Language Barriers Begin to Crumble As Initiatives Take Hold." *Dayton Daily News,* 30 July 2002, C1.

———. "Community Of 'Grande' Hope." *Dayton Daily News,* 22 August 2004, E1.

———. "Language Barrier." *Dayton Daily News,* 29 July 2002, E1.

———. "Neighborly Concerns." *Dayton Daily News*, 28 July 2002.

"Tenn. Driving Papers a Hot Item Nationally." *Washington Post*, 30 January 2006, A8.

Texeira, Eric. "Number of Mexican Immigrants Continues to Grow in the Northeast." (AP) *Buffalo News*, 1 August 2005, A7.

Thernstrom, Stephen. "Rediscovering the Melting Pot—Still Going Strong." In *Reinventing the Melting Pot*, ed. Tamar Jacoby, 47–59. New York: Penguin/Basic Books, 2004.

Thomas, Cal. "Politicians Refuse to Tell Truth about Immigrants." *Dayton Daily News*, 6 June 2007, A15.

———. "Tuberculosis Being Carried across Borders." *Dayton Daily News*, 15 June 2005, A8.

Thompson, Ginger. "Corruption Hampers Mexican Police in Border Drug War." *New York Times*, 5 July 2005, A3.

———. "Mexico: Meeting Set on Fox's Comment." *New York Times*, 18 May 2005, A11.

———. "Trying to Stop Surge of Illegal Migrants, Mexican Authorities Meet Them at the Airport." *New York Times*, 8 August 2004, 12.

Thompson, Richelle. "Latino Ministry Revived and Thriving." *Interchange: News from the Episcopal Diocese of Southern Ohio*, June 2004, 1.

Thornburgh, Nathan. "Inside the Life of the Migrants Next Door." *Time*, 6 February 2006, 34–45.

Tierney, John. "Sense and Sandwiches." *New York Times*, 2 May 2006, A27.

Tobar, Héctor. *Translation Nation: Defining a New American Identity in the Spanish-Speaking United States.* New York: Riverhead/Penguin, 2005.

Tolson, Jay. "An Education in Muslim Integration." *U.S. News & World Report*, 21 November 2005, 37–38.

Tompkins, Wayne. "Hispanics Changing Area Profile." *Louisville Courier-Journal*, 2 March 2003. http://www.courier-journal.com;localnews/2003/03/03/ke030203s374642.htm.

Tunarosa, Andrea. "Houses of Worship: Spreading the Word—Fast." *Wall Street Journal*, 28 July 2006, W11.

"Tyson Chicken, 41 Infected with Tuberculosis in Processing." 4 May 2005. http://www.groupsrv.com/science/about95902.html.

"Tyson Foods Indicted for Illegal Aliens." *Farmed Animal Watch*, no. 46 (20 December 2001).

"An Underclass Rebellion." *The Economist*, 12 November 2005, 24.

United States Conference of Catholic Bishops, Inc. and Conferencia del Episcopado Mexicano. "A Pastoral Letter Concerning Migration from the Catholic Bishops of Mexico and the United States." 22 January 2003.

"Urgen a crear una estrategia contra la 'fuga de cerebros.'" *El Universal.com*, 30 May 2006. http://www.eluniversal.commx/nacion/vi_138891.html.

Urrea, Luis Alberto. *The Devil's Highway.* New York: Little, Brown and Co., 2004.

U.S. Environmental Protection Agency. "United States Files Amended Complaint and Consent Decree Resolving Clean Air Act Violations at Buckeye Egg Farm." *Enforcement Action Summary FY 2004—State of Ohio.*

"U.S. Hispanic Purchasing Power: 1978–2010." Research Market. http://www.researchandmarkets.com/reports75036/75036.htm.

"U.S.: Terrorists May Cross Mexico Border." *Dayton Daily News*, 8 October 2004, A5.

"Utah Senate Approves Immigrant Driver's Card." *New York Times*, 20 February 2005, N25.

Vaca, Nicolás C. *The Presumed Alliance: The Unspoken Conflict between Latinos and Blacks and What It Means for America*. New York: HarperCollins, 2004.

Voell, Paula. "Effort Shows Humanity Knows No Borders." *Buffalo News*, 2 July 2005, C1.

Wadhwani, Anita. "Negativism about Hispanics Rising, Poll Says." *Tennessean*, 14 November 2004. http://www.tennessean.com/local/archives/02/11/25263988.

Wagner, Dennis. "Mexicans Go to Ariz. for Medical Help." *USA Today*, 18 May 2005, 3A.

Waldinger, Roger, "The 21st Century: An Entirely New Story." In *Reinventing the Melting Pot*, ed. Tamar Jacoby. New York: Penguin/Basic Books, 2004.

Waldman, Amy. "British Bombers' Rage Formed in a Caldron of Discontent." *New York Times*, 31 July 2005, 1.

Walsh, James H. "Sanctuary Cities, States: Undermining the American Republic." *The Social Contract* (Spring 2005): 196. www.thesocialcontract.com/pdf/fifteen-three/xv-3-192.pdf

Ward, Kathy. Letter to the editor. *Palm Beach Post*, 27 February 2004, 19A.

Warner, R. Stephen. "Coming to America: Immigrants and the Faith They Bring." *Christian Century*, 10 February 2004, 20–23.

Watson, Ginny. "The Rights of Workers and Illegal Immigrants: The State of Worker's Compensation." *Avance* (September/October 2005): 43–45.

Wei, William. "The Chinese-American Experience: An Introduction." http://www.immigrants. harpweek.com/ChineseAmericans/1Introduction/BillWeiIntro.htm.

Weissert, Will. "Illegal Immigrants Flown to Mexico. (AP) *HoustonChronicle.com*, 12 July 2004. http://www.freerepublic.com/focus/f-news/1170306/posts.

"What Meat Means." *New York Times*, 6 February 2005, 12.

"Why Are Latinos Leading Blacks in the Job Market?" *Business Week*, 15 March 2004, 70.

Wides, Laura. "Task of Deporting Illegal Immigrants Too Big." (AP) *Dayton Daily News*, 19 September 2004.

Wilcox, Bruce. Letter to the editor. *USA Today*, 10 May 2006, 11A.

Williams, Kissah. "Salvadorans Buying Up Stakes in the Homeland: Expatriates Reshape Housing Market." *Washington Post*, 28 November 2004, A1.

Williams, Sherri. "Need Rises for Immigrant Prenatal Care." *Columbus Dispatch*, 18 July 2005, B1.

Winerap, Michael. "Essays in Search of Happy Endings." *New York Times*, 10 August 2005, A15.

Winton, Richard, and Daniel Yi. "Police Split on Plan for Migrant Checks." *Los Angeles Times*, 23 January 2006, B1.

Wolfe, Alan. "Native Son: Samuel Huntington Defends the Homeland." *Foreign Affairs* (May/June 2004).

Wright, Bruce. Letter to the editor. *Foreign Policy* (May/June 2004): 13.

Yzaguirre, Raul. Letter to the editor. *Foreign Policy* (May/June 2004): 4.

Zagier, Alan Scher. "Missouri Town Rallies around Illegal Immigrant." (AP) *Dayton Daily News*, 9 October 2005, A19.

Zuckerman, Mortimer B. "Land of Opportunity." *U.S. News & World Report*, 20 June 2005, 64. Review essay on *Who Are We? The Challenges to America's National Identity*, by Samuel P. Huntington (*Foreign Affairs* [May/June 2004]: 120–25).

Zurita, Brenda, "Christians Shine the Light on Sex Trafficking," *Family Voice* (July–August 2005).

INTERVIEWS AND PERSONAL COMMUNICATIONS

Berry, Amelia. (Project Coordinator of Alliance for Battered and Abused International Women.) Interview of 17 January 2006, Cincinnati, Ohio.

Bissell, Margot. (Public Use Assistant, Cabeza Prieta National Wildlife Refuge.) Interview of 23 April 2006, Ajo, Arizona.

Burton, Paula. (Patient Representative, Miami Valley Hospital.) Interview of 20 October 2005, Dayton, Ohio.

DeWine, Michael. (U.S. Senator.) Conversation of 19 May 2006, Dayton, Ohio.

Ericson, Peter. (Political Counselor, Embassy of Sweden.) Interview of 1 February 2006, Washington, DC.

Escudero, Ezra. (Executive Director of the Ohio Commission on Hispanic/Latino Affairs.) Interview of 20 October 2004, Columbus, Ohio.

Gerace, Joseph A. (Sheriff of Chautauqua County, New York.) Interview of 22 July 2004, Mayville, New York.

Gómez-Arnau, Remedios. (Mexican Consul for Georgia, Tennessee, Alabama, and Mississippi.) Interview of 17 October 2006, Atlanta, Georgia.

Graham, Nolan. (Principal, Kennedy-Patterson Elementary School.) Interview of 13 January 2006, Dayton, Ohio.

Green, Chris. (Patient Representative, Miami Valley Hospital.) Interview of 20 October 2005, Dayton, Ohio.

Heck, Mathias. (Montgomery County Prosecutor.) Telephone conversation, 18 August 2004, Dayton, Ohio.

Hopkins, Kathleen. (Center Director, Agri-Business Child Development, Migrant Head Start.) Interview of 20 July 2004, Fredonia, New York.

Jones, Richard K. (Sheriff of Butler County, Ohio.) Interview of 17 January 2006, Hamilton, Ohio.

Kelly, Alison. (Counselor, Embassy of Ireland.) Interview of 1 February 2005, Washington, DC.

Korn, Richard. (Hispanic Missioner, Episcopal Diocese of Southern Ohio.) Interview of 17 June 2005, Columbus, Ohio.

Lambert, Lourdes de Pilar Otero. (Principal, East End Community School.) Interview of 24 August 2005, Dayton, Ohio.

LePore-Jentleson, Jan. (Director, East End Community Services.) Interview of 21 April 2004.

Lydell, Carmen. (Physician, Joint Neighborhood Project, Jamestown, New York.) Interview of 28 July 2004, Jamestown, New York.

Merz, Judge Michael. (Federal Magistrate, Dayton, Ohio). Interview of 23 August 2004, Dayton, Ohio.

Moss, Thomas. (Former Deputy Commissioner of Human Services in Minnesota and member of Gov. Jesse Ventura's staff, member of Hispanic Episcopal Church, St. Paul, Minnesota.) Interview of 7 July 2004, Chautauqua, New York.

Nichols, Sandra. (Research Analyst, California Institute for Rural Studies, Davis, California.) Telephone Interview of 18 October 2004.

Pawelski, John D. (Founder and President, the Latino Connection.) Interview of 27 August 2004, Dayton, Ohio.

Pham, Huyen. (Associate Professor of Law, University of Missouri-Columbia). Personal communication, 18 November 2006.

Santana, Benjamin. (Episcopal Priest who ministers to Hispanic congregation.) Interview of 8 July 2004, Jamestown, New York.

Silva, Carolina. (Program Management and Evaluation, East End Community Services Corporation.) Interview of 22 September 2004, Dayton, Ohio.

Stacy, Sister Maria Francine. (Director of Catholic Hispanic Ministry of Dayton, Ohio.) Interview of 24 February 2004, Dayton, Ohio.

Stough, Gina. (Latino Family Advocate, East End Community Services Corporation.) Interview of 24 August 2005, Dayton, Ohio.

Thomas, Lucie. (Rector, St. Andrew's Episcopal Church, Nogales, Arizona.) Telephone conversation of 26 August 2004.

Thornton, William. (President, Miami Valley Hospital.) Interview of 5 October 2005.

Toonkel, Robert. (Communications Director and Senior Researcher, U.S. English.) Interview of 29 September 2004, Washington, DC.

Tristan, Stephanie. (Catholic Social Services.) Interview of 21 September 2004, Dayton, Ohio.

Vargas, Daniel. (Director, Vargas & Amigos Latino advertising agency, Atlanta, Georgia.) Telephone interview of 26 January 2007.

Virola, Minerva (Police Officer, Community Relations Department, Louisville, Kentucky). Interview of 30 August 2004, Louisville, Kentucky.

Wagner, Jean. (English as a Second Language Teacher.) Interview of 6 October 2004, Centerville, Ohio.

Wolfe, James (Management Consultant, member of Jackson, WY, community forum.) Conversation of 22 May 2007.

*   *   *

Barbara (American, registered nurse, suburban hospital, Ohio)

Bill (American, plasterer, Ohio)

Carlos Martinez (Mexican, construction worker, Georgia)

Carmen (Mexican, student, New York)

Gabriel (Mexican, laborer, Ohio)

Isabel (Mexican, chambermaid, North Carolina)

Jesús Perez (Guatemalan, construction worker, Florida)

John (American, roofer, Ohio)

José (Ecuadorean, skilled worker, Ohio)

Luis (Mexican, restaurant worker, Ohio)

Lupe (Mexican, chambermaid, North Carolina)

Marta (Mexican, restaurant worker, Ohio)

Miguel (Mexican, landscape worker, Ohio)

Pedro (Mexican, laborer, Ohio)

Silvia (Mexican, chambermaid, North Carolina)

Steve (American, carpenter, Ohio)

INDEX